ADVANCE

NEW LANDSCAPES OF POPULATION CHANGE

"A must-read book if you want a clear-eyed view into the global impacts of ongoing, unprecedented demographic shifts. In this comprehensive tour de force, Dr. Hayutin brings to bear lens-changing data and the inexorable trends that must be understood and incorporated now into our national security strategies. An unmatched and invaluable resource."

—General Jim Mattis, US Marines (ret.)
and twenty-sixth Secretary of Defense

"While 'democracy is destiny' is an overstatement, anyone interested in national or global economic, financial, labor market, and political history and future challenges must understand demographic trends and their applications. Adele Hayutin's insightful, beautifully illustrated *New Landscapes of Population Change* is the invaluable best place to start."

—Michael J. Boskin, Tully M. Friedman Professor of Economics and
Wohlford Family Senior Fellow, Hoover Institution, Stanford University;
and former chair, President's Council of Economic Advisers

"As Adele Hayutin shows in this stunning and vividly illustrated analysis, historic shifts are under way in global population dynamics. Wealthier countries will see their populations age and shrink due to declining fertility, while today's poorer countries will continue to experience rapid population growth for decades to come. These changes will heavily influence employment needs and opportunities, migration patterns, economic growth, environmental sustainability, political power, and social stability. Policy makers, business leaders, and thoughtful citizens worldwide will benefit enormously from reading this work."

—Larry Diamond, senior fellow, Hoover Institution; and Mosbacher
Senior Fellow in Global Democracy, Freeman Spogli Institute for
International Studies, Stanford University

"Population changes and demographics will change all our lives. The analyses are critical, and the demographic trends and figures are riveting. It is a view into the future, for business, policy, development, and foreign affairs leaders and students."

—Henrietta Fore, former executive director of UNICEF, former
administrator of USAID, and former director of foreign assistance,
US Department of State

"The author has provided us with an invaluable source of easily accessible data on the world's demographic future. As a real estate and urban economist, I have long considered demographic data the key to any medium- or long-term projections on economic and real estate markets on a metropolitan and countrywide basis. The author's analysis showing the explosive population growth projected for Africa and projected dramatic decline in population for Europe, China, and Japan should be a critical input for business leaders and policy makers. I especially like the graphics showing the role of alternative assumptions for Africa. The author's work begs for an interactive version with an ability to simulate different assumptions and policy levers that may change a country's 'demographic destiny.' This book is essential reading for any global business and policy leader."

—Ken Rosen, chairman of the Fisher Center for Real Estate and Urban Economics, Haas School of Business, University of California–Berkeley

"With the deft perception of an experienced analyst, Hayutin lays out population and age structure data and insights within and across nations. The demographics reveal critical risks and opportunities and inform possibilities and priorities from finance and markets to agriculture and industry to policy and politics."

—Sue Wagner, co-founder, BlackRock

"I dare you to read the first five pages of this document. I guarantee that if you do, you won't be able to put it down. . . . This report features characters and plot that give any page-turner a run for its money. But this is no work of fiction: it is truth—or as close to it as the UN data allow. The plot is fascinating and full of suspense. But what is most compelling is that this tale has no ending. . . . Ultimately, we are the authors of this story."

—George P. Shultz, former secretary of state, on a precursor to *New Landscapes of Population Change*

NEW LANDSCAPES OF POPULATION CHANGE

NEW LANDSCAPES OF POPULATION CHANGE

A Demographic World Tour

ADELE M. HAYUTIN

HOOVER INSTITUTION PRESS
STANFORD UNIVERSITY | STANFORD, CALIFORNIA

hoover.org

Hoover Institution Press Publication No. 727

Hoover Institution at Leland Stanford Junior University
Stanford, California 94305-6003

Cover illustration by Howie Severson, based on Adele Hayutin's chart of the global landscape of workforce growth (see figure 7.10).

First printing 2022
28 27 26 25 24 23 22   7 6 5 4 3 2 1

Manufactured in the United States of America
Printed on acid-free, archival-quality paper

Cataloging-in-Publication Data is available from the Library of Congress.
ISBN: 978-0-8179-2535-2 (pbk)
ISBN: 978-0-8179-2536-9 (epub)
ISBN: 978-0-8179-2538-3 (PDF)

In memory of George P. Shultz
with gratitude for his inspiration
and constant encouragement

and

for Elena, Leo, Bianca, Chloe,
and Luca—my five grandniblings—
who have taught me so much.
I hope you will be inspired to explore
the trends shaping your future
and to apply your creativity
to global problems.

CONTENTS

PART IV

NOTE TO THE READER ON DATA SOURCES AND NOMENCLATURE

Except where noted, this book uses population estimates and projections from the United Nations, *World Population Prospects 2019*, medium variant. The analysis in the book relies on the UN's classification of geographic regions and subregions as well as aggregations for income and development groups. For ease of reference, this book uses familiar names for selected geographic areas and countries, for example, East Asia instead of Eastern Asia, and South Korea instead of Republic of Korea. See the Appendix for the UN classification of countries by region and subregion.

The ***medium-variant projection*** used throughout the book represents the results of the UN's statistical modeling of key demographic variables for more than 200 countries and areas. In addition to the medium variant, which is treated here as the most likely scenario, the UN produces other variants with alternative assumptions of key variables, including fertility, life expectancy, and migration. These alternative scenarios can illustrate differences that arise if key assumptions change. In addition to showing the sensitivity of the medium variant to changes in the underlying assumptions, these variants are useful in highlighting a range of outcomes rather than just one trajectory.

This book considers alternative fertility variants for Africa and illustrates a range of population outcomes under varied assumptions. Similarly, the book evaluates the implications of two alternative migration scenarios for population growth in the large economies.

Most of the UN data is reported in five-year increments. For variables that are reported for a five-year period, this book uses the ending year as the reference point. For example, fertility data reported for 2015–20 is treated here as data for 2020.

The data for countries and areas is aggregated by geographic region, development group, and income group, as described below.

The *six geographic regions* include: Africa; Asia; Europe; Latin America and the Caribbean; Northern America; and Oceania. Two clarifications about the UN regional specifications will be useful to readers. According to the UN regional definitions, Northern America includes Canada and the United States, but not Mexico, which the UN categorizes as part of Central America, a subregion of Latin America. Also, according to the UN specifications, the Western Asia subregion of Asia extends from Turkey to Yemen and includes many countries generally thought of as part of the Middle East.

To facilitate historical comparisons of the development regions, the UN continues its long-used development segmentation and presents demographic data for more developed and less developed regions. *More developed regions* comprise Europe, Northern America, Australia and New Zealand, and Japan. *Less developed regions* include all regions of Africa, Asia (except Japan), and Latin America and the Caribbean, plus Melanesia, Micronesia, and Polynesia.

In 1971, the UN created a new subcategory, the *least developed countries*, to identify the most vulnerable and disadvantaged countries. The designation reflects evaluation on specific criteria, including income, health, education, and vulnerability to economic and environmental shocks. The UN regularly reevaluates the countries to determine if their designation should be changed. In 2019, this development group included 47 countries. See the Appendix for the UN's list of least developed countries.

The UN aggregates the remaining countries of the less developed regions into a subcategory designated as *other less developed countries*, comprising all countries in the less developed regions minus the least developed countries.

For *income groups*, the UN's 2019 Revision uses the June 2018 World Bank segmentation of countries by gross national income per capita. Historical trends by income or development group reflect the patterns for that specific group of countries, regardless of past income or development status. Similarly, the projections assume the group members will remain the same in the future. See the Appendix for the classification of countries by income level.

The book also uses data from two other sources: United Nations, *International Migrant Stock 2019*; and International Labour Organization, ILOSTAT.

LIST OF FIGURES AND TABLES

CHAPTER 3 DECLINING FERTILITY

CHAPTER 4 INCREASING LIFE EXPECTANCY

CHAPTER 5 INCREASING INTERNATIONAL MIGRATION

CHAPTER 6 POPULATION AGING

CHAPTER 7 SHRINKING WORKFORCES

CHAPTER 8 THE SHAPE OF THINGS TO COME

ACKNOWLEDGMENTS

I've benefited from three decades of conversations and collaboration with the late George P. Shultz, starting from my days at Bechtel Investments. I profited greatly from his wisdom about the world, and I have grown wiser from his commentary and stories and from developing answers to his many questions. He was my mentor, colleague—and chief distributor, taking my demographic briefings around the world to various gatherings of business leaders and foreign policy experts. He often advised that people might think they know demographics but could be using them more effectively to better understand world events. George read early versions of many chapters in this book and was always enthusiastic about the comparative analyses in my presentations to the Hoover Project on Governance in an Emerging New World and to the discussion group he started in week two of the COVID pandemic. I am terribly saddened by his passing but grateful for his wisdom and the opportunity to work with him over so many years.

David Fedor, a member of the Shultz team, offered invaluable advice on the content and graphics. He read early versions of all the chapters and helped shape my thinking about how to make the book useful to a variety of readers. I profited from our weekly discussions and especially appreciated his advice on making the graphics more compelling, the captions more powerful, and my writing more pointed.

Many other Hoover colleagues from the Governance project and the Shultz "salon" were especially helpful. Michael Boskin met with me several times during my research and writing and offered useful comments along the way and at the finish line about the content, as well as the visuals. Larry Diamond's appreciation of my basic premise served as an inspiration throughout the writing. He reviewed the final manuscript and made helpful suggestions for strengthening my message.

Also instrumental in the publication were Chris Dauer, Barbara Arellano, Danica Michels Hodge, Alison Law, and John O'Rourke from Hoover Institution Press, copy editor Mike Iveson, and book designer Howie Severson. I thank you all for your guidance and fine tuning. I am deeply grateful to the Hoover Institution for supporting my work and hosting me as a visiting fellow.

My interest in demographics grew over the course of my career, and I deeply appreciate the many people who influenced my thinking, including Alan Dachs at the Fremont Group, who prompted me to explore the impacts of changing demographics; and Laura Carstensen, who invited me to join the newly established Stanford Center on Longevity to research the implications of global aging.

I am especially grateful to my family and friends for their constant encouragement. My interest in world events was fueled in my early school days, when my parents installed a large world map on our family room wall and encouraged all of us kids to keep up on the news and pay attention to important current events. I fondly recall many conversations with my late brother, Marc, who regularly read and eagerly commented on my briefings and reports, including many that became part of this book; my sister-in-law Stephanie; my late sister Randi; and my sister Diane, who reviewed all the chapters and lovingly suggested improvements. Sue and Bill Gould, my longtime friends and traveling companions, have listened to my demographic comments in all the countries we visited, and they closely read and commented on all the chapters of this book. Several other friends were especially helpful throughout the project, including Barbara Casey, Barbara Creed, and Julie McHenry. I also want to thank Ken Rosen, a longtime friend and mentor, for his encouragement and intellectual support.

Many people have helped me with various parts of producing the book. Jane Anne Staw, known as a "horse whisperer for writers," offered editorial advice and invaluable guidance; and Andrea Lepcio, a former colleague from Salomon Brothers, read many iterations of all the chapters and provided helpful suggestions as well as enthusiasm. Ted Horsch, a freelance programmer, helped me enormously by automating some of the comparative analysis.

I benefited from the graphics work of two Stanford students, Lilla Petruska and Nineveh O'Connell. I especially appreciate Nineveh's additional fine tuning of many figures and maps during the editing phase of the book.

Miranda Dietz and Lily Mitchell at the Stanford Center on Longevity were true collaborators on many projects that led to ideas in this book. I fondly remember our data jackpot celebrations. Before coming to Stanford, I was lucky to work with Michelle Angier at the Fremont Group, who helped me field those early questions from George Shultz and worked with me to develop a system for organizing the data and the results.

Finally, I am grateful for the many opportunities I have had to present my work, both formally at conferences and informally with colleagues. Much of the fine tuning is the result of the questions and comments arising from those discussions. Special thanks go to the Wellesley Business Leadership Council, the International Women's Forum of Northern California, the Carol Marshall-Susan Hyatt Salon, and of course, the George Shultz Salon.

Adele Hayutin
April 2022

PART

INTRODUCTION

1 UNCHARTED TERRITORY

"Long Slide Looms for World Population, with Sweeping Ramifications"
New York Times, by Choe Sang-Hun, May 24, 2021

"Stitched Up by Robots: The Threat to Emerging Economies"
Financial Times, by Kiran Stacey and Anna Nicolaou, July 18, 2017

"After Half a Century of Success, the Asian Tigers Must Reinvent Themselves"
The Economist, December 7, 2019

"A Shift in Global Power: Is It Time?"
Forbes Business Council Post, by Sarah Dusek, June 5, 2020

THE SITUATION

We are in uncharted demographic territory. Across the globe, some populations are starting to shrink, and others are growing explosively. The world has more old people than ever before, and fewer and fewer children are being born. These demographic trends in population change and age structure have enormous implications for economic growth and stability, as well as for national power.

Already, many countries have more old people than children. Workforce growth is reversing in many places and slowing almost everywhere else. Indeed, we have begun hearing about worker shortages, and we have already read about the burdens of graying populations throughout the advanced economies. In reaction, we are seeing older people working longer even while some younger people disengage. Many countries have proposed politically fraught policies to raise their retirement ages, while others have encouraged greater immigration. Still others have adopted pronatal policies to increase the number of babies.

To make matters worse, this unprecedented demographic upheaval is occurring in a world grappling with political and economic turmoil. Global problems compound whatever national challenges countries already face within their own borders. Besides the threat of the COVID-19 pandemic, we face the existential threats of climate change and nuclear proliferation—not to make light of the great-power competition, the rise of China, cybersecurity threats, and political shifts all over the world, including threats to democracy and the specter of authoritarianism.

In this context of global turmoil, countries will be balancing their own priorities for economic growth and political stability. And as we think about our allies and adversaries, we must pay attention to their differing national priorities. Attention to the divergent demographics behind these priorities will be critical for our understanding of how the world is changing. It's more imperative than ever to grasp the impact of the unprecedented demographic shifts under way around the world. And it's especially important for us to appreciate how the changes affect our allies and adversaries.

The good news is that we have tools and forecasts that allow us to anticipate the coming developments. In fact, we have a reliable set of projections for navigating this uncharted demographic territory. These projections provide guideposts and warnings, and they help us identify the questions and uncertainties we need to address. Demographics can be a window into our future, and we should use it.

It is important to understand that many of the startling demographic changes now under way throughout the world stem from population trends set in motion as far back as the 1960s and 1970s. During those years, we saw dramatic declines in the number of births per woman, and at the same time, we also saw huge gains in life expectancy. These trends evolved differently around the world, with major variations in the timing and pace of change across countries.

In some places the impacts of these two fundamental trends are already evident, as reflected, for example, in the aging populations and slower-growing workforces in Europe. But in many places, the impacts are just starting to be felt, even though they have been unfolding over decades. China's workforce decline is one example. In other places, the changes were more gradual, and therefore the workforce declines will also be more gradual, as in India and Mexico. While most of the future impacts can be anticipated, the speed of changes makes effective adjustments even more challenging. The burdens will be especially great for developing countries facing these rapid demographic shifts with limited economic and political resources.

These global changes in age structure are dramatic, unprecedented, and consequential. The well-being of millions of people and their homelands is at stake. For those who care about world events and the US role, it will be increasingly important to understand the demographics behind the news headlines. Such consideration will in turn shed light on the global transformation, and help cut through the ever-increasing volume of stories and opinions.

A GUIDEBOOK FOR
UNDERSTANDING POPULATION CHANGE

To help you digest the flood of information, this book provides you with a framework for understanding the demography behind the news, and it provides a perspective for thinking about global developments through the lens of population. It will arm you with facts that should inform your opinions.

As you read, you will be guided through consequential demographic changes around the world—some that have already occurred as well as some that will soon unfold. The premise is this: to understand current global events, you should understand the demography of about 20 important countries, including the largest economies, selected emerging economies, fast-growing populations, and any major political hot spots. The book will take you on a demographic tour of those countries.

Rather than embarking on a single world tour from country to country, you will take several round-the-world tours, each with a different focus, and each using a comparative perspective. This will be useful for several reasons. First, using a comparative approach can be much more compelling than drilling down on an individual country. You can always access information on single countries, but understanding how countries stack up is an effective way to develop a broad global perspective and helps to illuminate different national priorities.

Also, because the demographics are evolving differently around the world, a comparative perspective will be useful for understanding the divergent changes. The regional and country comparisons illuminate some surprising and unexpected differences, as well as similarities among countries. The comparisons also provide a framework for digesting information and putting each country's situation within a larger context. Considering countries in relation to each other helps you better understand each one and highlights the interconnectedness of the trends. Another advantage of this comparative approach is that it will help you deepen what you already know.

And last, besides being helpful, the comparisons can be fun, both fueling and satisfying your curiosity, as you gather pieces of information to fill in the puzzle.

The comparisons of China and India are particularly striking. By highlighting the demographic weaknesses and strengths of the world's two most populous countries, the comparisons shed light on the different challenges faced by each: China is rapidly aging and faces a shrinking workforce, while India is still relatively young and growing. Both need to figure out how to leverage their changing working-age populations.

Another key feature of this book is its long horizon: it starts in 1950, highlights developments expected by midcentury, and extends to 2100. The historical framework illuminates the divergent timing of important changes and reveals how variations in the timing affect the nature of the population shifts now taking hold. Perhaps at first glance this seems to be too long a perspective based on our more immediate concerns, but the long-term projections serve to highlight some of the uncertainties we should consider, as well as underlying assumptions that we should question. Without this long horizon, you could well miss the major inflection points in workforce growth and population aging. These are events we can be preparing for now, but only if we see them coming. Furthermore, we can use the long-term projections to more fully understand what kind of world we are leaving for future generations. Baby boomer readers can calculate that your grandchildren and grandnephews and -nieces will be reaching their prime working ages around midcentury, and your great-grandchildren will be expected to live well past the end of the century.

The world tours in the book rely heavily on visual displays to synthesize the data and illuminate the comparisons. These graphics allow you to see the contrasts at a glance and to better understand the countries within a regional or global context. The visuals are designed to highlight the pace of change and the urgency of addressing the coming changes. To underscore the timing of these changes, most of the figures in the book include vertical indicators for the years 2020 and 2050. The 2020 vertical line marks the beginning of the projections, allowing you to clearly see how the future is expected to unfold differently from the past. Additionally, within the long perspective that takes us to 2100, the book focuses on changes expected over the 30 years from 2020 to 2050. The two vertical markers draw attention to those changes in particular while still illustrating the longer trajectory.

THE TOURS

Part I of this book starts with a population overview and highlights the overall population shift to Africa. Part II turns to the three demographic drivers—fertility, life expectancy, and migration. In Part III, the focus is on two critical challenges: population aging and shrinking workforces. Part IV gives you guidance for thinking about the future and outlines issues and uncertainties to watch for.

The tours follow a similar itinerary. Each one starts with a global overview that showcases key regional differences—for example, a shrinking Europe and an explosively growing Africa. It is revealing to see that Africa's population at 1.3 billion in 2020 makes it smaller than China, but due to its high fertility rates, Africa will skyrocket past China's population, nearly doubling to 2.6 billion by midcentury. Africa's population is projected to triple to 4.2 billion by the end of the century, while China's will shrink by one-quarter.

Following the regional overview, each tour looks at differences across the major income groups. We will see that today's poorest countries are the world's fastest growing and account for nearly all the projected population growth, while the rich countries are growing more slowly, shrinking in both size and share of world population. Surprisingly, the upper-middle-income countries—the economic core of the emerging economies—are also projected to lose population.

After these broad comparisons, each tour turns to focus on individual countries, grouped to underscore similarities and differences regarding the timing and pace of their changes. For example, we will see that China wasn't alone in its steep fertility decline. Other countries, such as South Korea and Thailand, experienced significant declines around the same time, even without imposing draconian one-child policies. It's surprising to see that Iran's fertility decline was as steep as China's, though it occurred 20 years later. The tours highlight different countries to illustrate particular trends, but always in a comparative framework.

TRENDS YOU WILL SEE ON THE TOURS

Globally, we are seeing fewer and fewer children, but the fertility declines across countries have been mixed. Most of the advanced economies have experienced decades of below-replacement-rate fertility, which has resulted in aging populations and slower workforce growth. In some of these countries, workforce growth has reversed, and total populations have already declined. Among the advanced economies, the United States has fared better than most, with immigration fueling its workforce and population growth.

In contrast, in many developing countries, including China, fertility rates have steeply declined, leading to dramatic slowdowns in working-age population. Although China only recently began promoting three-child families, many other countries have been trying for decades to boost their birth rates. At the same time, births per woman remain stubbornly high in many African countries, leading to continued explosive population growth in the poorest, least developed parts of the world. This shift in global population poses economic and political challenges we have not encountered before.

The global increase in life expectancy over the past century has been a remarkable success story, with more children surviving childhood and more people enjoying longer, healthier lives. Over the past decades, most countries have benefited from increasing life expectancy, even though the upward trend has been interrupted by wars, famine, and disease. Countries differ markedly in their responses to such disruptions. While some countries were able to get back on the same upward track after a temporary drop, others ended up on a lower trajectory. Even in the United States, life expectancy has declined for the last few years, due largely to the opioid epidemic. And now, due to the COVID-19 pandemic, we face the possibility that life expectancy could decline globally.

We know that the fertility and life expectancy changes already under way globally will shape the future in ways completely different from what we have come to understand from past demographic changes. It is clear that the future will not be a simple extrapolation of the past, but will reflect the divergent trends unfolding around the world. We already know that countries aren't aging the way they used to. Today's young countries are aging much faster than the old European stalwarts and the relatively young United States. The changes for these faster-aging countries will likely be much more disruptive to social cohesion and economic growth. Many of these youngster countries are on the cusp of economic development, just as they get their population growth under control. Yet, they are now said to be getting old before they get rich. But it isn't too late. They still have time to prepare—many are indeed adopting education, immigration, and labor policies to meet today's changing economic interdependence. Still, many of the world's poorest countries with limited economic prospects continue to face the challenges of high population growth.

By the end of the tours, you will have a global perspective on the key demographic drivers and challenges. You will understand the competitive demographic advantage of the United States, as well as the major demographic challenges faced by China, Russia, and Iran. You will have a clear picture of how the population shift toward Africa is likely to unfold and why Nigeria will rapidly overtake the United States to become the world's third most populous country. You will understand the way demographic drivers affect population aging and workforce changes, and you will also gain an appreciation for why the impacts that took so long to emerge now appear more sudden. You will see that demographics affects all aspects of our lives.

While the book doesn't recommend particular policies, the tours will arm you with information and insights about the demographics that drive important key policy decisions, from migration and refugee policy to family-friendly policies such as day care assistance and home health care. You will be able to hone your opinions about pronatal policies, family-planning programs, free education, higher retirement ages, and increased migration.

To prompt your thinking, the book ends with a long watch list of questions you might want to consider as you read the news. The 11 categories of questions include education, economic growth, technology and innovation, migration, climate change, health care and wellness, the role of the family, population aging, women's rights, national security, and governance and civil society. If you care about any of these topics, you will want to pay attention to demographics. Armed with such information, you will be able to foresee important changes. Most important, you will not be taken by surprise when you see alarming demographic headlines.

2 THE BIG PICTURE OF GLOBAL POPULATION GROWTH

"This Century Will See Massive Shifts in the Global Population, Economy, and Power"
SingularityHub, by Vanessa Bates Ramirez, July 16, 2020

"World Population Likely to Shrink after Mid-century, Forecasting Major Shifts in Global Population and Economic Power"
ScienceDaily, July 15, 2020

"The African Century: Africa Is Changing So Rapidly It Is Becoming Hard to Ignore. Rapid Economic and Social Change Will Give the Continent a Bigger Role in World Affairs"
The Economist, March 28, 2020

For years, many of us were panicked by population explosion, worrying that the world would become overpopulated, with insufficient resources to support everyone. Yet more recently, we're being warned about just the opposite problem: shrinking populations. Whichever of these outcomes concerns you the most, you are right to worry. It turns out, paradoxically, we can expect a combination of both outcomes. Both of these startling trends are already under way in different regions and countries, and in combination, they will lead to population shifts that will have enormous social, economic, and political consequences. This chapter points to some of the more alarming changes we can anticipate.

Our world tour of global demographics starts with an overview of total population by region and country, highlighting broad changes we can expect to see over the coming decades. I use the wide lens of total population to show the outcomes you will see as the demographic drivers take hold in diverse ways around the world.

I give you this big picture before delving into the details of how each driver works—and how they work together—to produce these changing population totals. I'm presenting the results to you in advance for several reasons. If you see the results first and understand the broad population shifts, it will be easier to develop your own view of how the world is changing. Equally important, you will have an overall framework for making sense of the coming changes, and you will better understand how the three demographic drivers—fertility, life expectancy, and migration—work together to produce these changes.

It's true: total population has continued to expand, but as we will see, country and regional trajectories are unfolding differently than they have in the past. World population reached a milestone of 7 billion in 2011 and is on track to reach 10 billion by 2050 and 11 billion by 2100. However, while the total population continues to grow, the pace of growth is slowing dramatically, mainly due to the worldwide decline in births per woman. Despite this slowdown, the prospect of world population reaching nearly 11 billion by the end of the century elicits mixed reactions: many are worried about adding any more people to the planet, while others celebrate the remarkable success of more infants surviving into childhood and more people living longer. Still others recognize that the changing regional composition of the population and changing age structures will have important global consequences—some negative, some positive. For example, the further population shift to developing countries changes the global economic landscape by dramatically increasing labor supply in those regions, while aging populations and shrinking workforces threaten economic well-being in the advanced economies.

The trajectory to 11 billion has several notable characteristics. First, despite the continued population increase, the pace of growth will slow dramatically everywhere—although at different rates, as the impacts of declining and persistently low fertility rates take hold.

A second noteworthy element of the global trajectory is that Africa's growth, though much slower than in the past, will still be much faster than growth in other developing regions. As a result, Africa will account for an increasing share of global growth. This global population shift toward Africa will accelerate from now through the end of the century.

Third, most of the global population growth will occur in the most vulnerable, least developed countries, those that have the fewest resources for adapting to the challenges of rapid population growth. Perhaps not surprisingly, most of these countries are African.

A fourth feature of the demographic trajectory is the upward shift in the age composition of the population. Populations around the world will see increased median ages as fewer children are born, and as more people reach older ages. As part of the upward shift in age, working-age population will increase more slowly, and, in many places, workforces will shrink, creating economic challenges for many countries. At the same time, there will be more older people than ever before, and their share of total population will increase dramatically.

Another important element of the global population shift is that an increasing number of countries will experience shrinking populations over the coming years. Population decline is uncommon in the modern world, and in the past has been associated with specific disruptive events, such as wars, famines, or epidemics. But the population decline projected for the coming years results, not from a particular event or series of events, but from longer-term structural demographic changes, including declining number of births and increased life expectancy. Most of our culture and our economic models have been built on the assumption of continued population growth, so this new structural impact is particularly challenging. The conventional premise was that continued population growth would fuel labor force growth, which would in turn fuel economic growth. Now, seemingly all of a sudden, the assumption of continued labor force growth is no longer justified. This shift will most certainly require adapting to and rethinking how we increase and maintain economic well-being.

A sixth element of the global population shift is that country growth will be uneven—even within geographic regions. So it is necessary to consider how the divergent patterns of fertility decline and life expectancy gains affect population dynamics in individual countries, especially as some neighboring countries have embraced different economic policies and social practices, from migration to family-planning policies, that have led to divergent demographic outcomes.

Finally, the projected demographic changes are not extrapolations of past trends. They are the result of dramatic changes in the underlying demographics that have been unfolding over the past few decades. The combined impact of key drivers—declining births per woman and increasing life expectancy—is an especially powerful force in countries where the changes have been large and rapid. In these countries, the combination of drivers is leading to an inflection point in population growth and age structure. In some cases, the inflection point marks a change in direction, for example when a population begins to decline. In other cases, the combination of forces bolsters a trend already under way, such as continued strong growth, so the impact might be more difficult to observe.

With these elements of change in mind, it will be easier to understand both how we got to our current global population of just under 8 billion and how the population trajectory to 11 billion will unfold. As I said above, I'm giving you the results at the beginning of the book so you can better and more deeply understand how the demographic processes lead to these results. Then in Part II of the book, you will see how each driver has contributed to population growth differently in each region and country.

GLOBAL GROWTH AND
THE POPULATION SHIFT TO AFRICA

According to the UN's most likely scenario, over the 30 years from 2020 to 2050, global population will grow by 1.9 billion, and over the subsequent 50 years, from 2050 to 2100, will add another 1.1 billion. The total addition of 3.1 billion by the end of the century represents a 40% increase from the 2020 level. While the increase is worrisome in itself, the distribution of the growth across the world is especially consequential. Figure 2.1 shows how the regional population distribution is projected to change.

FIGURE 2.1 The global population shift to Africa accelerates.

Population by Region, in Billions

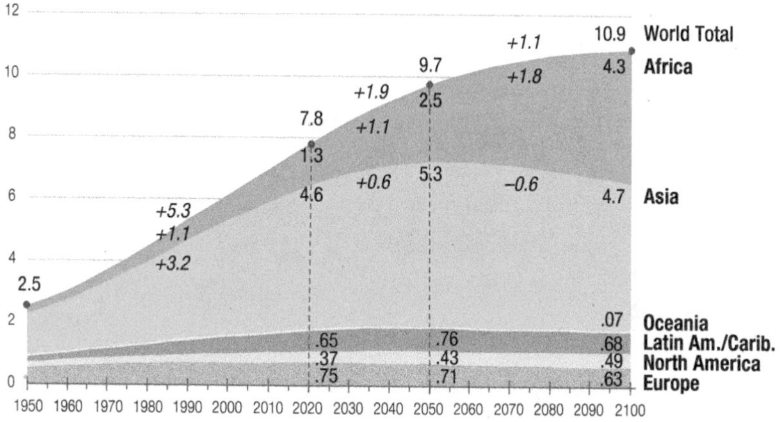

Data source: United Nations, *World Population Prospects 2019*, medium variant.

A critically important and startling demographic trend is the continued explosive population growth in Africa and the shifting regional composition of the world's population. Another startling projection is that Asia is declining in share of world population, not just because it is projected to grow much more slowly than Africa, but because the total population of Asia is projected to decline by nearly 600 million people over the second half of this century. Even more surprising is that most of this decline will occur in China. While some people are aware that India will soon overtake China as the world's most populous country, few realize that China's population, which steadily increased for so many years, is projected to actually decline beginning around 2030.

In the coming years, the global population shift to Africa will accelerate as Africa's population explodes and other regions decline. As a result of its disproportionate growth, Africa's share of world population is projected to increase from 17% in 2020 to 26% by midcentury and 39% by the end of the century, while Asia's population share will decrease from 60% to 43%. Europe's share of global population has already dropped by more than half, from 22% in 1950 to 10% in 2020. Europe and Latin America are each projected to decline to 6% of world population by century's end, while North America's continued growth keeps it at 5% of the world's total.

The 70-year picture of historical growth provides an important perspective on the divergent population patterns, especially when considering the developing regions. Since 1950, Asia's population has more than tripled, Latin America's has nearly quadrupled, and Africa's has increased nearly sixfold. In contrast, the number of people in North America doubled while Europe's population increased by just a third.

Population growth in all the developing regions has already started to slow from the high-growth years, and this trend will continue. Even the high growth rate projected for Africa will be slower than what has occurred over the past few decades. While population growth in Asia and Latin America will follow an arc, peaking around midcentury and then declining, Europe's population has already peaked and is projected to slowly decline. In contrast, North America and Oceania, fueled by immigration, are projected to continue growing well past the time that the other regions start to decline.

Despite a slower pace, total global population is projected to increase by 25% by midcentury. During this time, Africa's population is projected to nearly double. Africa will continue to far outpace growth in other regions and will account for a growing share of global growth. As shown in Figure 2.1, Africa will add 1.1 billion people over the 30 years from 2020 to 2050 and another 1.8 billion by the end of the century.

The population trajectories in other regions differ sharply from Africa's explosive growth. Population growth in Asia and Latin America has been slowing since the peak growth years of the 1960s, and rates will continue to slow, with growth turning negative around midcentury. Asia's population is projected to peak at 5.3 billion and Latin America's at 768 million, with population declines setting in after that.

The growth trajectory for North America, though slowing from previous rates, has been and will continue to be much more stable than growth in the other regions. Most significantly, unlike in other regions except for Africa, population growth in North America, fueled by immigration, is projected to remain positive.

Europe's population growth rate, already the lowest of all the regions, has been slowing since the 1960s. Although the growth has recently fluctuated, Europe's total population was projected to peak around 2020 at 748 million, with continued declines after that.

Before turning to the geographic patterns of population growth, I want to show two other helpful perspectives on global growth.

POPULATION SHIFT BY DEVELOPMENT GROUP AND INCOME LEVEL

Almost all the projected global population growth will occur in developing countries, and more importantly, an increasing share of that growth will occur in the least developed countries, while population in the other less developed countries will stabilize. The UN defines the least developed countries as those most vulnerable to poverty, disease, and environmental damage—and as you might surmise, they have limited human and capital resources for building infrastructure for education, health care, and other social services critical for economic growth and development. In 2019 this development group included 47 such countries. The group referred to as other less developed countries includes the remaining countries in the less developed regions.

Over the 30 years from 1990 to 2020, population in the group of 47 least developed countries doubled from 500 million to 1.1 billion, accounting for 22% of world population growth. As you can see in Figure 2.2, over the subsequent 30 years, from 2020 to 2050, the combined population of these 47 countries is projected to increase by more than 800 million people, accounting for 42% of global growth. After midcentury, as most other countries face stable or shrinking populations, these least developed countries will continue to have explosive growth and will account for the entire global population increase.

FIGURE 2.2   Least developed countries account for an increasing share of global growth.

Population by Development Group, in Billions

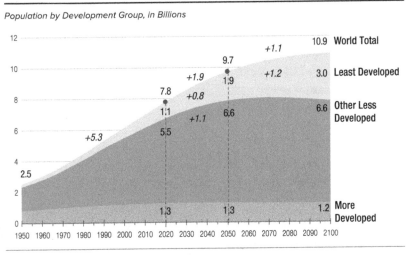

Note: The UN defines the least developed countries as those most vulnerable to poverty, disease, and environmental damage. In 2019, this subgroup included 47 countries. A second subgroup, designated as other less developed countries, includes the remaining less developed countries.

Data source: United Nations, *World Population Prospects 2019,* medium variant.

As a result of the disproportionately high growth rate, the least developed countries, which accounted for 14% of world population in 2020, are projected to increase their share of total to 19% by 2050 and 28% by century's end. Their increasing population share is particularly concerning because these countries have the fewest resources for adapting to the challenges of rapid population growth.

In contrast to this continued rapid population growth in the least developed countries, population in the other less developed countries is projected to stabilize near 6.6 billion around midcentury. This pattern reflects the continued demographic transition: as fertility rates go down, population growth slows and then begins to decline as the population of childbearing women decreases.

While the less developed regions, fueled by high fertility and increasing life expectancy, have been rapidly growing, total population of the more developed countries has grown slowly since 1950, largely due to decades of below-replacement fertility. As shown in

Figure 2.2, total population of the more developed countries will remain stable at around 1.3 billion, at least through midcentury, although many individual countries, including Japan, Russia, and Italy, will see declining total populations. At the end of World War II, the more developed countries accounted for a third of the world's population. The share has declined by half since then and is projected to fall to just 13% by midcentury.

The dichotomy of more and less developed, based on geography, was helpful in the past, when countries in each group had similar demographics. But over time, the characteristics have diverged: developing countries have become more varied, and the number and location of rich countries has expanded beyond the original regional definition. To address this, the United Nations recently started reporting demographic data by per capita income. This breakdown is especially useful because it allows us to clearly see the connection between income level and population growth. The segmentation by income mirrors the trends by development group and shows that most of the world's population growth and the fastest growth is projected to occur in the lower-income groups, those with the fewest financial resources for adapting to the challenges of rapid population growth.

The population growth patterns illustrated in Figure 2.3 reflect what we would expect based on the divergent fertility patterns of the income groups. The high-income countries have seen low fertility for decades, and their populations are either stable or declining. At the opposite end of the scale, in the low-income countries, which generally have the highest fertility rates, the populations are exploding. Many of these countries are also among the UN's group of least developed countries.

The growth patterns for the two middle-income groups start to diverge around 2000, reflecting their different patterns of fertility decline. The upper-middle-income group generally includes countries that experienced steep fertility declines during the 1970s, and now have low fertility rates. These lower fertility rates will lead to an arc of slower population growth followed by population decline. In contrast, the lower-middle-income group saw more

FIGURE 2.3 Population trends in the two middle-income groups started to diverge in 2000, as growth in the lower-middle-income countries accelerated.

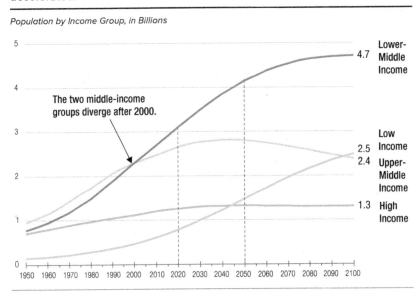

Population by Income Group, in Billions

The two middle-income groups diverge after 2000.

Lower-Middle Income — 4.7

Low Income — 2.5

Upper-Middle Income — 2.4

High Income — 1.3

Data source: United Nations, *World Population Prospects 2019*, medium variant.

gradual fertility declines and demonstrates a population growth rate that is still high, though slowing. The divergent population trajectories of the two middle-income groups demonstrate that the higher incomes typically associated with economic growth and development are also correlated with slower population growth.

You can see the first of these divergent trends in the ***low-income*** countries. Due to continued high fertility rates, this group of countries is projected to have the fastest population growth. With growth of 2.2% per year, this population will increase from 776 million in 2020 to 1.5 billion in 2050, rising from 10% to 15% of world population in just 30 years. Continued high growth over the second half of the century will add another 1 billion people to this group of low-income countries, increasing their share of world population to 23%.

The ***lower-middle-income*** group, the most populous of the income groups, is projected to grow at 1% per year between 2020 and 2050, adding 1 billion to its population. After 2050 growth will slow. The two lower-income groups together accounted for half the world population in 2020, and by 2050, their combined share of global population will total 57%, increasing to 66% by the end of the century as their disproportionately fast growth continues.

In contrast, the ***upper-middle-income*** group of countries generally had steep fertility declines from 1970 to 2000 and is projected to face a 5% decline in total population by midcentury, with the decline accelerating during the second half of the century. Population growth rates of the individual countries in this group diverge, depending mainly on the timing of the fertility declines. This upper-middle-income group is projected to decline from 34% of world population in 2020 to 29% in 2050, and just 22% by 2100.

Finally, as you might now expect, the ***high-income*** group of countries, which has experienced below-replacement fertility since 1990, is projected to stabilize at around 1.3 billion. As we have seen, many high-income countries, including Japan, Russia, and Germany, will have large population losses, while others, such as the United States, Canada, and the United Kingdom, all of which have been fueled by immigration, are projected to continue growing. Overall, the high-income group is projected to slowly decline in share of world population, from 16% in 2020, to 14% in 2050 and 12% by end of the century.

REGIONAL POPULATION GROWTH

So far, you have seen the projected shift to Africa and the accelerating population growth in lower-income countries. Now we turn to detailed analysis of the changes projected for each region.

AFRICA

Fueled by extremely high fertility, Africa's explosive population growth will continue, and its high growth rate will remain well above population growth rates in other regions. As a result of this disproportionately fast growth, the world's population distribution will shift markedly toward Africa, with Africa's share of global population increasing dramatically while Asia's share declines.

The comparison to other developing regions is striking. Africa's population has grown from a sliver of the world's total to a large—and growing—share of it. As shown by the orange line in Figure 2.4, Africa's population has increased nearly sixfold since 1950, from just 228 million to 1.3 billion in 2020. Just over the past 30 years, Africa's population more than doubled, from 630 million to 1.3 billion, and it is projected to nearly double again over the next 30 years, increasing to 2.5 billion by 2050. By the century's end, Africa will have a total population of 4.3 billion, more than three times its 2020 population.

This pattern of Africa outpacing other regions in population growth will continue, even though growth will be slower. Figure 2.5 shows how Africa's population growth rate (orange line) accelerated over the 1960s and 1970s, and peaked during the 1980s, even as other developing regions started to slow. While over the 30 years from 1990 to 2020 Africa's population growth slowed, averaging 2.5% per year, its rate of increase was still more than twice that of

FIGURE 2.4 Africa's population is on track to nearly double to 2.5 billion by midcentury.

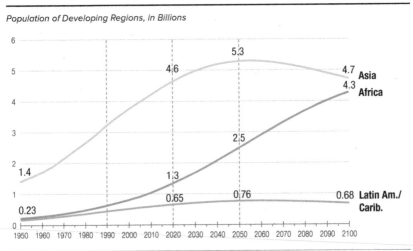

Population of Developing Regions, in Billions

Data source: United Nations, *World Population Prospects 2019*, medium variant.

FIGURE 2.5   The population growth rate in Africa is projected to remain far higher than everywhere else.

Average Annual Population Growth, by Region, % per Year

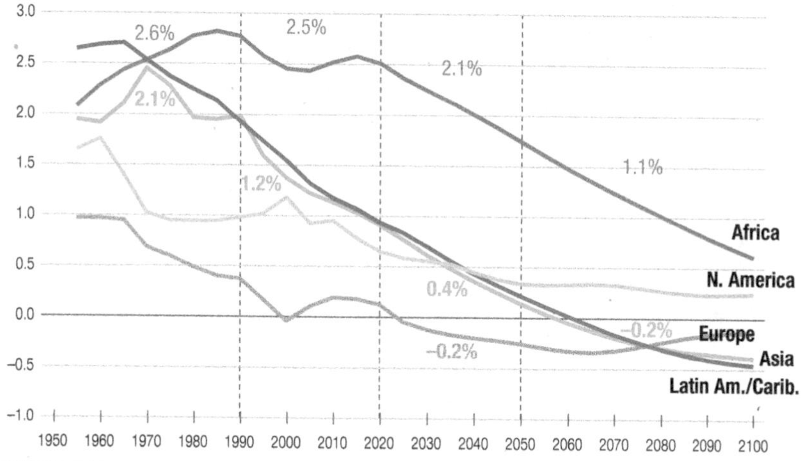

Data source: United Nations, *World Population Prospects 2019*, medium variant.

Asia and Latin America. And the population growth rate, though still extremely high, will continue to slow due to declining fertility. Africa's population growth is projected to slow further to 2.1% per year over the next 30 years. The trend is not universal across Africa. While the regionwide growth is projected to slow, many countries, as you will see later in the chapter, are on pace to see growth rates exceeding 3%.

Over the second half of this century, growth in Africa is projected to slow by half, decreasing to 1.1% per year. But even at this slower pace, Africa is projected to add another 1.8 billion people between 2050 and 2100. In contrast, Asia, Europe, and Latin America will all have declining populations during this period, which means that Africa will account for a shocking 157% of the global increase.

Africa's explosive population growth is driven mainly by its stubbornly high fertility rate. Although fertility has declined from its peak of 6.7 births per woman in 1970, the 2020 rate of 4.4 is more than twice the fertility rates for Asia and Latin America. The size of the future fertility decline is a critical determinant of population growth. An accelerated decline would further dampen the population growth, while a stall or slowing of the fertility decline would fuel even faster population growth.

Increasing life expectancy has also added to population, as fewer people die at younger ages. Life expectancy gains fueled by notable declines in child mortality have been significant throughout Africa, and with the greater survival of children, life expectancy at birth increased from 37 years in 1950 to 63 in 2020. Even so, Africa's life expectancy at birth is still well below the average in Asia (73 years) and Latin America (75 years).

Pace of Fertility Decline

To assess the impacts of different rates of fertility decline, the UN presents alternatives to its most likely case. Under the UN's medium variant projection—the most likely case—Africa's fertility rate is projected to decline to 3.1 births per woman by 2050, down sharply from 4.4 in 2020. This leads to a projected total population on the continent of 2.5 billion in 2050, growing to 4.3 billion by the century's end, as you can see above in Figure 2.4. The alternative projections, shown in Figure 2.6, assume variations in the births per woman of one-half child, higher or lower.

Under the high-fertility scenario, with fertility falling more slowly, Africa's total population would reach 5.9 billion by the end of the century. This slower fertility decline under the high-fertility variant adds 1.6 billion more people. Conversely, in the low-fertility variant, if the fertility decline accelerates, total population would reach only 3.0 billion by century's end, 1.3 billion less than in the medium variant. Finally, a decline to replacement rate, not a likely scenario but considered for illustrative purposes, would lead to much slower growth. Even in this scenario of replacement-rate fertility, total population would continue to grow over the short term due to the population momentum of a youthful population; this occurs when a high share of young women leads to a higher number of families, even though average family size would be smaller.

As you can guess, these alternative fertility assumptions lead to vastly different population trajectories. Figure 2.6 shows how

FIGURE 2.6   A faster decline in Africa's fertility rate would significantly dampen its population growth.

Africa's Population under Alternative Fertility Scenarios, in Billions

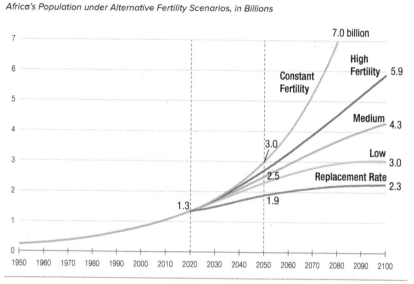

Data source: United Nations, *World Population Prospects 2019*, medium variant.

the differences may appear small over the next 30 years, but the impacts of each fertility scenario accumulate, and the differences widen as the fertility rate patterns take hold. The increasing difference over time underscores the urgency of making short-term policy changes to reduce fertility, if indeed slower population growth is desired. It is not surprising that a key policy lever for achieving lower fertility is the education of high school girls.

Population Growth Is Concentrated

As mentioned earlier, fertility declines will differ across countries, and therefore, population growth across Africa will be uneven, with the highest growth occurring chiefly in sub-Saharan countries. Nearly half the population gain in Africa over the next 30 years is projected to occur in just six countries: Nigeria, the Democratic Republic of the Congo (DRC), Ethiopia, Tanzania, Egypt, and Angola. These gains range from 195 million in Nigeria to 45 million in Angola. The total growth of 562 million in these six countries represents 49% of Africa's gain and a startling 29% of the world's population growth over the next 30 years.

It is especially important to understand these countries where growth is concentrated, not just because they are Africa's most populous, but because their rapid population growth poses enormous challenges to their economic and political stability. These countries, through government policy and private economic activity, will need to provide education, employment, and housing opportunities to youthful populations seeking economic prospects and social stability in geographic areas that suffer from significant economic, political, and climate vulnerabilities.

Ten Most Populous

Figure 2.7 illustrates the dramatic population trajectories for the 10 most populous African countries as of 2020. Nigeria, with 200 million people, is by far the most populous country in Africa, nearly double the size of Ethiopia, the second largest. Nigeria, the world's seventh most populous country in 2020, is projected to double its population and surpass the US population before midcentury, becoming the third largest and bumping the US to fourth largest.

Of the 10 most populous African countries, five are projected to at least triple their populations by 2100. Tanzania and the DRC are projected to more than quadruple in population. Niger and Angola, shown with dashed lines, are among the fastest-growing countries and will soon join Africa's top 10 ranking. Niger has the world's highest fertility rate, 7.0 births per woman in 2020, and its population is projected to increase nearly sevenfold, from 24 million in 2020 to 165 million by 2100; Angola is projected to increase nearly sixfold, from 33 million to 188 million.

The population shift to Africa you have been reading about here is important: First, because it means that an increasing share of global population growth will occur in the most vulnerable populations—those with the lowest life expectancy, lowest incomes, and poorest education. Also, the dim economic prospects in tandem with environmental threats will continue to fuel large-scale out-migration, which

FIGURE 2.7 Nigeria is on pace to double over the next 30 years, surpassing US population by midcentury.

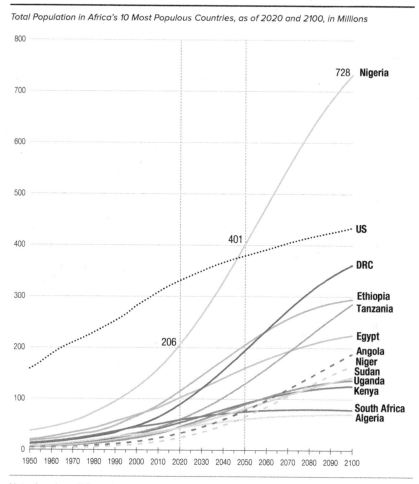

Total Population in Africa's 10 Most Populous Countries, as of 2020 and 2100, in Millions

Note: Angola and Niger, shown with dashed lines, join the top 10 after 2050.

Data source: United Nations, *World Population Prospects 2019*, medium variant.

will in turn affect other countries. The political instability associated with out-migration combined with poor economic prospects make this region a major threat to global stability.

While Africa will certainly be a source of political, social, and environmental challenges, on a more positive note, Africa is a new frontier for many investors and could be a source of economic growth and innovation. Most of the worldwide growth in working-age population will occur in Africa, so there are vast opportunities for productive employment. Much, of course, depends on education, especially for young women. At the same time, as mentioned above, Africa will likely also be a huge source of out-migration as people flee environmental challenges. Whether these migrants can provide needed labor elsewhere is another critical uncertainty.

ASIA

Asia's Population Growth Is Slowing and Will Soon Decline

In contrast to Africa's continued explosive growth, Asia's population growth will slow dramatically and then start declining after mid-century. These vastly different trajectories, as you see in Figure 2.4 above, largely reflect the divergent timing and pace of fertility declines in these two regions. While Africa's fertility rate remains extremely high, averaging 4.4 births per woman in 2020, the fertility decline that occurred in Asia, falling to 2.2 births per woman in 2020, has resulted in slower population growth, with declines projected to occur in countries throughout Asia.

More specifically, Asia's population is projected to peak around 2055, then begin to decline, ending the century at 4.7 billion, close to its size in 2020. Due to its disproportionately slower growth, Asia's share of global population is projected to decline from 60% in 2020 to 54% by 2050, falling to 43% by the end of the century, while Africa's share increases to 39%.

Demographic Milestones: China and India Diverge

Several demographic milestones in the coming decades will transform many of our current perspectives. Around 2027, India will overtake China to become the world's most populous country, and around that same time, Africa's population will soar past both. Figure 2.8 provides a useful perspective on the rapid pace of Africa's population growth as it passes the 1 billion mark and is on track to more than triple its current population.

FIGURE 2.8   Population milestones in 2030 include India surpassing China and Africa soaring past both.

Population of China, India, and Africa, in Billions

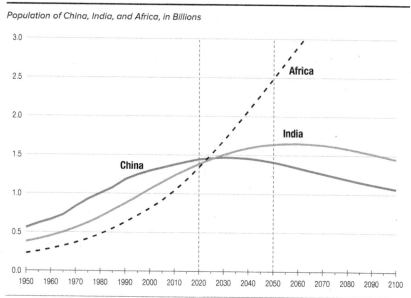

Data source: United Nations, *World Population Prospects 2019,* medium variant.

You might be interested to note that the world's two most populous countries—China and India—are contributing very differently to Asia's overall population trajectory. China's population is projected to decline after 2030, while India's population is projected to continue growing until around 2060. China's low fertility rate has resulted in a decreasing number of children, a rapidly aging population, a shrinking workforce, and a soon-to-be-shrinking total population. In contrast, India's fertility rate has declined more gradually than China's and is still above replacement rate. India's population will continue to grow for another 40 years, and the aging of its population will occur more gradually.

Both China and India are projected to see significant population declines during the second half of the century, with China declining by 337 million and India by 189 million. China is projected to end the century at 1.065 billion, 26% smaller than in 2020 and approximately equal to its 1985 population. Despite its own population

decline, India is projected to end the century one-third more populous than China. At 1.45 billion, India's century-end population
will be down significantly from the projected 2059 peak, but up
slightly from its 2020 level. In addition to their different population trajectories, their age distributions will follow divergent patterns, with India's workforce continuing to expand while China's
will shrink.

Most Populous Countries

As in China and India, most Asian countries will see an arc of population growth, with growth slowing and then declining in the second half of the century. We saw that China's population is projected
to peak in the next few years, while India's population arc extends
higher and longer, peaking after midcentury. Figure 2.9 shows the
varied timing of the slowdowns and declines of the other most populous Asian countries. Population has already started declining in
Japan. Growth is slowing in Indonesia, Bangladesh, and Vietnam,
with all three projected to have declining populations after 2050.
Iran is projected to grow slightly faster than Turkey and Vietnam,
with its population peaking at just over 105 million around 2060.
Pakistan is the notable exception and is projected to see continued
explosive growth. Driven by high fertility, Pakistan's population
increased nearly sixfold over the past 70 years, from 38 million to
221 million in 2020. With a fertility rate of 3.6 births per woman in
2020, the population of Pakistan is projected to surpass Indonesia's
by 2050 and to nearly double to 400 million by 2100.

With an increase of 259 million people over the next 30 years,
India will be the world's largest population gainer by far, and will
account for 40% of Asia's growth and 13% of global population growth.
India, Pakistan, and Indonesia, the three largest population gainers in Asia, will together account for two-thirds of Asia's population
growth over the next 30 years, and 22% of global growth. In contrast,
during this same time, China's population will decline by 37 million.

Figure 2.10 contrasts the population growth of Pakistan and
Bangladesh, along with Nigeria—three countries with similar population profiles until around 2000. Driven by divergent patterns of

FIGURE 2.9 Patterns diverge, but growth is slowing in Asia's most populous countries.

Total Population, Eight Most Populous Asian Countries after China and India, in Millions

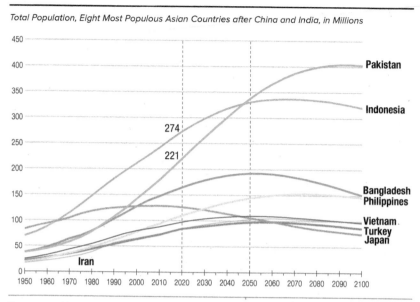

Data source: United Nations, *World Population Prospects 2019*, medium variant.

FIGURE 2.10 Divergent fertility declines set in motion vastly different population trajectories.

Total Population in Bangladesh, Pakistan, and Nigeria, in Millions

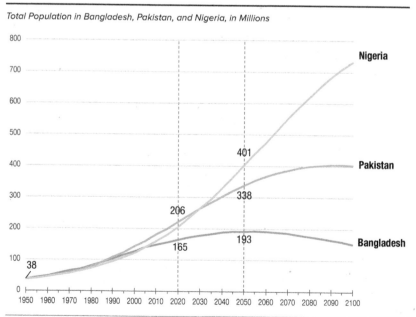

Data source: United Nations, *World Population Prospects 2019*, medium variant.

fertility rate declines, their population trajectories have already taken vastly different shapes over just the past 20 years, and the variations among them will increase over the coming decades. Due to a family-planning program that dramatically reduced its fertility rate from nearly 7.0 births per woman to 2.0, Bangladesh's population growth has already slowed and is projected to peak soon after midcentury. In contrast to Bangladesh's below-replacement-rate fertility, the UN projects that Pakistan's fertility rate, 3.6 in 2020, will fall to 2.4 births per woman by 2050, while Nigeria's fertility rate is projected to remain extremely high, falling only slowly to 3.6 by 2050. As a result, Nigeria's population is projected to grow three times faster than Pakistan's, reaching 400 million by 2050, and more than 700 million by 2100. Pakistan's population is projected to double to 400 million by the century's end, with the arc of population decline starting to show. China and India are the only other countries that have ever been this populous, and they reached their totals with much slower growth than what is projected for either Nigeria or Pakistan. This underscores concerns about whether these countries can effectively manage their newfound large size and rapid growth.

Asia's Largest Economies Will See Population Decline

While Asia's total population is on pace to grow by 14% over the next 30 years, three of its largest economies are projected to see continued population decline. With a projected drop of 37 million, China will have the region's largest absolute decline over the next 30 years. Japan will have the largest relative decline, with a 16% decline (a drop of 21 million), followed by South Korea, with a 9% decline (a drop of nearly 5 million). Thailand and Taiwan are projected to see population declines of around 6%. After midcentury, shrinking total populations will be the norm rather than the exception for most of Asia.

The Population Shift to South Asia

In the past, East Asia was the most populous subregion of the continent, accounting for more than 40% of Asia's total population. The population concentration, however, has shifted in recent years to South Asia. As population growth diverges across the continent, the population shift from East Asia to South Asia will accelerate, driven by large gains in India and Pakistan, and large declines in China and Japan. South Asia has consistently been growing faster than East Asia, increasing to 42% of Asia's total population in 2020, while East Asia's share of the region has declined from nearly half in 1950 to just 36% in 2020. As shown in Figure 2.11, the trajectories differ markedly: East Asia's population is nearing its peak, while South Asia's population will continue growing until around 2070, then slowly decline.

This population decline in East Asia is important for several reasons. China and Japan are the second- and third-largest economies in the world, so how they adapt to the challenge of declining population and shrinking workforces will be important for the global economy.

FIGURE 2.11   The population shift to South Asia will accelerate as East Asia's powerhouse shrinks.

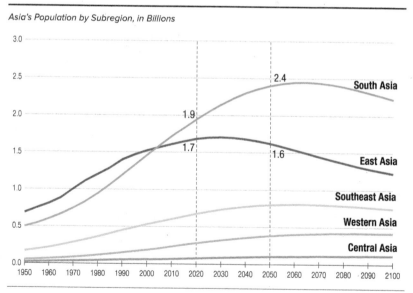

Asia's Population by Subregion, in Billions

Note: South Asia includes, in order of population, India, Pakistan, Bangladesh, Iran, Afghanistan, Nepal, Sri Lanka, Bhutan, and Maldives. East Asia includes, in order of population, China, Japan, South Korea, North Korea, Taiwan, Hong Kong, Mongolia, and Macao. Western Asia extends from Turkey to Yemen and includes many countries that are generally thought of as part of the Middle East.

Data source: United Nations, *World Population Prospects 2019,* medium variant.

This region is also home to several of the most rapidly aging economies in the world, including China, Japan, South Korea, and Hong Kong. In Chapter 6, you will read about the demographics of population aging and learn about the varied patterns of aging.

Of Asia's five subregions, Western Asia has grown the fastest. Although its growth will slow, its current population of 280 million is projected to increase by two-thirds, reaching over 400 million by 2100. This is a relatively small subregion, but it is home to some of the most volatile populations. Over the next 30 years, Western Asia is projected to add 103 million people, with the largest gains projected to occur in Iraq (an addition of 31 million) and Yemen (18 million). Other large gains are projected for Syria (16 million), Turkey (13 million), and Saudi Arabia (10 million). Iraq's growth trajectory is particularly astonishing: from a 1950 population of less than 6 million, Iraq's population increased more than sixfold to 40 million in 2020 and is projected to reach 71 million by 2050 and end the century at 108 million, approaching three times its 2020 size.

LATIN AMERICA AND THE CARIBBEAN

Latin America, though much smaller than Asia, will have a similar demographic trajectory. Both regions experienced rapid population growth over the past 70 years, but that growth is now slowing dramatically, and after midcentury, their total populations will start declining. Although the main driver for the population slowdown in these two regions is their declining fertility rate, there are some key differences in the underlying demographics. Latin America's overall fertility rate decline has closely tracked Asia's, but Latin America has enjoyed a higher life expectancy, and as a result, its population growth rate has been slightly higher, as illustrated in Figure 2.5. Over the next 30 years, growth will slow in both regions, falling to near zero by 2050. Both regions will see their populations peak around midcentury, then decline, falling almost back to their 2020 levels by the end of the century.

With 654 million people, Latin America accounts for just 8% of global population. Comparison with other developing regions offers a useful perspective on its growth: Latin America's 2020 population is about one-seventh the size of Asia's population, and about half the size of Africa's. This population difference will increase noticeably by century's end, as Africa's population triples and Latin America's stabilizes. By that time, Latin America's population is projected to be one-sixth the size of Africa's, and its share of global population will decrease to 6%.

Population Is Projected to Decline after Midcentury in All Three Subregions

Latin America and the Caribbean includes three subregions: Central America, the Caribbean, and South America. As shown in Figure 2.12, each of the three subregions is projected to display an arc of slowing population growth followed by decline after midcentury. Despite the general similarity, certain differences across the subregions have important economic and political implications. South

FIGURE 2.12 Population is projected to decline after midcentury in all three subregions of Latin America.

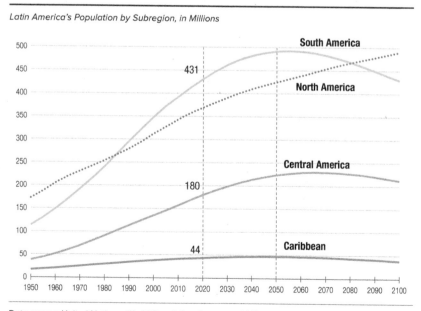

Latin America's Population by Subregion, in Millions

Data source: United Nations, *World Population Prospects 2019,* medium variant.

America, the largest subregion, will see the steepest population arc, with population starting to decline soon after midcentury. In contrast, Central America will continue to have the fastest growth, and will see only a gradual population decline beginning toward the end of the century. North America, shown here for reference, is projected to have continued population growth, fueled by immigration—in part from Latin America.

With a 2020 population of 180 million, *Central America* accounts for 27% of the region's population. It will continue to grow faster than both South America and the Caribbean, and it is projected to account for a disproportionate 40% of the regional growth over the next 30 years. This subregion includes Mexico, with 129 million people; the three Northern Triangle countries—Guatemala, Honduras, and El Salvador—with a combined total of 34 million; plus four other small countries—Nicaragua, Costa Rica, Panama, and Belize.

Over the next 30 years, Central America is projected to add 44 million people. Mexico, with a gain of 26 million people, will be the largest contributor to population growth by 2050. But the fastest growth is projected to occur in Guatemala, at 1.4% per year, and Honduras, 1.1% per year, compared with 0.6% average annual growth in Mexico and 0.5% for Latin America overall. This means Guatemala's total population will increase by 50%, from 18 million in 2020 to 27 million in 2050. As shown in Figure 2.13, the three Northern Triangle countries combined will see an increase of 14 million from 2020 to 2050. This growth is particularly worrisome because it brings challenges that may lead to political violence and economic weakness, potentially increasing pressure on residents to migrate, both internally and northward to Mexico and the United States.

South America has a 2020 population of 431 million and accounts for two-thirds of Latin America's total. Over the next 30 years South America is projected to add 61 million people, but the total number of people will shrink by a similar amount during the second half of the century. As a result, South America is projected to end the century at about the same population as in 2020.

FIGURE 2.13   Guatemala's population is projected to grow by 50% over the next 30 years, gaining 9 million.

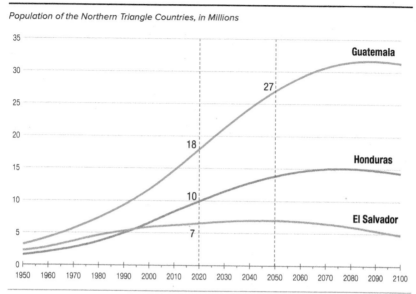

Population of the Northern Triangle Countries, in Millions

Data source: United Nations, *World Population Prospects 2019*, medium variant.

Figure 2.14 shows population growth for the eight most populous countries in Latin America. Brazil, with 213 million people, is the world's sixth most populous country and by far the most populous country in Latin America, followed by Mexico. The two next most populous countries are much smaller. Colombia, with 51 million, and Argentina, with 45 million, are each less than half the size of Mexico, and their trajectories of population growth differ dramatically. For Brazil, the projected arc of population decline is steep, with a projected gain of 8% (16 million more people) over the next 30 years, followed by a decline of 21% (48 million fewer people) by century's end. For Mexico, population growth over the next 30 years at 20% will be faster than in Brazil, and the decline after 2050 will be slower, just 9%.

Like Brazil and Mexico, most countries in Latin America will face population declines after 2050. Argentina and Guatemala are exceptions to this pattern and are expected to see continued population

FIGURE 2.14   Brazil faces a 21% population decline after midcentury, a loss of 48 million.

Total Population, Most Populous Countries in Latin America, in Millions

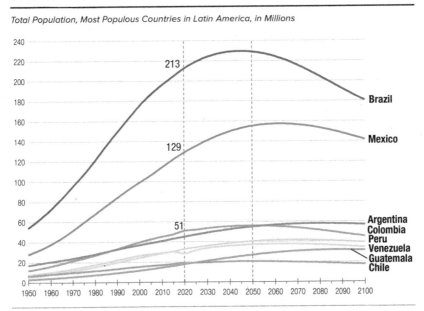

Data source: United Nations, *World Population Prospects 2019,* medium variant.

growth, with the timing of their fertility declines accounting for most of the differences. Mexico, Brazil, Colombia, and Chile all had large fertility declines that will contribute to the projected slowdown in population growth.

Turning to the region's largest economies, the population decline is important because it will play out in shrinking workforces and aging populations, as you will see in later chapters. The exception is Argentina, the region's third-largest economy. Unlike most other Latin American countries, Argentina has had a low fertility rate since the 1950s and did not experience the steep fertility declines that will reduce population growth among its neighbors. Also, Argentina has had a relatively high life expectancy, which also contributes to its population increase.

Migration and other population changes associated with political and economic upheaval are difficult to anticipate and forecast, but it is possible to at least understand the current population trajectories and assumptions. It is important to consider several events in Latin America. As mentioned above, the Northern Triangle countries of Central America, though small in total population, are the fastest-growing countries in the region. This is potentially worrisome from a national security point of view, as these countries continue to be a politically fraught source of migrant flows to Mexico and the United States. Secondly, the recent population dip in Venezuela reflects the massive out-migration stemming from its economic and political crises. The UN projection shown in Figure 2.14 assumes the population will recover to its previous level. Another political impact that you should consider for its longer-term implications is the massive internal displacement and out-migration that occurred in Colombia as the civil conflict associated with the FARC militant group escalated in the 1990s.

The third subregion of Latin America, the *Caribbean*, has a 2020 population of 44 million, or 7% of Latin America's total. The subregion includes three large countries of about 11 million each— Haiti, Cuba, and the Dominican Republic—plus 25 small island nations and territories. Cuba's population is already shrinking and rapidly aging, and is projected to decline by 10% by midcentury. In contrast, Haiti, the poorest and fastest-growing country in the region, is projected to grow by 30%, to 15 million, by midcentury, before leveling off. Most of the 25 small island nations and territories are rapidly aging and are projected to have declining populations. Notably, Puerto Rico's population has been declining since 2000, falling 22% from 3.7 to 2.9 million in just 20 years, with further declines projected.

NORTH AMERICA

Largely due to immigration, North America will deviate from the pattern of population decline seen in most advanced economies. Instead, despite decades of low fertility, North America will see continued population growth. The region, which includes the United States and Canada, has a 2020 population of 369 million, representing just 5% of the global population. It is currently about half the size of Europe's population and slightly more than half of Latin America's.

The United States, with about 330 million people, accounts for 90% of the region's total, with Canada comprising the remaining 10%. Figure 2.15 shows the population projections for these two countries with Brazil and Mexico, the two most populous countries in Latin America, included for reference and comparison.

It is important to understand that these population projections for North America depend on continued immigration. Given the recent discussions and restrictive policies already implemented, there is reason to question the likelihood of this growth trajectory. Because immigration plays such a key role in this region, understanding its contribution to total population growth is critical. According to the UN's medium-variant assumptions, the United States will add about 50 million people over the next 30 years and another 50 million over the second half of the century. The *natural increase*, equal to the

FIGURE 2.15   Unlike other large economies, the US and Canada are projected to see continued population growth.

Total Population, North America and Its Most Populous Neighbors, in Millions

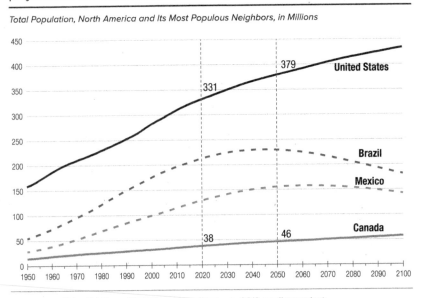

Data source: United Nations, *World Population Prospects 2019*, medium variant.

difference between births and deaths, is projected to slow dramatically, while the current level of ***net migration***, about 1 million per year, is projected to continue. (Net migration equals the number of cross-border arrivals minus the number of people leaving.) This means that over the next 30 years, the natural increase will add about 18 million people, while net migration is projected to contribute 31 million to the population, 64% of the total.

Figure 2.16 shows you how the two components of growth combine. As illustrated in Panel A, the average number of births (the light blue dashed line) peaked at 4.3 million per year in the early 1960s, near the height of the post–World War II baby boom. After falling during the baby bust, the number of births rebounded during the 1980s and 1990s, as the baby boomers had children of their own, a time that became known as the echo boom. Since around 1990, with the fertility rate hovering around replacement rate, the number of births averaged around 4 million per year. At the same time, due mainly to aging of the population, the number of deaths (the solid black line) was increasing. Around 2010, the natural population increase, represented by the gray bars in the figure, began declining. The UN projects that while the number of births will remain high, the increasing death rate will reduce the natural increase, causing it to slowly decline to near zero by midcentury. The UN also projects that net migration, which has averaged 1 million people per year, will continue at the same level. You can see this in the blue bars in Panel B.

Panel C combines the two components, showing that immigration becomes an increasingly important contributor to population growth in the United States. The final panel shows that immigration as a share of total population gain will increase sharply over the next 30 years. According to the UN projection, by 2050, net migration will account for 90% of all population growth, assuming immigration will continue at its current level. In a 2020 analysis of alternative immigration scenarios, the US Census Bureau concluded that if immigration falls to zero, total population growth in the United States will stall and possibly turn negative.

FIGURE 2.16   US population growth is driven by immigration. In 2020, net migration accounted for about half of its total population growth.

United States: Components of Population Growth, Five-Year Annual Average

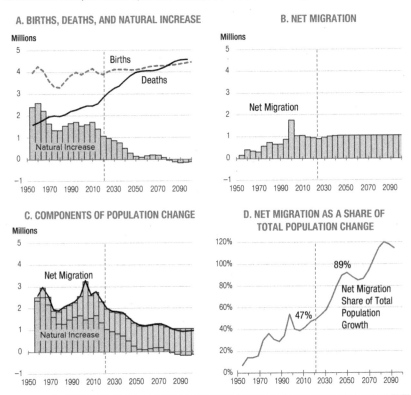

Note: Natural increase equals births minus deaths. Net migration equals the number of cross-border arrivals minus the number of people leaving.

Data source: United Nations, *World Population Prospects 2019,* medium variant.

EUROPE

Since at least World War II, Europe has been the slowest-growing region, and it will be the first region to see its population start to decline. (See Figure 2.5 above for a comparison of regional population growth rates.) At 748 million in 2020, Europe's population is projected to shrink by 37 million, or 5% by midcentury. This population loss places Europe about 30 years ahead of Latin America and Asia in its arc of population decline. Immediately after World War II, Europe accounted for almost a quarter of the world's population. Since then, world population has more than tripled, but Europe's population has increased by only 36%. As a result, Europe's share of world population declined to just 10% in 2020. The projected decrease of more than 100 million people by century's end will reduce Europe's population to 630 million, or just 6% of the world's total.

Growth Differs by Subregion

The direction and patterns of population growth are projected to vary across Europe's four subregions. The population changes over the next 30 years range from an 11% decline in Eastern Europe to an 8% gain in Northern Europe. As shown in Figure 2.17, the population losses over the next 30 years will be concentrated in Eastern Europe (a drop of 31 million) and Southern Europe (16 million). These two subregions will each see a decline of around 10%. In contrast, Northern Europe is projected to see an 8% population gain

FIGURE 2.17   Europe's population losses are concentrated in Eastern and Southern Europe.

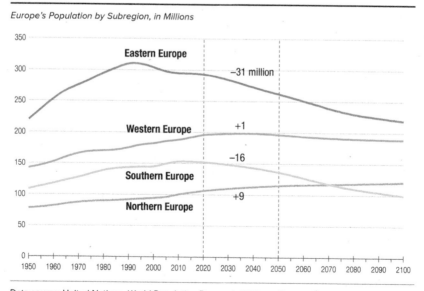

Europe's Population by Subregion, in Millions

Data source: United Nations, *World Population Prospects 2019,* medium variant.

(an addition of 9 million), while Western Europe's population will stabilize. Each of the subregions has one or two large countries that dominate the population trends for that area, but with only a few exceptions, most of the other countries within each region generally follow similar trends. The subregion patterns and the country exceptions are profiled below.

All European countries have experienced decades of below-replacement-rate fertility, even though some have recently seen slight gains. Most of Europe is rapidly aging, and as the population ages, the death rate increases. Due to the increasing death rate, the natural increase, equal to birth minus deaths, has rapidly declined in most European countries. In the face of this slowing or declining natural increase, net migration has become the primary driver of population growth in many countries. The projections generally assume continued low fertility and continued migration. The level of migration is an important uncertainty, which you will read about in a later chapter.

Eastern Europe, with 293 million people, accounts for nearly 40% of Europe's total population, and its population is projected to decline by more than 10%, or 31 million people, over the next 30 years, with continued declines after that. Russia, with 146 million people, is by far the most populous country in Eastern Europe, and accounts for half the region's total population. Despite a recent uptick, Russia's population is projected to decline by 10 million over the next 30 years. Population in almost all the Eastern European countries has already peaked and will steadily decline. Notably, Poland, with a 2020 population of 38 million, is projected to see a 12% decline. These population decreases in Eastern Europe are primarily fueled by extremely low fertility rates and increasing death rates. The fertility rates throughout Eastern Europe fell sharply after 1990, and although the rates have risen slightly over the past decade, they are still well below replacement rate.

Southern Europe, which is about half the size of Eastern Europe, is projected to have a 10% decline by midcentury, losing 16 million people. Italy, with 60 million people, is the most populous in the subregion and is projected to see a 10% decline by midcentury, followed by an even steeper decline after that. Spain, the region's next most populous at 47 million people, follows a similar pattern. Many of the Balkan countries—Serbia, Croatia, Bosnia and Herzegovina, and Albania—have already been declining in population, and that trend will continue. As noted above, the losses generally stem from extremely low fertility rates. Italy and Spain both had steep fertility declines during the 1980s, with rates reaching as low as 1.2 births per woman by 2000. Despite recent upticks to 1.4, fertility rates in both countries fell back to 1.3 as of 2020, contributing further to their population declines.

Unlike its neighbors to the east and south, **Western Europe**, which accounts for a quarter of Europe's population, has been steadily growing since around 1980. The population, currently 196 million, is projected to stabilize over the next few decades, with only small declines occurring after midcentury. Germany, the most populous country in Western Europe, is projected to see a small decline of about 4 million, or 4%, over the next 30 years. Most other Western European countries, including France, will see continued, albeit small, population gains until at least midcentury.

The two largest countries in Western Europe, Germany and France, have different demographic profiles, which in turn lead to these divergent patterns. Although all European countries have below-replacement-rate fertility, France in 2020 had one of the higher rates at 1.85 births per woman, compared with just 1.59 in Germany. Possibly reflecting the success of its pronatal policies, the fertility rate in France has been hovering near 2.0 for the last 10 years, after falling to a low of 1.7 in 1995. In contrast to the moderate decline in France, Germany's fertility rate fell to a low of 1.3 in 1995, and the recent uptick raised the rate to only 1.59. At the same time as the number of children was declining, both the number and share of older people were rapidly increasing, and now, both countries face aging populations and a rising number of deaths. As a result, the natural increase in population is slowing, and in the case of Germany, turned negative in 1975, when deaths exceeded births.

Until recently net migration has compensated for the natural population decline in Germany. According to the UN projection, after 2020, net migration will no longer offset the accelerating natural population decline, so Germany's total population will decrease. The pattern differs in France, where both natural increase and net migration are adding to total population growth. According to the UN projection, natural increase will remain positive until around 2040; after that, net migration will offset the natural decline until around 2050.

Finally, we see that ***Northern Europe***, which is currently about half the size of Western Europe, is the one area of Europe projected to continue growing until the century's end, driven by population gains in the United Kingdom. With a 2020 population of 68 million, the UK is by far the largest country in Northern Europe, accounting for 64% of the subregion's total population of 106 million. It is projected to add 6 million people before midcentury, with net migration contributing nearly 80% of this gain—4.9 million out of 6.2 million. The next most populous country in Northern Europe is Sweden, with just 10 million people. The combined population of the five Nordic countries—Sweden, Denmark, Norway, Finland, and Iceland—reached 27 million in 2020, or 26% of Northern Europe's total. The recent strong population growth in the Nordics is expected to slow but remain positive through the rest of the century. In contrast, the only countries in Northern Europe with populations that have not been growing are the three small Baltic states—Estonia, Latvia, and Lithuania—where the population decline already under way is projected to continue.

Europe's 10 Most Populous Countries

As noted above, the population trajectories differ across Europe's subregions, with the largest countries in each region establishing the overall trend. Figure 2.18 illustrates these differences. Over the next 30 years Europe's total population is projected to decline by 37 million. The largest population declines are projected to occur in Russia (a drop of 10 million), Ukraine (9 million), Italy (6 million), Poland (5 million), Germany (4 million), and Spain (3 million). Among the most populous countries, the only countries with projected

FIGURE 2.18   Among Europe's large populations, only the UK and France are projected to grow.

Europe's 10 Most Populous Countries, Population in Millions

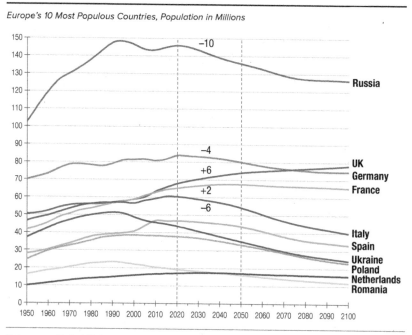

Data source: United Nations, *World Population Prospects 2019,* medium variant.

population growth are the UK (an addition of 6 million) and France (2 million), with increases fueled mainly by net migration. Although their populations are small, several other countries are projected to have large percentage gains, including Sweden, Norway, Switzerland, and Ireland.

It is important for you to understand the different drivers behind these population shifts. The steep declines in Russia and Ukraine are not surprising, given the low fertility rates and increasing death rates. What is more notable is that Germany's population appears relatively stable, with only a 4% decline by 2050, a loss of less than 4 million. Up until recently, net migration more than compensated for Germany's natural population decrease, but as the natural decline expands, migration will fall short, leading to the projected population decline. The situation differs for the UK and France, where net migration is projected to offset the natural declines.

OCEANIA

Oceania, which includes Australia, New Zealand, and numerous Pacific islands, is a tiny but strategically important region. With a total population of 43 million, it accounts for less than 1% of the world's population. It is a region of economic and geographic diversity, including two high-income advanced economies—Australia and New Zealand; one low-income, developing country—Papua New Guinea; one continent—Australia; and many small island nations and territories, including the US territory of Guam. Because of its small population, geographic location, and economic ties with Asia, Oceania is often analyzed as part of Asia, but because of its strategic location and alliances with the United States, I treat the region separately.

Moreover, several demographic differences distinguish the countries and subregions of Oceania from the surrounding geographic area. The region overall is growing faster than Asia, and the population drivers differ. Net migration contributes significantly to population growth in Australia and New Zealand, while high fertility fuels population growth in Papua New Guinea and many of the small islands.

Australia, the world's 14th largest economy, with 25 million people in 2020, accounted for 60% of the region's total population. Population growth here has been faster than in other advanced economies for two reasons: First, even though it hovers below replacement rate, fertility there is higher than in other advanced economies. Since 1980, the rate has stayed close to replacement, and the natural increase of births minus deaths has remained positive. Second, as in the United States, net migration has accounted for a large share of Australia's population growth. Over the last 30 years population growth in Australia has been almost evenly split between natural increase and net migration. With a declining natural increase, net migration at the same level over the next 30 years will account for a growing share of total population gain, projected to average nearly 60%. As a result of these drivers, Australia is projected to have the fastest workforce growth of all the large high-income economies.

Papua New Guinea, which gained independence from Australia in 1975, is the second most populous country in the region, nearly double the size of New Zealand. Its 9 million people account for 21% of Oceania's regional population. Occupying the eastern half of the island of New Guinea, Papua New Guinea is a low-income, rapidly growing developing country, whose population growth is fueled by a high fertility rate. Growing much faster than its neighbors—Indonesia and the Philippines—Papua New Guinea is more like the fast-growing countries of Africa. More importantly, Papua New Guinea has a strategic location near the edge of Asia and attracts significant foreign investment in its vast natural resources.

Overall, during the next 30 years, Oceania is projected to grow by one-third, adding 15 million people, with Australia accounting for about half of that growth. Although the United States and Australia have similar demographic profiles, Australia's population is projected to grow twice as fast as that of the United States over the next 30 years, increasing by nearly 30%, while the United States is projected to increase by 15%. Although both countries have a history of immigration, Australia will likely have an increasingly significant role in future global population growth, as global migration accelerates and anti-immigration attitudes in many other countries strengthen.

UNEVEN COUNTRY GROWTH

By looking at individual countries within their regions, you have seen dramatic differences in the trajectories of population growth. The comparisons below highlight additional striking changes.

CHANGE IN THE TOP 10 MOST POPULOUS

The ranking of the world's most populous countries will change significantly over the coming years. While all the newcomers to the list of 10 most populous countries are in Africa, the departing countries are more geographically diverse. Figure 2.19 shows the population growth of the world's most populous countries after India and China. It captures the explosive growth among African countries and the arc of population slowing or declining elsewhere across the globe.

We have known for a while that India would overtake China to become the world's most populous country by 2030. This will occur shortly after China's total population starts declining, due largely

FIGURE 2.19   Several fast-growing African countries will soon join the world's 10 most populous.

World's Most Populous Countries after China and India, Population in Millions

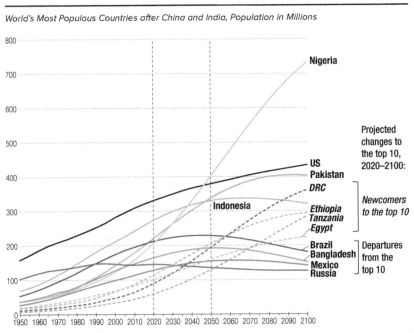

Data source: United Nations, *World Population Prospects 2019*, medium variant.

to the effect of its steep fertility decline. In contrast, India's population will continue to grow until around 2060.

Another striking change apparent in the demographic reshuffling is that by midcentury, Nigeria, the seventh most populous in 2020, will skyrocket past the United States to become the third most populous country. While the US population continues to gradually increase, Nigeria's population is projected to double from 200 million to 400 million by midcentury, and then nearly double again by the end of the century.

In addition to the re-ranking of 2020's most populous countries, several fast-growing African countries will soon join the top 10. By midcentury, Ethiopia and the DRC will join the list, and by the end of the century, Egypt and Tanzania will be included.

Many other countries will fall in the ranking, as their population growth slows or declines. The four departures from the top 10 are Russia, Mexico, Brazil, and Bangladesh. Note that Japan, while it was the fifth most populous nation in 1950, had already dropped to 11th most populous by 2020.

The change in rankings highlights the dramatic shifts that are projected to occur and that should frame our thinking about population growth. In addition, the varied patterns of population growth and decline highlight important challenges. How Nigeria, the DRC, and other fast-growing African countries will manage their rapid growth is one of the biggest conundrums. Another is how well the declining countries will anticipate and plan for their shrinking populations and shrinking workforces. Russia's continued population decline points to further questions about how it will adapt its national security strategy to a falling population.

Table 2.1 highlights changes in the rankings of the most populous countries. You can see the re-ranking of the historically large countries, as well as the many newcomers projected to join the lists in 2050 and 2100.

You may be struck by how concentrated the world's population is. In 2020, the 10 most populous countries accounted for nearly 60% of the world's population, and the 25 most populous accounted for

TABLE 2.1 A look at the changing ranks of the 25 most populous countries shows that most newcomers joining the list after 2020 are African countries.

Total Population, in Millions

Country	2020 Rank	2020 Pop.	2050 Rank	2050 Pop.	2100 Rank	2100 Pop.
China	1	1,439.3	2	1,402.4	2	1,065.0
India	2	1,380.0	1	1,639.2	1	1,450.4
United States	3	331.0	4	379.4	4	433.9
Indonesia	4	273.5	6	330.9	7	320.8
Pakistan	5	220.9	5	338.0	5	403.1
Brazil	6	212.6	7	229.0	12	180.7
Nigeria	7	206.1	3	401.3	3	732.9
Bangladesh	8	164.7	10	192.6	14	151.4
Russia	9	145.9	14	135.8	19	126.1
Mexico	10	128.9	12	155.2	17	141.5
Japan	11	126.5	17	105.8	36	75.0
Ethiopia	12	115.0	8	205.4	8	294.4
Philippines	13	109.6	13	144.5	15	146.3
Egypt	14	102.3	11	160.0	10	224.7
Vietnam	15	97.3	16	109.6	25	97.4
DRC	16	89.6	9	194.5	6	362.0
Turkey	17	84.3	19	97.1	28	86.2
Iran	18	84.0	18	103.1	24	98.6
Germany	19	83.8	23	80.1	38	74.7
Thailand	20	69.8	29	65.9	50	46.0
United Kingdom	21	67.9	26	74.1	34	78.1
France	22	65.3	28	67.6	41	65.5
Italy	23	60.5	37	54.4	58	40.0
Tanzania	24	59.7	15	129.4	9	285.7
South Africa	25	59.3	25	75.5	32	79.2
Countries in Top 25 for 2050 and 2100, but not in Top 25 in 2020						
Kenya	27	53.8	20	91.6	20	125.4
Uganda	31	45.7	21	89.4	18	136.8
Sudan	34	43.8	22	81.2	16	142.3
Angola	44	32.9	24	77.4	11	188.3
Iraq	36	40.2	27	70.9	22	107.7
Mozambique	46	31.3	31	65.3	21	123.6
Madagascar	51	27.7	38	54.0	23	100.0
Niger	56	24.2	30	65.6	13	164.9
World Total		7,794.8		9,735.0		10,874.9
10 Most Populous		4,503.0		5,312.7		5,572.9
Share of World Total		58%		55%		51%
25 Most Populous		5,777.8		6,948.4		7,604.1
Share of World Total		74%		71%		70%

Data source: United Nations, *World Population Prospects 2019*, medium variant.

74% of the total. What is also startling is that half of all the world's countries have populations of less than 10 million! And these smallest 100 countries account for less than 5% of the total.

BIGGEST GAINERS

As you have seen, projected population growth over the next 30 years is highly concentrated in a few countries. The eight countries with the largest projected gains account for nearly half of the world's population growth. India alone, with its projected increase of 259 million people, accounts for 13%, followed by Nigeria, whose growth of 195 million equals 10% of the world's projected growth. The other large gainers include Pakistan, the DRC, Ethiopia, Tanzania, Egypt, and Indonesia. Five of these large gainers are fast-growing African countries and three are Asian countries. The United States, with a projected population increase of 48 million, would be the ninth-largest gainer. Notably missing from the list of large population gainers is China, which instead, is the largest decliner, losing 37 million over the next 30 years.

Three of the African countries on this list are projected to more than double in population over the next 30 years. As shown above in Figure 2.19, Nigeria is projected to increase from 206 million to 402 million by 2050, and nearly double again by 2100, reaching 732 million. This makes Nigeria the only country that would come even close to reaching the size of China and India. Both the DRC and Tanzania are also projected to double by 2050, and approximately double again by 2100.

There is nothing new about population growth being concentrated among a few countries; we have historically had a small number of extremely large populations, which in the past have grown rapidly. For example, over the past 30 years, just seven countries, most of them in Asia, accounted for half of the world's population growth. China and India together accounted for nearly one-third of the globe's population growth after 1990. Other large contributors to recent population growth include Pakistan, Nigeria, Indonesia, and the US.

What is different looking forward is that the countries responsible for most of the projected growth are primarily African countries, not Asian. This trend will persist as Asian countries start to see their populations decline, while African countries continue to grow rapidly. Over the 30 years from 2020 to 2050, Africa is projected to account for nearly 60% of global growth, and during the second half of the century, for more than 150% of global growth.

BIGGEST DECLINERS

National population declines have been unusual in modern history, but according to the UN projections, an increasing number of countries will face population declines over the coming years. This is a startling development, given that continued population rise has been a key assumption in our models of economic growth.

Recall that the projected net population gain from 2020 to 2050 totals 1.9 billion: this includes absolute population gains of over 2 billion, mostly concentrated in African countries, and population declines of 122 million occurring in 46 countries, primarily in Asia and Europe. China tops the list, with a projected decline of 37 million (a drop of 3%), followed by Japan with a decline of 21 million, or 16%. Other countries with large population losses include Russia (a decrease of 10 million people), Ukraine (9 million), Italy, and Poland.

During the second half of the century the number of countries with population losses will increase to more than 100—nearly half of all countries are projected to have shrinking populations even as global population continues to increase. It's interesting to note that while growth is concentrated in a few countries, population declines are projected for many countries. China, with a projected decrease of 337 million people from 2050 to 2100, continues to top the list of population decliners, but is joined by India (189 million), Brazil, Bangladesh, and Japan.

One of the key features of the population changes you've been reading about is that population growth will slow globally—even the fast-growing countries will grow more slowly. And countries that previously followed similar paths are suddenly diverging. You saw that the population growth patterns of China and India have already diverged, while Pakistan and Nigeria are on pace to diverge around 2030. Now that you have explored the various patterns of population growth, we turn to analyzing the drivers behind these changes—some gradual and some sudden. As you read the following chapters, you will see how the drivers combine to produce such divergent results.

DEMOGRAPHIC DRIVERS

3 | DECLINING FERTILITY

"The Struggle to Reverse a Shrinking Population Hits Some Nations Harder"
Wall Street Journal, by Ian Lovett, September 13, 2021

"China Got Its Economy Growing Again, but a Shortfall in Babies Will Be Harder to Fix"
Wall Street Journal, by Liyan Qi, February 28, 2021

"Thanks to Education, Global Fertility Could Fall Faster Than Expected"
The Economist, February 2, 2019

The global decline in fertility, or births per woman, is one of the most transformative demographic developments of the past century. Declining fertility rates around the world have dramatically slowed population growth, and by reducing the number of children born per woman, these lower fertility rates have substantially altered the overall age mix: we see a rising median age and an overall shift to older age brackets, and in turn, a higher share of older people, and in many places, a declining share of working-age people.

Worldwide, the number of births per woman has dropped by half over the past 55 years, falling from a peak of 5.0 in 1965 to 2.5 in 2020. Though the rates have declined almost everywhere, they remain high in sub-Saharan Africa, where the average fertility rate only recently fell below 5.0.

While fertility has dropped worldwide, the timing, pace, and size of the fertility declines vary greatly across countries. And as you might guess, these differences have contributed to uneven population growth and dramatic variations in population age mix. In turn, these divergent demographic outcomes have major social, economic, and political implications. Understanding how the drivers behind these outcomes differ around the world will help in planning for anticipated developments, many of which pose huge economic and social challenges. Understanding the underlying drivers will also shed light on unexpected results and vulnerabilities that might arise from global developments, such as regional conflicts or global pandemics.

GLOBAL OVERVIEW: BIG PICTURE OF FERTILITY DECLINE

The fertility rate, or average number of births per woman, is the standard indicator for understanding changes in fertility trends over time and for making international comparisons of changing birth rates. Akin to family size or number of children per family, this number is useful as an indicator of whether a population is growing, declining, or just replacing itself. Statistically, replacement-rate fertility, 2.1 births per woman, means that if a woman has 2.1 children, she will be replacing herself and her mate. The additional fraction accounts for the probability that not all infants will survive.

Replacement-rate fertility is a useful benchmark for comparing countries, but as you will see, it might take a generation or two for the impact of a fertility decline to take full effect, depending largely on the current age mix of the population. In a relatively young country with a large proportion of women of childbearing age, the total population could continue to grow long after fertility falls to 2.1 births per woman. The average births per woman could be 2.1, but because of past high fertility, the number of women having children would have increased, which means that population will continue to grow. Using the family model, we might see smaller families, but the number of families would be increasing. This "population momentum" arising from a youthful age mix explains why we see situations where young countries with steep fertility declines might continue to see high population growth rates for several decades. Thus, in these cases, a certain amount of population growth is already baked into the future, even if the fertility rate falls. China is a good example. Even though China's fertility fell below replacement rate in 1995, the total population is projected to continue growing until around 2030. This explains why it would be easy to celebrate declining fertility for its role in reducing explosive population growth, but it is critical to understand that the full impact may take a generation or two to be revealed.

MAPPING THE WORLDWIDE FERTILITY DECLINE

The two world maps in Figure 3.1 show the dramatic changes in fertility over the past 55 years, starting with 1965, the global peak. In 1965, when the global fertility rate peaked at 5.0, almost all countries had high fertility rates—shown in red and orange on the map. Low fertility rates, shown in blue, occurred only in a few European countries and in Japan.

The 2020 fertility map looks dramatically different. Low fertility is no longer just a Japanese or European phenomenon, but now occurs widely around the world. Shades of blue, showing low fertility rates, occur in all the regions except Africa. In 2020 half the world's population lives in low-fertility countries. Intermediate fertility, in yellow, ranging from 2.2 to 3.5 births per woman, occurs throughout the developing regions. Most striking is that North America and Europe are solid with below-replacement fertility. Latin America and Asia each have a combination of low- and intermediate-fertility countries, reflecting their diverse patterns of fertility decline. The highest fertility rates—red and orange—remain concentrated in Africa, though many African countries have already achieved significant fertility declines.

The changes from 1965 to 2020 are striking but varied. Many countries have experienced steep fertility declines over just a few decades, while others have had more gradual declines. Some already low-fertility countries have had minimal declines, while many high-fertility countries are just at the beginning of their fertility declines.

FIGURE 3.1   In 1965, low fertility rates occurred only in Europe and Japan. By 2020, half the world's population lived in low-fertility countries.

Fertility Rate (Births per Woman)

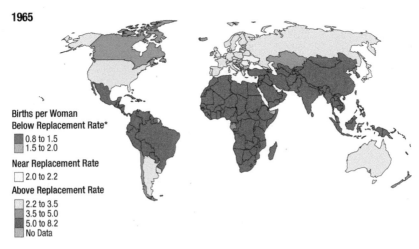

1965

Births per Woman
Below Replacement Rate*
■ 0.8 to 1.5
□ 1.5 to 2.0

Near Replacement Rate
□ 2.0 to 2.2

Above Replacement Rate
■ 2.2 to 3.5
■ 3.5 to 5.0
■ 5.0 to 8.2
■ No Data

* Replacement Rate = 2.1 births per woman

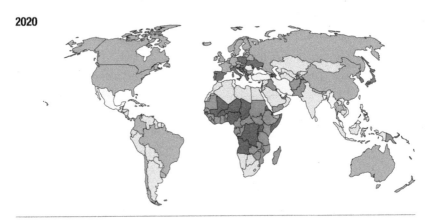

2020

Data source: United Nations, *World Population Prospects 2019*, medium variant.

DIVERGENT FERTILITY PATTERNS FOR SELECTED COUNTRIES

From the maps, you can see that fertility has plummeted almost everywhere, even though the timing and pace of decline varies greatly across countries. To illustrate key differences, Figure 3.2 shows

FIGURE 3.2   Fertility has plummeted almost everywhere. Variations in timing and pace lead to stark differences in population growth and age mix.

Fertility Rate (Births per Woman)

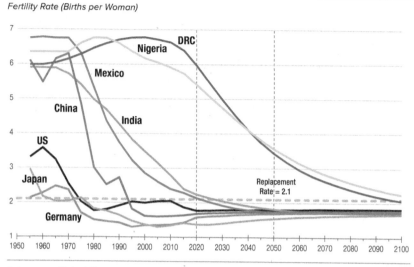

Data source: United Nations, *World Population Prospects 2019,* medium variant.

a sampling of countries with varied fertility declines. You can see several distinct patterns based on the timing and pace of the declines.

Three of the world's largest economies—the United States, Japan, and Germany, shown at the bottom of the figure—had post–World War II baby booms, but have had below-replacement fertility rates since the 1970s. Although fertility rates have ticked up in the United States and Germany, you can see they remain below replacement rate, represented here by the dashed gray line.

The developing countries shown in the middle of the figure have experienced large fertility declines, but the pace of decline has varied. China, the world's second-largest economy, joined the countries with below-replacement-rate fertility around 1995, after its fertility rate fell sharply from over 6.0 births per woman. If we compare the world's two most populous countries, we can see key differences in the pattern of fertility decline: China's fertility fell below replacement in 1995 after a steep decline, while India's fertility decline has been smoother and more gradual. These differences in fertility declines have different consequences for each country and have resulted in divergent population growth rates and age structures. Most notably, China's total population will begin declining after around 2030, while India's will continue growing; also, China is now one the fastest-aging countries, while India remains relatively young. Mexico generally followed China's pattern of fertility decline, but started a few years later from a higher level.

Nigeria and the DRC, shown at the top of the figure, are examples of countries with very high fertility rates and divergent patterns of decline. Fertility rates increased in both during the 1970s and 1980s, while most other countries were seeing fertility rate declines. Nigeria's fertility rate peaked in 1985, while the DRC's fertility continued increasing until around 2000. Although their fertility rates have recently declined, these countries rank among the top 10 highest-fertility countries.

WHY DOES FERTILITY FALL?

Many related factors have contributed to the global fertility decline, and scholars continue to analyze which factors are most significant. Arguably the most important impetus for fertility decline is economic development: as societies become more industrialized and less agrarian, fewer children are needed to support a family's livelihood. Then, as countries continue to modernize and more women become economically empowered, the economics of child-rearing change again. In many cases this further reduces the desired number of children.

The decline in infant and child mortality associated with economic development is another factor that contributes directly to the fertility decline: more children survive, so fewer live births are needed to achieve the desired family size.

Beginning as early as the 1950s, global family planning and reproductive health programs were aimed at reducing population growth, and many observers credit these programs for their success in lowering family size. These population programs were varied, ranging from slogans to reproductive health education. Many programs also provided contraceptives. Although cultural influences and social pressures are clearly important, some economists suggest the provision of contraceptives was the most effective element of the family planning programs.

While many of these early family planning programs focused on education and social pressure to reduce the number of children, China's one-child policy, implemented in 1980, officially restricted the number of children.

Many cultural and religious practices also influence a society's fertility rates. Cultural preference for male children has been responsible for female infanticide in many countries, including China, as well as for selective abortion in other countries. At the same time, cultural preference for large families may be a key factor constraining fertility decline in Africa. Other factors that contribute to fewer children include later marriage and greater spacing between births.

While many view worldwide family planning efforts as a remarkable success, continued fertility declines have not been universally welcomed. Many countries, including China, are now seeking to reverse their fertility declines through a variety of pronatal policies, such as direct financial incentives for having more children; provision of public services, such as childcare, that reduce the cost of raising children; and business adoption of family-friendly policies and practices. So far, there is little evidence that such pronatal programs are effective.

GLOBAL PERSPECTIVES ON CHANGING FERTILITY

Before comparing individual countries in greater detail, it is revealing to look at patterns of global change from several perspectives, including geographic region, development group, and income level. Although regional and economic aggregates can hide consequential country trends, these perspectives point to broad trends and provide a useful framework for understanding the global context of major changes.

FERTILITY BY REGION

Fertility rates have been declining globally, but the patterns of decline differ dramatically across regions. Globally, the fertility rate has declined by half, from 5.0 births per woman in 1965 to 2.5 births per woman in 2020. As you can see in Figure 3.3, fertility rates remain the highest by far in Africa. As of 2020 the region's fertility rate was 4.4 children per woman, down from 6.7 in 1975, a level that had persisted for several decades. The rate is projected to decline to 3.1 by midcentury, but remain above the replacement rate until the end of the century. This high fertility rate will fuel the continued explosive population growth in Africa, projected at 2.1% per year from 2020 to midcentury, compared with 0.4% for Asia.

Although there is considerable variation across countries, the region-wide fertility declines in Asia and Latin America closely tracked each other, beginning with a steep decline in the 1970s, from around 6.0 births per woman, and by 2020, falling below 2.1 in

FIGURE 3.3   Africa is the one region where fertility rates remain stubbornly high. In contrast, steep fertility declines have occurred in Asia and Latin America.

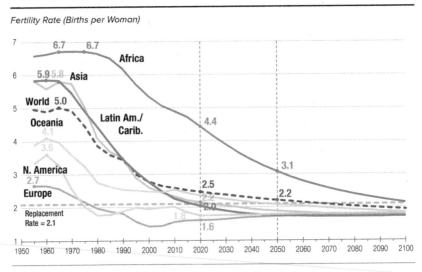

Data source: United Nations, *World Population Prospects 2019*, medium variant.

Latin America and near replacement in Asia. Fertility in these two regions is projected to continue declining. As a result, these two regions will see slowing population growth with population declines beginning around midcentury.

Fertility in Oceania fell from around 4.0 births per woman in the 1960s to 2.4 in 2020, with continued declines projected. Both Australia and New Zealand, which together account for 71% of Oceania's population, have seen several decades of below-replacement-rate fertility, but continued high fertility in the region's developing countries has kept regional fertility above replacement. Papua New Guinea, by far the largest developing country in the region with 21% of the region's population, registered 2020 fertility of 3.6 births per woman.

Turning now to the two major developed regions, we see that fertility in North America peaked in the 1960s, during the postwar baby boom, at 3.6 births per woman. The rate fell below replacement rate in 1975, reaching a low of 1.8 in 1980 before ticking up. Since then, the rate has hovered around 2.0, largely due to immigration, but declined slightly to 1.8 in 2020. Although slight increases are projected, fertility will likely remain below replacement rate.

Europe has the lowest fertility of any region, with average fertility registering just 1.6 in 2020. The region had already registered the world's lowest fertility rate by 1950, and the rate continued to decline to a low of 1.43 in 2000. In contrast to declines in the other regions, fertility in Europe has increased slightly over the past 20 years, reaching 1.6 in 2020. Although this rate is still below replacement, projections point to increases over the coming decades. The recent increase is being carefully researched, with two trends thought to be fueling the change. First, many governments are seeking to increase fertility by adopting pronatal and family-friendly policies that provide financial incentives and social services to encourage women to have more children. Second, some of the fertility increase may stem from the higher fertility rates of foreign-born women who immigrate from high-fertility countries.

This graph of regional differences rests on two critical assumptions that significantly affect the population forecasts. First is the pace of fertility decline in Africa. The projection shows a decline from

4.4 in 2020 to 3.1 by 2050. Given the uncertainty around this projection, we should consider what might happen if the fertility decline slows. It makes sense that a further stalling of the decline, such that fertility stays high for a longer time, would raise the population forecast. Conversely, a faster-than-projected fertility decline would lead to slower population growth.

By considering alternative fertility-rate assumptions, we can see how different fertility levels lead to varied population outcomes. According to the UN's alternative population projections for Africa, higher fertility by an additional 0.5 births per woman would add 1.6 billion more people by century's end, bringing Africa's total population to 5.9 billion rather than the 4.3 billion in the medium variant. In contrast, a faster decline in fertility would reduce projected growth by 1.3 billion, bringing Africa's total population to 3.0 billion by century's end—half the level seen in the high-fertility scenario. (Figure 2.6 in Chapter 2 shows how a faster decline in Africa's fertility rate would significantly dampen its population growth.)

A second major assumption in Figure 3.3 is that fertility rates outside of Africa will converge at just below replacement rate. That means fertility will increase slightly in North America and Europe, and that the steep fertility declines in Asia and Latin America will level off, with only slight declines continuing. The assumed clustering of fertility around 1.8 births per woman has important implications for how fast the populations will grow—or more likely shrink—and how fast they will age. Understanding what is behind these assumptions of increased fertility is important in shaping expectations about future population growth. Although many countries have tried various pronatal policies, the effectiveness of such policies is still questionable.

Few countries have experienced long periods of below-replacement-rate fertility, so we are now entering uncharted territory, with a record number of countries projected to experience sustained below-replacement fertility. How countries and regions adapt to their slower-growing and shrinking populations may indeed become the most important demographic challenge we face.

FERTILITY BY DEVELOPMENT GROUP

You saw in Chapter 2 that developing countries are projected to account for almost all the world's future population growth. And you also learned that the subgroup of least developed countries is projected to account for a disproportionate share of this growth. We can better understand this huge population shift if we look closely at the fertility rates of the two subgroups of developing countries.

As shown in Figure 3.4, fertility in the least developed countries has declined to 4.0 births per woman, down from a peak of 6.8 in 1965. In contrast, fertility in the other less developed countries has fallen much more sharply, and in 2020 averaged 2.3 births per woman.

The fertility decline for the least developed countries may be a welcome trend, but with their fertility rates projected to remain high,

FIGURE 3.4   The subgroup of 47 least developed countries stands out for its high fertility rate of 4.0 births per woman, compared with 2.3 for other less developed countries.

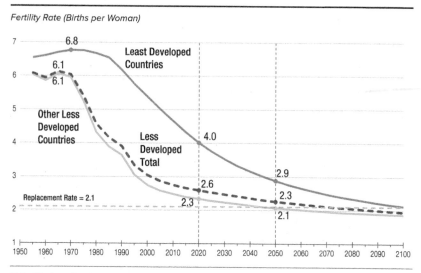

Note: The less developed total includes two subgroups: The first is the UN-designated group of 47 least developed countries. The second subgroup, other less developed countries, comprises all countries in the less developed regions minus the 47 least developed countries.

Data source: United Nations, *World Population Prospects 2019*, medium variant.

the population of this group is projected to grow at nearly 2% per year over the next 30 years, three times faster than other less developed countries. According to the UN projections, the least developed countries will account for 42% of world population growth from 2020 to 2050 and 103% of world population growth from 2050 to 2100. This means that the least developed countries will increase from 14% of world population in 2020 to 19% by 2050, and to 28% by 2100.

As for the other less developed countries, their total population is projected to stabilize by midcentury at around 5.6 billion, with their share of total population projected to slowly decline, from 70% in 2020 to 61% by century's end.

As you saw in Chapter 2, the population shift toward this most vulnerable group is a major global challenge, posing economic, social, and political threats to stability. While many reports lump all the developing countries together, it is revealing to focus on the subgroup that poses the most significant challenges to global economic and political stability.

FERTILITY BY INCOME LEVEL

You learned in Chapter 2 that population growth differs dramatically by income group, with a large divergence occurring between the two middle-income groups. The two lower-income groups are projected to have disproportionately faster population growth and register increasing shares of global population. The fertility rate differences shown in Figure 3.5 shed light on what drives the divergent population growth trajectories.

As we might expect, the segmentation by income level points to the correlation between economic development and fertility decline. We can see from Figure 3.5 that higher-income countries are associated with lower or falling fertility rates. The low-income group of countries, shown by the orange line at the top in Figure 3.5, has the highest 2020 fertility rate, 4.5 births per woman. Although this rate has been decreasing, the decline for this low-income group started later than in other developing countries and has happened

FIGURE 3.5 Lower-income countries continue to have the highest fertility and the slowest fertility declines. Upper-middle-income countries have had the steepest declines.

Fertility Rate (Births per Woman)

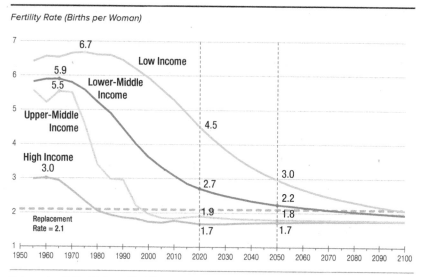

Data source: United Nations, *World Population Prospects 2019,* medium variant.

more slowly. And although the pace of this decline is projected to accelerate, with fertility dropping to 3.0 by midcentury, this group of 34 low-income countries is projected to account for a dispropor- tionate share of global population growth. Low-income countries accounted for just 10% of the world's population in 2020, but are projected to account for 36% of population growth by midcentury, thus increasing their share to 15% by that time. The most popu- lous countries in this income group as of 2020 include Ethiopia, the DRC, Tanzania, Uganda, and Afghanistan. (You can read more about their fertility patterns later in the chapter.)

The two middle-income groups show an important variation in fertility decline. Fertility for the lower-middle-income group, the orange line in Figure 3.5, declined from nearly 6.0 births per woman in 1965 to just 2.7 births per woman in 2020. The fertility decline has been gradual, but substantial, totaling 3.2 births per woman. The most populous countries in this group include India, Indonesia,

Pakistan, Nigeria, and Bangladesh. Nigeria is an outlier in this classification, with an income in the lower-middle range, but an extremely high fertility rate of 5.42 in 2020.

Most notable in this comparison is that the upper-middle-income group, the light blue line in Figure 3.5, saw the steepest overall decline and has experienced nearly 20 years of below-replacement-rate fertility. Fertility in this group declined from a peak of 5.5 in 1965 to 1.9 in 2020, a decline of 3.6 births per woman. The rate fell below replacement in the late 1990s and has been hovering around 1.9 for the past 20 years. The most populous countries in the group include China, Brazil, Russia, Mexico, Iran, and Turkey. The two middle-income lines reflect the divergent patterns of demographic change occurring in the world's two most populous countries: China's fertility decline was steep, typical of upper-middle-income countries, while India's was more gradual, typical of lower-middle-income countries.

It won't surprise you that the high-income countries at the bottom of the chart have the lowest fertility rates. As a group, these countries have had below-replacement fertility rates for more than 40 years. The group includes the United States, Japan, Germany, the United Kingdom, France, and Italy.

DIVERGENT TRENDS ACROSS COUNTRIES

While the previous discussion focused on fertility differences across various regions and groups, the following sections focus on divergent fertility trends across individual countries. The differences in timing, pace, and magnitude of the fertility declines lead to divergent changes in total population, changes in working-age population, and aging of the population. Understanding the underlying fertility differences will help us anticipate the divergent outcomes likely to unfold.

By way of introduction to country differences, Table 3.1 gives you a quick look at the countries with the lowest and highest fertility rates as of 2020.

East Asia and Europe dominate the ranking of low-fertility countries. South Korea has the lowest 2020 fertility at 1.11 births per

TABLE 3.1 The Asian Tigers have the world's lowest fertility rates; sub-Saharan Africa is home to all the highest fertility countries.

Fertility Rate (Births per Woman), Lowest and Highest					
Lowest Fertility Countries			**Highest Fertility Countries**		
Rank	Country	2020 Fertility	Rank	Country	2020 Fertility
1	South Korea	1.11	1	Niger	6.95
2	Taiwan	1.15	2	Somalia	6.12
3	Macao	1.20	3	DRC	5.96
4	Singapore	1.21	4	Mali	5.92
5	Moldova	1.26	5	Chad	5.80
6	Bosnia and Herzegov.	1.27	6	Angola	5.55
7	Portugal	1.29	7	Burundi	5.45
8	Greece	1.30	8	Nigeria	5.42
9	Hong Kong	1.33	9	Gambia	5.25
10	Spain	1.33	10	Burkina Faso	5.23
11	Italy	1.33	11	Uganda	5.01
12	Cyprus	1.34	12	Tanzania	4.92
13	Japan	1.37	13	Mozambique	4.89
14	Mauritius	1.39	14	Benin	4.87
15	UAE	1.42	15	Central African Rep.	4.75
16	Poland	1.42	16	Guinea	4.74
17	Ukraine	1.44	17	South Sudan	4.74
18	Saint Lucia	1.44	18	Côte d'Ivoire	4.68
19	Croatia	1.45	19	Zambia	4.66
20	Luxembourg	1.45	20	Senegal	4.65

Note: The Asian Tigers are South Korea, Taiwan, Singapore, and Hong Kong.
Data source: United Nations, *World Population Prospects* 2019, medium variant.

woman and is closely followed by the other three Asian Tigers—Taiwan, Singapore, and Hong Kong. At 1.4, Japan's fertility rate is higher than those of the Asian Tigers, and closer to the low fertility of many European countries. Most of the other lowest-fertility countries are in Europe, with concentrations in Southern and Eastern Europe. Many other European countries are close behind. Note that most of these low fertility countries are countries with high per capita income, according to the World Bank rankings.

In contrast, all 20 of the highest-fertility countries are sub-Saharan. As you have read, Niger has the world's highest fertility rate, at 7.0 births per woman, down from its peak of 7.9 in 1985. Niger is one of many African countries that had increasing fertility from 1955 to the late 1990s. As expected, these high-fertility countries are projected to have explosive population growth over the coming decades. What is particularly concerning is that the list includes four of Africa's most populous countries—Nigeria, the DRC, Tanzania, and Uganda—which, as we will see, are projected to add enormously to the world's total population.

Now that we see the 2020 ranking of countries according to their fertility rate, we can look at historical trends that led to these rates and consider what is projected for the coming years. We turn first to the large economies.

LARGE ECONOMIES—TWO DISTINCT PATTERNS

Most of the large economies are high-income countries and most have experienced below-replacement fertility for several decades. The 15 largest economies show two distinct patterns of fertility decline. The first group includes 10 low-fertility industrialized economies that already had relatively low fertility rates during the 1950s and 1960s, and have since had decades of below-replacement fertility. The second group includes five emerging economies that had high post–World War II fertility rates followed by significant declines.

The six *large, industrialized economies* shown in Figure 3.6 have all had below-replacement fertility for three to four decades. The individual trajectories differ, but most had post–World War II baby booms followed by fertility declines that put them below replacement rate. Three of these large economies, including the US, France, and the UK, have fertility rates that have been hovering just below replacement rate since around 1980, while Germany, Japan, and Russia saw further declines.

Fueled by its postwar baby boom, the United States saw higher fertility during the 1960s than most other industrialized economies, and as a result of these new births, now has a relatively younger

FIGURE 3.6 The large, industrialized economies have had sustained low fertility since the 1970s, with many experiencing rates well below replacement level.

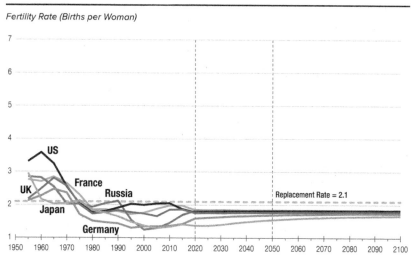

Fertility Rate (Births per Woman)

Data source: United Nations, *World Population Prospects 2019*, medium variant.

population profile, coupled with higher workforce and population growth. Fertility in the United States peaked at 3.6 births per woman in 1957, but fell by half, to 1.8, just 20 years later. The rapid fertility decline led to a baby bust during the 1970s, but as baby boomers started to have their own children, an echo boom occurred. The fertility rate rose slightly during the 1980s, with the total number of births reaching 4 million per year—a number not seen since the peak baby boom years.

Several other large economies, including Japan, Germany, Spain, and Italy, experienced fertility rates that fell well below replacement, with the low points ranging from 1.2 to 1.3. The rates have ticked up a bit in each country, but all four countries will remain well below replacement rate.

Japan had a short postwar baby boom from 1947 to 1949 with a peak fertility of around 4.4 births per woman and total number of births averaging 2.5 million per year. Fertility fell sharply after that, reaching replacement rate in the 1960s. After hovering near replacement, the rate declined again beginning in the late 1970s, falling to a low of 1.3 in 2005. The rate has recently been hovering around 1.4 births per woman. The early drop and persistently low fertility rate give Japan the distinction of having one of the longest periods of below-replacement-rate fertility and has turned Japan into one of the fastest-aging populations in the world. The total population has already started declining from its peak of 128.6 million in 2009, and the total number of births has been steadily declining since the 1970s echo-boom peak of 2 million per year. Even though widely expected, the 2016 drop in total number of births below 1 million per year was covered in the press as a worrisome milestone for the country's demography. The continued decline has generated more support for pronatal policies and possible relaxation of immigration policies.

Germany's postwar fertility rate rose to 2.5 in 1965 but quickly dropped well below replacement rate. After falling to 1.3 births per woman, fertility increased to 1.6 births per woman in 2020, with a slight increase projected for the coming decades. The steep decline and continued low fertility led to a sharp decline in number of births, and by 1975, deaths exceeded births, so the natural population increase turned negative. However, since 1975, international migration has offset most of the natural decline. The UN projects that after 2020, immigration will no longer offset the natural decline in Germany.

Russia's fertility pattern is notable because its decline occurred later than in other large economies. The rate hovered around replacement level from 1970 to 1990, but after the collapse of the Soviet Union, fertility fell to a low of 1.25 in 2000. As living conditions improved, the rate increased to 1.8, but is projected to remain below replacement.

The second group of large economies includes the five *emerging economies* shown in Figure 3.7, all of which experienced large fertility declines. The declines were especially large and steep in China, South Korea, and Mexico. South Korea, then one of the newly industrializing Asian Tigers, saw the earliest decline of these five emerging economies, starting in 1960, and falling below replacement

FIGURE 3.7   The large emerging economies had significant fertility declines beginning in the 1970s that pushed them toward or below replacement rate in more recent decades.

Fertility Rate (Births per Woman)

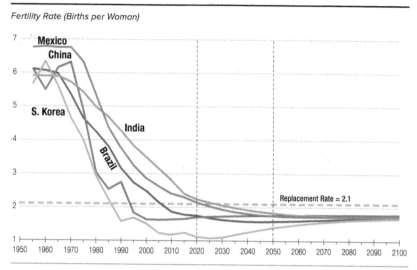

Data source: United Nations, *World Population Prospects 2019*, medium variant.

around 1985. China's fertility decline started later, but as reflected in the steeper line during the 1970s, moved faster than South Korea's decline.

China is well known for its one-child policy implemented in 1980. What is less well known is that China's fertility rate had already been steeply declining well before this policy came into effect. Prior to imposing the one-child restrictions, China had various family-planning programs, including a campaign for "Late, Long, and Few," that spurred the steep fertility decline that began in the 1970s. Since 1970, China has had one of the fastest drops in fertility, as births per woman fell from 6.3 in 1970 to 1.6 in 2000, a drop of 4.7 births per woman over 30 years. Fertility has since increased slightly to 1.7 in 2020, but is projected to remain below replacement level. China dropped its one-child policy in 2016, with the goal of boosting the number of children. After nearly five years of a two-child policy and seeing little change in the birth rate, China adopted a three-child policy in 2021. So far, there is little evidence of any impact on the number of births.

Compared to the declines in South Korea and China, Mexico's fertility decline was not quite as large or as fast, but its decline is even more remarkable because it started later and from a higher level. With a decline that did not accelerate until after 1975, Mexico looks like a newcomer to fertility decline. Although the pace of decline slowed after 1985, fertility fell to replacement rate by 2020 and is expected to continue declining. In contrast, India and Brazil had much more gradual declines, with India's a bit slower.

Understanding these fertility differences is important for anticipating divergent projections of population growth and specifically working-age population growth. As we know, fertility declines will eventually lead to slower workforce growth. The 2020 snapshot of fertility in the largest economies in Figure 3.8 shows that rates range from 1.1 births per woman in South Korea to 2.2 in India. Eight of these large economies, highlighted in gray, are projected to have shrinking workforces over the next 20 years, due largely to their low fertility rates. Among the 15 largest economies, only Mexico and India have 2020 fertility rates above replacement rate. These two countries are projected to see continued but slowing workforce growth until around 2050. After that, workforce growth turns negative as the impact of the declining fertility sets in.

The long and increasing period of low fertility, especially for the large, industrialized countries, is uncharted territory, but the different patterns of decline point to divergent impacts on the working-age population. The already older industrialized countries have seen low fertility for decades, and have adapted to the more gradual impacts. In contrast, the emerging economies with steep fertility decreases will face more abrupt changes in total population and age structure. The faster fertility declines will contribute to faster declines in the working-age population and faster aging of the total population. You will read about the impact of fertility declines on workforce size and population aging in Chapters 6 and 7.

FIGURE 3.8   Most of the 15 largest economies had below-replacement fertility in 2020. Eight of these large economies face shrinking workforces over the next 20 years.

Fertility Rate (Births per Woman), 15 Largest Economies, 2020

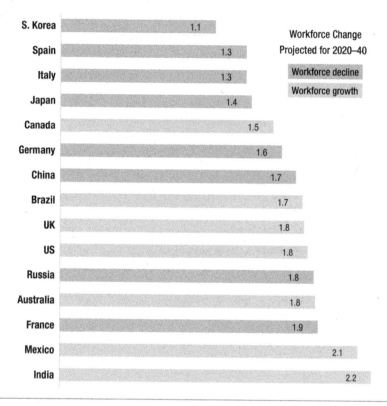

Data source: United Nations, *World Population Prospects 2019,* medium variant.

HIGH-INCOME COUNTRIES WITH STEEP FERTILITY DECLINES: ASIAN TIGERS AND GULF OIL STATES

As you saw above in Figure 3.5, distinct patterns of fertility decline are associated with the four per capita income levels. In the next few sections, you will see selected countries within each income group, starting with the high-income countries.

Most high-income countries are industrialized economies with three to four decades of below-replacement fertility. Like the largest industrialized economies shown above in Figure 3.6, most high-income countries had relatively low post–World War II fertility rates, followed by continued slow declines. For the high-income group overall, fertility fell from around 3.0 in 1955 to 1.7 in 2020, an average decline of 1.3 births per woman over the six decades. However, there are several important exceptions to this long pattern of sustained low fertility.

The first exception includes the four Asian Tigers, which were newly industrializing during the 1960s. As you can see in Figure 3.9, all four—Taiwan, Singapore, South Korea, and Hong Kong—had experienced large and rapid fertility declines that began in the 1960s and accompanied their rapid industrialization. Singapore's steep drop to replacement rate is especially notable because of its magnitude and speed: a decline of nearly 5.0 births per woman over less than 25 years. Taiwan's drop was similar in size but slightly slower.

FIGURE 3.9   Steep fertility declines accompanied rapid industrialization of the Asian Tigers.

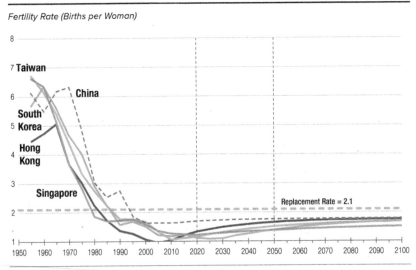

Fertility Rate (Births per Woman)

Note: China, though not a high-income Asian Tiger, is included for reference.

Data source: United Nations, *World Population Prospects 2019*, medium variant.

All four saw continued fertility declines, and have now had three to four decades of below-replacement fertility. It is not surprising that the four Asian Tigers rank among the world's lowest fertility countries. As of 2020, South Korea's fertility rate, at 1.11 births per woman, is the world's lowest, followed by Taiwan's, at 1.15. Hong Kong and Singapore are not far behind. Because of their sharp declines, all are among the world's most rapidly aging countries.

Figure 3.9 includes China for comparison, even though it is not a high-income country. Seen in the context of the Asian Tigers, the steep decline in China doesn't seem all that surprising, except that its economy was much less industrialized than that of the Asian Tigers. Compared with South Korea, China's fertility decline was faster, but not as large. China's initial fertility decline started 10 years later than South Korea's, but was steeper, falling from 6.3 to 3.0 in just 10 years, compared with 20 years for the same drop in South Korea. After 1980, China's fertility rate fluctuated, but then fell to a low of 1.61 in 2005, rising to 1.69 in 2020.

A second group of high-income countries with steep fertility declines includes oil-rich Middle Eastern countries, such as Kuwait, Qatar, the United Arab Emirates (UAE), and Saudi Arabia. During the 1960s, these currently rich countries had persistently high fertility rates of around 7.0 births per woman, but as their oil-rich economies grew, their fertility rates fell sharply. By 2020, fertility had fallen to 2.3 in Saudi Arabia, and well below replacement in the UAE.

Figure 3.10 shows three waves of fertility decline. Compared with the Asian Tigers, the declines in the Persian Gulf states started later and from higher peaks. The Asian Tigers have already had decades of low fertility, while the rich Gulf states have only recently approached replacement fertility. Notably, the fertility decline in Saudi Arabia, the most populous, started later and remains above replacement. Other countries in the greater Middle East with steep fertility declines include Iran, Turkey, Libya, and Tunisia.

We know that the steep fertility declines in these countries will lead to rapid changes in age structures; the most critical consequences to anticipate include slower-growing or shrinking workforces, and rapid aging of the population. Adapting to a smaller

FIGURE 3.10   Three waves of fertility decline occurred in the newly rich countries. Many oil-rich countries had steep fertility declines like the Asian Tigers, but 20 to 30 years later.

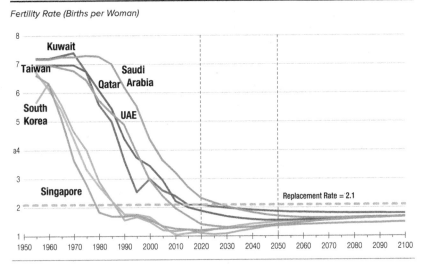

Fertility Rate (Births per Woman)

Data source: United Nations, *World Population Prospects 2019*, medium variant.

share of young people will be an especially important challenge in these countries.

There is a third exception to the pattern of continued low fertility among rich industrialized countries: Israel, with 2020 fertility of 3.0 births per woman, has the highest fertility rate among the high-income countries. Israel's fertility fell from a peak of 4.3 in 1955 to 3.1 in 1985, and has been hovering around 3.0 births per woman for the past 30 years. Fertility rates vary greatly across the religious and ethnic groups, but it is notable that the secular population of Israel has had a relatively high fertility rate.

UPPER-MIDDLE-INCOME COUNTRIES: STEEP FERTILITY DECLINES

Most of the 56 upper-middle-income countries have achieved large fertility declines since the 1960s. Almost half now have fertility at or below replacement rate, and many of these—including China,

Thailand, and several Eastern European countries—have seen several decades of below-replacement fertility. Most of the other upper-middle-income countries have had substantial fertility declines, but have 2020 fertility rates between 2.0 and 3.0 births per woman. Only a few countries in this income group still have fertility rates above 3.0 births per woman.

Like the high-income Asian Tigers, many countries in this income group were able to achieve large fertility declines without the draconian features of China's one-child policy. Although their per capita incomes have increased, they have not yet achieved the high-income success of the Asian Tigers. Figure 3.11 shows several upper-middle-income countries with steep declines like China's, even though the timing has been different. Like China, due largely to their steep fertility declines, these countries will see rapid aging of their populations and declining working-age populations within a few decades.

FIGURE 3.11   Many upper-middle-income countries have had large and rapid fertility declines; Iran's decline was even faster than China's.

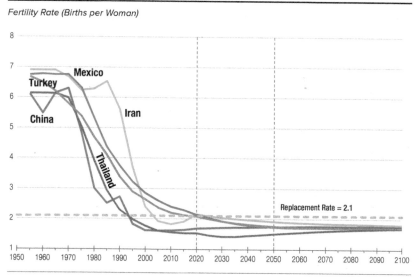

Data source: United Nations, *World Population Prospects 2019,* medium variant.

Thailand's rapid fertility drop—from 6.1 in 1965 to 1.5 by 2020—was prompted by major family-planning efforts and serves as an early example of how population policy could lead to fertility-rate declines.

Turkey and Mexico each had large fertility declines, starting from the same high level but with different timing. Turkey's decline started earlier, falling from 6.7 in 1955 to replacement rate in 2020. In contrast, Mexico's fertility remained above 6.7 for another 15 years, until 1970. Though its decline started later than Turkey's, it was much steeper in the early years. Since 1970, Mexico's fertility has dropped by 4.6 births per woman, reaching 2.1 by 2020.

Iran's fertility decline is perhaps the most surprising. Although it started later than those of many other upper-income countries, Iran's drop-off in fertility has been one of the world's steepest, down 4.7 births per woman. Iran is one of many upper-middle-income countries that experienced steep fertility declines resembling the rapid decreases in China and South Korea. Iran's most recent decline was just as steep as China's, but it started in 1985, about 15 years later than China's. Several other differences are notable and will shape future demographics. Iran had an uninterrupted fertility decline from 1985 to 2010 as its fertility rates fell from 6.5 in 1985 to just 1.82 in 2010. In addition, Iran has had one of the largest total fertility declines, a total decline of 5.1 births per woman from its 1965 peak of 6.91 to its 2010 trough of 2.18. As you can see in Figure 3.11, the fertility rate had ticked back up to replacement rate by 2020.

Iran's fertility pattern reflects several reversals in its population policies. The initial, but small, fertility decline from 6.9 to 6.2 births per woman in the 1960s and 1970s occurred during the family-planning era of the Shah, when policies were designed to slow population growth. Following the 1979 revolution, Ayatollah Khomeini reversed the family-planning policies of the Shah, and introduced a pronatal strategy to encourage population growth, suggesting a strategic goal of 100 million people, which would almost triple the 1979 population of 36 million. By the mid-1980s, as the population was nearing 50 million, the Iranian government became concerned that the baby boom and its accelerating population growth would hinder economic development. So, with the support of key clerics, the government introduced a national family-planning program to again slow population growth. In the face of a steep fertility decline, these policies were reversed in 2014 and once again replaced with pronatal policies aimed at stimulating population growth and slowing the pace of population aging. While there was a slight increase in the fertility rate, a much further increase would be necessary to slow the increase in median age and dampen projected growth in the share of older people.

There are many research projects under way analyzing the demographic transition and evaluating the effectiveness of family-planning programs in reducing fertility rates. Although providing contraceptives is effective in reducing fertility, many researchers argue that fertility decline is achieved primarily through economic development and improved education, especially for women and girls, along with programs that provide great opportunities for women. In addition to considering the impacts of education and greater opportunities for women in reducing fertility, researchers are now also focused on understanding which, if any, pronatal policies are effective in increasing the number of children.

LOWER-MIDDLE-INCOME COUNTRIES: GRADUAL FERTILITY DECLINES

In line with the global pattern, fertility has declined in all the lower-middle-income countries, but the declines in general have been smaller and more gradual than the declines described above for richer countries such as China and Iran. While some of the 46 lower-middle-income countries have achieved large fertility declines since the 1960s, almost half still have fertility rates of 3.0 or higher, and two still have fertility rates of 5.0 or more births per woman, including Nigeria, the world's seventh most populous country. Figure 3.12 shows the six most populous countries in this income group and illustrates some notable differences in the pace and timing of fertility decline.

India's fertility declined gradually from nearly 6.0 births per woman in 1965 to 2.2 births by 2020. The comparison with China

FIGURE 3.12   Most lower-middle-income countries have had gradual fertility declines. Bangladesh is a notable exception, with one of the largest and fastest declines.

Fertility Rate (Births per Woman)

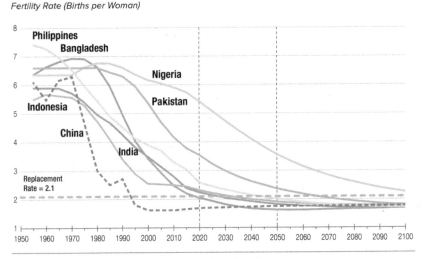

Note: China, an upper-middle-income country, is shown for reference.

Data source: United Nations, *World Population Prospects 2019*, medium variant.

points to some key features that lead to different outcomes. India's fertility decline has been much more gradual than China's, with India's fertility remaining slightly above replacement rate. In contrast, China's fertility declined further and from a higher peak, and has been below replacement rate since the early 1990s. Due largely to its higher fertility rate, India's population growth will continue longer, and the population will remain relatively younger than China's. Sometime around 2030, India will overtake China as the world's most populous country; after that, India's population is projected to increase by about 200 million, before peaking around 2060. Growth in working-age population will continue for several decades in India, while in China, the working-age population is already shrinking.

Among this group of six large developing countries, Bangladesh has had the fastest fertility decline, as births per woman fell from a peak of 6.9 in 1970 to below replacement, 2.05, in 2020. The steepness of the line is notable because the fertility rate had increased during the 1960s before the decline set in. This steep fertility decline has already dampened population growth in what had been a fast-growing country. Fertility in Bangladesh is projected to decline even further.

In contrast to the long steep fertility decline in Bangladesh, the fertility decline in Pakistan started later and has been slower. The decline slowed in 2010, reaching 3.6 in 2020. Although continued declines are projected, fertility is expected to remain well above replacement rate until at least midcentury. Fueled by high fertility, Pakistan's population is projected to increase by 53% by 2050, compared to just 17% for Bangladesh.

Almost as steep as that of Bangladesh, Indonesia's fertility decline stalled around 2000. The rate has hovered around 2.5 since 2000, before falling to 2.3 in 2020.

The fertility decline in the Philippines is especially remarkable because the decline started earlier than elsewhere and from a higher peak. The initially rapid decline from a high peak slowed after 1985, but fell to 2.6 births per woman in 2020, and is projected to reach replacement rate before midcentury.

You won't be surprised that Nigeria is an outlier in this group. While it fits the income profile, it still had extremely high fertility of 5.42 in 2020. Nigeria's population is projected to double by 2050, reaching a total of 400 million and replacing the United States as the world's third most populous country.

While most lower-middle-income countries are in Africa and Asia, several Latin American countries fall in this group, including two countries in the Northern Triangle of Central America— El Salvador and Honduras. Guatemala, the third and largest, is now in the upper-middle-income group. Over the past several years these Northern Triangle countries have fueled a wave of economic migrants seeking better economic prospects, as well as political refugees fleeing from drug-related violence. As shown in Figure 3.13, all three of these countries have had large and relatively rapid declines in fertility since 1960, but past decades of high fertility will continue to fuel explosive population growth and will increase the numbers of young people seeking better economic prospects.

FIGURE 3.13   Fertility rates in the Northern Triangle of Central America have fallen by more than half, but decades of high fertility will continue to fuel explosive population growth.

Fertility Rate (Births per Woman)

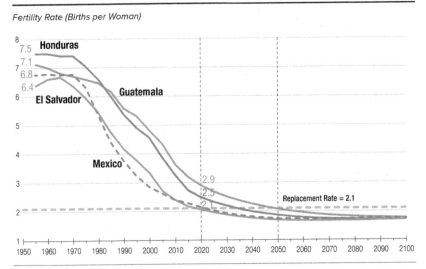

Note: The Northern Triangle countries of Central America are Guatemala, Honduras, and El Salvador. Mexico is shown for reference.

Data source: United Nations, *World Population Prospects 2019,* medium variant.

In all three Northern Triangle countries, and in Mexico as well, fertility rates have fallen significantly. They all saw peak rates between 6.0 and 8.0 births per woman during the 1960s, and since then have had large declines of 4.0 to 5.0 births per woman.

Guatemala, the most populous of the three Northern Triangle countries, with a 2020 population of 18 million, also has the highest 2020 fertility of the three, at 2.9 births per woman. Although its growth is slowing, Guatemala's population is projected to rise by 50% over the next 30 years, registering an average annual increase of 1.4%. The number of children will stabilize, but the working-age population is projected to increase due to past high fertility rates. Like Guatemala, Honduras also faces continued strong population growth that is forecasted to slow after midcentury as the effects of lower fertility take hold. El Salvador, with 6.5 million people, is the least populous of the Northern Triangle countries, and the only one of the three to have below-replacement fertility. Due to its early and steep fertility decline, the number of children has already started shrinking, and growth in the working-age population has slowed.

The fertility declines in Honduras and Guatemala are especially notable, not just because of the size of the declines, but because of the high rates during the 1960s. Although births per woman have declined significantly, the total populations will continue to rapidly increase, at least for a generation or two, until the impacts of the fertility declines are fully reflected. This will continue to fuel the working-age populations and most likely increase the numbers of people seeking better economic prospects in the United States.

LOW-INCOME COUNTRIES: STILL HIGH FERTILITY

Low-income countries generally have the world's highest fertility rates and have seen the smallest and latest declines. Twenty-seven of the 34 low-income countries have fertility rates of 4.0 births per woman or higher, with the highest occurring in Niger at 7.0 and Somalia at 6.1. While most other countries had fertility declines beginning in the 1960s and 1970s, most low-income countries experienced sustained high fertility, with many even seeing increasing fertility rates well into the 1990s. Over the past few decades, the patterns of fertility decline in these countries varied, but most declines have been small and gradual, with a few exceptions discussed below.

Figure 3.14 shows fertility rates for the five most populous low-income countries as of 2020. You can see examples of increases in already high fertility, sustained high fertility, and gradual fertility decline.

Ethiopia, the most populous of the low-income countries, saw its fertility rate increase during the 1970s and 1980s, peaking at 7.4 in 1985. By 2020 it had declined to 4.3. Fertility in the DRC also increased substantially, from 6.0 to 6.8, and has only recently ticked down to 6.0 births per woman, the same level as in 1955. At 6.0, the DRC has the third-highest fertility rate in the world, behind the much less populous Niger and Somalia.

Afghanistan and Uganda had very high and unchanged fertility rates until around 2000. In Afghanistan, fertility stabilized at

FIGURE 3.14   Decades of high fertility in the most populous low-income countries will fuel continued explosive population growth, despite recent fertility declines.

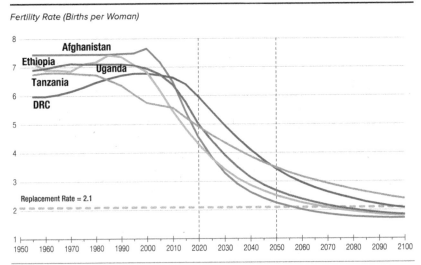

Fertility Rate (Births per Woman)

Data source: United Nations, *World Population Prospects 2019,* medium variant.

7.5 births per woman and didn't begin declining until after a brief uptick in 2000. Since then, it has declined by almost 3.0 births per woman, one of the largest declines among low-income countries.

Of the five, Tanzania saw the earliest fertility decline, but its pace has been slower and its decline smaller than in Afghanistan and Ethiopia.

What's important here is that although the fertility declines dampen their population growth rates, all five of these countries, and low-income countries overall, are projected to see continued explosive population growth. The DRC, Tanzania, and Uganda are projected to be among the fastest-growing populations worldwide, with their populations projected to double by 2050. Growth in Afghanistan and Ethiopia will be slower due to their larger fertility declines, but these two populations are still projected to nearly double by 2050.

To help you understand the importance of these countries, we can look at their disproportionate contribution to global population growth. These five most populous low-income countries have a combined 2020 population of 350 million, or about 4% of the world's population. Their projected near-doubling over the next 30 years adds another 334 million, which represents 17% of the projected worldwide growth. The DRC and Ethiopia each account for an astonishing 5% of projected growth, with even higher shares projected for the second half of the century.

CONCLUSION

You now have a good understanding of key differences in how fertility rates have changed around the world over the past 60 years. Although there is tremendous variation across countries, we can discern three distinct patterns of fertility decline.

First, most of the established industrialized economies already had low fertility at the end of World War II, and most have seen continued, small, steady declines and several decades of below-replacement fertility. Second, most developing countries with previously high fertility rates during the 1960s and 1970s have had significant fertility declines; some declines have been large and steep, while others have been more gradual. A third pattern emerges for high-fertility countries, mostly those in sub-Saharan Africa, that have only recently begun to see fertility declines.

We might be tempted to applaud these fertility declines for their role in dampening population growth, but that is only part of the story. It's true that fertility declines eventually blunt population growth, but they also lead to other significant outcomes that need to be considered, including aging populations and shrinking workforces.

After we consider the other two drivers—life expectancy and migration—you will be better able to understand the implications of these fertility declines for population growth and age structure. Most importantly, you will be able to see how differences in fertility declines unfold in the subsequent arcs of workforce change and the accelerated pace of population aging.

4 INCREASING LIFE EXPECTANCY

"Air Pollution Is Cutting Global Life Expectancy"
Worldhealth.net, November 18, 2018

"Middle Classes Drive Up Life Expectancy in Sub-Saharan Africa"
The Guardian, by Rebecca Ratcliffe, September 15, 2018

"India Plans Big Increase in Health-Care Spending to Catch Up to Rivals"
Washington Post, by Rama Lakshmi, March 9, 2012

For years we've been hearing about people living longer, and we've celebrated the increasing numbers of centenarians. But lately we have been hearing about declines in life expectancy stemming from several causes, including drug overdoses, drug violence, obesity, air pollution, and COVID-19, to name a few. Not to mention the already high death rates from gun violence, drunk driving, and suicide. Yet despite the more recent grim news, increased life expectancy over the past century represents a remarkable success story. Over the past 65 years, worldwide life expectancy at birth increased by 25 years, from 47 years in 1955 to 72 in 2020, with an increase to 77 projected for 2050. This worldwide gain in life expectancy is one of the most stunning success stories of the twentieth century, and you can look forward to promising future gains.

Though life expectancy has been increasing almost everywhere, as you've come to expect from reading this book, the levels and patterns of gain vary widely across regions and countries. The already high life expectancies in the more developed countries have steadily increased, averaging 79 years in 2020—up 14 years from 1955. In contrast, less developed countries starting from a lower base have

seen much larger and often sudden gains. Overall, developing countries have enjoyed a 29-year gain in life expectancy, from 42 years
in 1955 to 71 in 2020, with many countries experiencing even larger
gains.

In some places, life expectancy gains have slowed, and in other
countries, as we all know from the news, life expectancy has even
declined. The biggest increases generally stem from basic improvements in public health and sanitation, which contribute to overall
health improvements and dramatically reduce the number of child
and maternal deaths. Other gains result from ongoing improvement
in health care policies and practices, including new medications,
innovative medical devices, and behavioral changes. Conversely,
actual declines in life expectancy usually reflect specific negative
events, such as wars, epidemics, economic downturns, and other
political disruptions. Declines can also result from ongoing poor
health care. Some of these declines are short-term, while others have
long-lasting effects.

This chapter explores life expectancy trends across countries and
regions and shows how the gains have differed globally. The steep
increases in life expectancy in many developing countries will contribute to rapid population growth across all age brackets as well
as to continued changes in age structure. In contrast, for advanced
economies, the gains in life expectancy are likely to be concentrated in the older brackets and will contribute further to population aging. The steepness of the changes is particularly important
because it is linked to the speed of population growth. The chapter
also highlights deviations from the generally upward trend.

Before we dig into differences in how life expectancy has been
changing around the world, it will help to understand more fully
how life expectancy is defined and reported. Since life expectancy
might not mean what you think it does, here are some clarifications
for making sense of the data and understanding the significance of
the differences across countries.

Life expectancy at birth, the most common indicator for comparing mortality rates, is the average number of years a newborn
is expected to live if current age-specific mortality rates continue

to apply. For example, if the current death rates continue to apply throughout the baby's life, a baby born in the United States in 2020 is expected to live to 79 years. To reiterate, this definition assumes that the age-specific death rates at the time of birth—the *prevailing death rates*—will continue. It assumes that babies born today will face today's death rates as they reach successive age brackets, with no allowance for improvement during the person's life. Because it seems so unrealistic to assume there will be no future innovations that reduce death rates, this assumption may be difficult for many of us to accept. After all, most of us imagine that health care innovations and lifestyle changes would help individuals live longer. But with this definition, those prospects for future improvement are just that—they are prospects not yet observed in the actual death statistics. The measure used here is based only on applying observed data. To address future prospects, we would have to look to the models developed by innovators and scientists, which include formulas reflecting the likely or hoped for life-saving impacts of medical innovations, such as new drugs and technologies.

You might then wonder why we even use statistics based on prevailing death rates. The answer is that using prevailing rates allows us to make useful comparisons. Based on observed deaths, we can compare countries at a particular time. Then, when an innovation actually comes into play, the impact will show up in observed death rates, which will have improved. We can then compare countries and look at increases over time. So, statistics based on prevailing death rates allow us to compare the current—or then current— health of different countries and to assess how this health has changed over time.

To understand the usefulness of life expectancy statistics, it will help you to think of life expectancy as a *composite indicator*, incorporating current death rates at every age of the population. Viewed in this way, life expectancy at a specific age is a summary measure for people at that particular age, indicating the average age of death at a certain point in time. For example, estimated life expectancy at birth in 2020 incorporates information about 2020 death rates for people at every age, to create an estimate of number of years of life if those death rates prevail. Similarly, estimated life expectancy at age 65 in 2020 would combine information about the 2020 death rates of all individuals age 65 and older to create an estimate of the number of years of life remaining, if those death rates prevail. This view will also help you to distinguish between the technical definition, which uses prevailing death rates, and the more conceptual sense. Technically, life expectancy statistics are defined to reflect the prevailing death rates in a given population. Conceptually, life expectancy reflects the overall health of a population—the higher the life expectancy the better the health. There are other more detailed measures of health, but we can rely on this one as a general indicator.

You might also keep in mind that the term *expected* is a statistical measure of probability, which means something different in a demographic or statistical context than in general conversation. It does not mean "what is reasonable to anticipate based on what you might think is likely to happen or what you think is a reasonable outlook to plan around." Based on your family history or your personal characteristics, you might think you will live to 100, but that information and view of the future is not incorporated into the official life expectancy indicator, which uses only observed death statistics. Other models account for medical innovations and other changes and characteristics that affect mortality, but these are used for other types of projections and comparisons.

News reports that today's newborns could live to 100 is a good example of these two different perspectives on what is *expected*. If you look at the UN statistics on life expectancy at birth, you will see that a baby born in the United States in 2020 is, on average, expected to reach age 79. Remember, this perspective assumes no health improvements during a person's life. But by using a more inclusive lens that incorporates health care improvements and scientific advances, many researchers estimate that a large percentage of babies born in 2020 will benefit from major health improvements and will live to age 100. The first statistic assumes prevailing death rates continue, and the second assumes some promising new developments will come to fruition and reduce death rates.

Most of the analysis in this book considers historical changes in life expectancy and compares the increases over time. For example, in the US in 1955, life expectancy at birth was 69 years. That statistic was compiled using the 1955 death rates of people at every age from children to the oldest old. By 2020, the death rates had declined and life expectancy at birth had increased by 10 years—a baby born in the US in 2020 would be expected to live to 79 years.

Now, compare this to a country with much higher childhood death rates. For example, babies born in China in 1955, given the prevailing death rates, would have been expected to live to age 44. By 1970, life expectancy at birth in China had increased to age 55; and by 1980, another 10-year increase had occurred. These increases stem mainly from reduced child mortality rates, and most of the increase in childhood survival results from improved sanitation and other public health initiatives, such as better nutrition and health care. Once those childhood death rates start falling, life expectancy at birth increases. In addition, as more children survive childhood, the death rates at each age decline. So, once the probability of dying in childhood is reduced, life expectancy rises across the age spectrum.

While many low-income countries still suffer from high infant and child mortality, many others have made huge gains, which have contributed to rising life expectancy in those countries. Now we turn from generalities to specifics and explore how these gains have differed across countries and over time.

GLOBAL OVERVIEW:
BIG PICTURE OF LIFE EXPECTANCY

WORLD MAPS OF LIFE EXPECTANCY

The maps in Figure 4.1 show dramatic improvements in life expectancy throughout the world. In 1955 the highest life expectancies of 71 to 72 years occurred in just five countries in Northern Europe. As of 2020, relatively high life expectancies had spread throughout the world. More than 30 countries, most of them in Europe and East Asia, saw 2020 life expectancies of more than 80 years,

FIGURE 4.1   Life expectancy has increased worldwide, with more than 30 countries reaching life expectancies higher than 80 years. The lowest life expectancies remain concentrated in Africa.

Life Expectancy at Birth, in Years

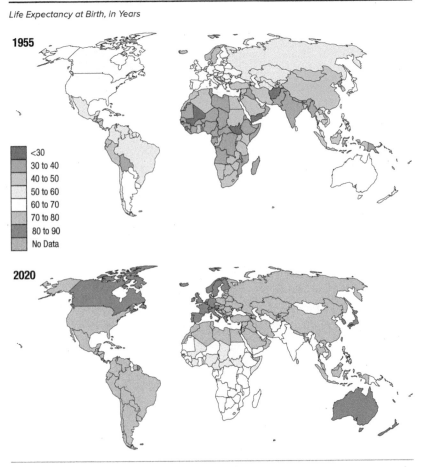

Data source: United Nations, *World Population Prospects 2019,* medium variant.

and more than half of all countries had a life expectancy of more than 70. As in the past, the lowest life expectancies continue to be concentrated in sub-Saharan Africa. Despite some gains, half of the 54 African countries had 2020 life expectancies of less than 63 years. Most startling is that this group includes three of the most populous and fast-growing countries—Nigeria with 2020 life expectancy at 54 years, the DRC at 60, and Uganda at 63.

DIVERGENT PATTERNS OF LIFE EXPECTANCY FOR SELECTED COUNTRIES

As you see in the world maps, life expectancy in 2020 varies widely across the world, and the changes in life expectancy over time have varied significantly across countries and regions. Figure 4.2 shows stark differences across selected countries of particular interest. The already high life expectancy in the more developed countries at the top of the chart has steadily increased, though at different rates. For example, life expectancy in Japan, at 84 years in 2020, increased sharply following World War II and surpassed life expectancy in the United States in the late 1960s. Interestingly, US life expectancy grew more slowly, falling short of other industrialized economies, reaching 79 years in 2015 and then dipping slightly.

In contrast to the slow but steady increases in the more developed countries, many less developed countries have experienced

FIGURE 4.2   Life expectancy has been increasing everywhere but remains extremely low in some of the fastest-growing populations, such as Nigeria and the DRC.

Life Expectancy at Birth, in Years, Selected Countries

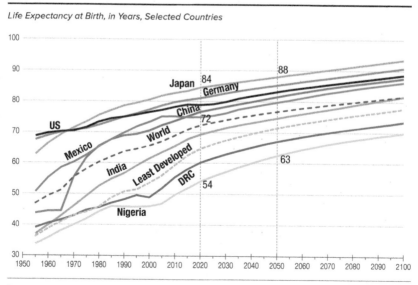

Data source: United Nations, *World Population Prospects 2019,* medium variant.

large and rapid gains in life expectancy. The increase in China's life expectancy was especially dramatic, improving from 45 years in 1965 to 69 in 1990, and reaching 77 by 2020. A further increase to 82 years is projected for 2050. Most of these gains stem from improvements in public health, including public sanitation and nutrition. You will see in Chapter 6 how the combination of increased life expectancy and a steep drop in fertility contributes to China's rapid aging.

India's life expectancy also improved significantly, but not as much or as rapidly as China's. As in China, the steepest gain in India occurred in the 1960s and 1970s, due largely to improvements in public health. Mexico is another example of a developing country with a large increase in life expectancy. As we will see later, it is also an example of where recent civil unrest and drug violence have dampened life expectancy gains.

The most startling data on life expectancy concerns the low level of life expectancy in the fast-growing populations of sub-Saharan Africa. Nigeria, the most populous country in Africa, and currently the seventh most populous in the world, with 206 million people, had a 2020 life expectancy of only 54 years—the fifth lowest in the world. This is particularly startling because Nigeria, fueled by high fertility, is projected to add nearly 200 million people over the next 30 years, boosting its 2050 population to 400 million. Nigeria alone is projected to account for 10% of the world's projected population growth between 2020 and 2050. The DRC, with a life expectancy of only 60 years and a projected population gain of 105 million, will account for another 5% of worldwide population growth.

GLOBAL PERSPECTIVES ON INCREASING LIFE EXPECTANCY

LIFE EXPECTANCY BY REGION

Looking at the global patterns of change gives us an overall context for understanding the wide variation across countries. You can see that although life expectancy has increased worldwide, there are significant differences in the amount and speed of increase across regions. As Figure 4.3 shows, the already high life expectancies in Europe and North America have risen since the 1950s, although the pace of improvement differed. The gap initially widened as Europe's gains slowed, but recently, US life expectancy has dipped while Europe's life expectancy has continued to grow. Regionally, North America has the highest life expectancy at 79 years, but many European countries rank well ahead of the North American average. While Europe is home to many of the highest-life-expectancy countries, the weak regional growth reflects the stagnation and poor gains in life expectancy in Russia and other Eastern European countries, which together account for almost 40% of Europe's total population. In 2020, life expectancy in Eastern Europe was 74 years, compared with 81 to 82 years for the other subregions. This is a good example of how regional averages hide important trends.

A striking feature of the regional comparison is that since 1950, all the developing regions have seen substantial gains in life expectancy and have narrowed the gap between them and the more

FIGURE 4.3   Asia had the largest gain in life expectancy and is now just two years behind Latin America. Despite its recent gains, Africa's life expectancy is almost 11 years below Asia's.

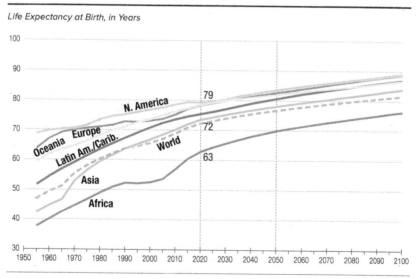

Life Expectancy at Birth, in Years

Data source: United Nations, *World Population Prospects 2019,* medium variant.

developed regions. Asia had the largest gain, 31 years, as life expectancy increased from 42 to almost 73. The steep increase beginning in 1965 reflects an especially large gain in China, as noted above. Steady gains continued in Latin America, where 2020 life expectancy reached 75, keeping the region a few years ahead of Asia.

Africa's life expectancy remains well below the global average, even though Africa too has narrowed the gap with the more developed regions. Life expectancy in Africa improved from just 37 years in 1955 to 52 years in 1990, when the gains were truncated, largely due to the AIDS epidemic. Average life expectancy for the region stagnated around 52 years for more than a decade before increasing again. Starting around 2005, life expectancy rose sharply to 63 years, but remains almost 11 years below Asia's.

According to the UN projections for 2020 to 2050, global life expectancy will increase from 72 to almost to 77 years, a 4.5-year gain. Africa will show the largest gain, with a seven-year increase, bringing Africa's life expectancy up to almost 70 years, still well below Latin America and Asia. Life expectancy in Latin America is projected to increase by slightly more than five years, and in Asia by slightly less than five years. The already high life expectancies in North America and Europe are projected to increase by slightly more than four years.

LIFE EXPECTANCY BY DEVELOPMENT GROUP

When we compare the progress in life expectancy by geographic regions, we see slow, steady gains in the developed regions of Europe and North America and steeper increases in the developing regions of Asia, Latin America, and Africa. The comparison by development group in Figure 4.4 gives us some additional insights into how gains in life expectancy affect population growth.

In the more developed regions, the already high life expectancy has steadily increased, reaching 79 years in 2020, a gain of 14 years since 1955. In contrast, the remarkable gains in the two less developed groups were nearly twice as large. Both subgroups had gains of at least 28 years, but along different trajectories.

FIGURE 4.4   Although gradually increasing, life expectancy in the 47 least developed countries lags seven years behind that in other less developed countries.

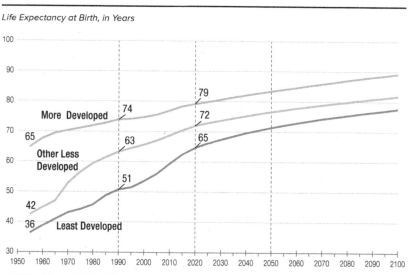

Data source: United Nations, *World Population Prospects 2019*, medium variant.

Since 1955, the least developed subgroup of 47 countries has experienced relatively steady increases in life expectancy, rising from 36 years in 1955 to 65 years in 2020. The gains slowed in the early 1990s due to the AIDS epidemic but accelerated after 2000. Although the gap with other countries has narrowed, the low life expectancy for this group is critical because it is the fastest-growing group. Fueled by these large life expectancy gains and still high fertility rates, the least developed countries will account for a disproportionate share of global population growth. In 1950, these 47 least developed countries accounted for 8% of the world's population, but that share grew to 14% by 2020. According to UN projections, this group of vulnerable countries will account for 42% of population growth over the next 30 years, and by 2050 will reach 19% of the global population. The most populous least developed countries include Bangladesh, Ethiopia, the DRC, Tanzania, and Uganda. These last three are also among the fastest-growing countries, each projected to grow by at least 2.3% per year over the next 30 years.

Since 1955, other less developed countries have enjoyed a 29-year gain in life expectancy, from 42 years in 1955 to 72 years in 2020. This group saw a particularly large gain from 1965 to 1990, with slower but steady increases continuing since then.

LIFE EXPECTANCY BY INCOME LEVEL

Figure 4.5 shows life expectancy by income group, and further explains the differential pattern of life expectancy gains: on average, countries with higher per-capita incomes have higher life expectancy.

The group of high-income countries has seen small, steady gains, with life expectancy reaching nearly 81 years in 2020. Unlike the steady gains in the high-income group, the upper-middle-income countries, led by China, showed significant gains from 1965 to 1990, with life expectancy reaching 75 in 2020, just five years below the high-income group. In contrast, the lower-middle-income countries, led by India, had more gradual gains in life expectancy. Finally, the

FIGURE 4.5   Upper-middle-income countries show a steep gain in life expectancy during the 1960s and 1970s. Lower-middle-income countries registered more gradual gains.

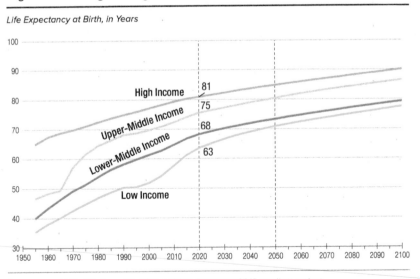

Life Expectancy at Birth, in Years

Data source: United Nations, *World Population Prospects 2019,* medium variant.

low-income countries, mainly located in sub-Saharan Africa, have enjoyed a 12 -year gain in life expectancy since 2000, bringing the 2020 level to 63 years, still nine years below the global average.

The two lower-income groups are the fastest-growing populations and account for a disproportionate share of population growth. Together, the two groups make up about half the world's total population, but are projected to account for almost 90% of the projected population growth over the next 30 years.

Knowing how the timing of life expectancy gains differs across groups will help you better understand how these improvements contribute to population growth. For example, the large increase in life expectancy in the upper-middle-income countries contributed to the high population growth several decades ago, with smaller contributions expected in the future as life expectancy gains decrease. Similarly, the recent gains in life expectancy for the low-income countries are now reflected in disproportionately rapid population growth. The combined population of the 34 low-income countries, 10% of the global total in 2020, is projected to nearly double to 1.5 billion in 2050, accounting for more than one-third of the global population increase.

DIVERGENT TRENDS ACROSS COUNTRIES

COUNTRIES WITH HIGHEST AND LOWEST LIFE EXPECTANCY

While the previous sections have analyzed the broad differences in life expectancy across regions and groups, we now turn to considering the divergent trends across individual countries. As you might recall from the 2020 map in Figure 4.1, due to the stunning increases over the past century, high life expectancy is now much more common throughout the world than it had been. Given that great progress, it might not surprise you that the list of high-life-expectancy countries in Table 4.1 is diverse, including large and small populations, large and small economies, and countries in diverse geographic locations, including four continents. One thing these highest-life-expectancy

TABLE 4.1 The 20 countries with the highest life expectancies are diverse in population, GDP, and geography; high per capita income is the common thread.

Top 20 Life Expectancies (at Birth, in Years), 2020				
2020 Rank	Country/Area	1955	2020	Change 1955–2020
1	Hong Kong	63.2	84.6	21.5
2	Japan	62.8	84.4	21.6
3	Macao	61.0	84.0	23.1
4	Switzerland	69.3	83.6	14.2
5	Singapore	60.2	83.4	23.2
6	Spain	64.6	83.4	18.8
7	Italy	66.5	83.3	16.8
8	Australia	69.4	83.2	13.8
9	Iceland	72.2	82.8	10.5
10	South Korea	41.9	82.8	40.8
11	Israel	68.9	82.7	13.9
12	Sweden	71.9	82.6	10.7
13	France	67.3	82.5	15.2
14	Malta	65.8	82.3	16.5
15	Canada	69.1	82.2	13.2
16	Norway	72.8	82.2	9.4
17	New Zealand	69.8	82.1	12.3
18	Netherlands	71.9	82.1	10.1
19	Ireland	66.9	82.0	15.2
20	Luxembourg	66.0	82.0	16.0
	Other			
	United States	68.7	78.8	10.1
	China	43.8	76.6	32.8
	Iran	40.6	76.3	35.8
	India	37.0	69.3	32.3
	WORLD	*47.0*	*72.3*	*25.3*

Data source: United Nations, *World Population Prospects 2019*, medium variant.

countries share is that they are all high-income countries. And all have 2020 life expectancies greater than the high-income average of 81 years. Also notable is the tight clustering at the top. Hong Kong has the highest 2020 life expectancy at 84.6 years and is closely followed by Japan and Macao. Another five countries, including Switzerland, Singapore, Spain, Italy, and Australia, are close contenders, having achieved life expectancies of between 83 and 84 years.

Propelled by large gains in life expectancy, Japan and Hong Kong joined the top-ranked countries in the late 1970s, and by 1985, Japan had the world's highest life expectancy. Hong Kong recently edged out Japan, with a 2020 life expectancy of 84.6 compared with Japan's 84.4. Though similar small increases have reshuffled the overall ranking, it is remarkable to see that so many countries have achieved such high life expectancy. It is also notable that many of these countries have had especially large gains in life expectancy. As shown in Table 4.1, of these 20 high-life-expectancy countries, the East Asian countries saw the largest gains. These large gains combined with their steep fertility declines will contribute to the rapid aging we will see in many of these countries.

The geography of high life expectancy is interesting: three East Asian economies—Hong Kong, Japan, and Macao—outrank all the European economies. While European countries have consistently ranked among the highest life expectancies, East Asian countries are relatively new to the list.

Figure 4.6 illustrates the history of some of the highest-life-expectancy countries. While their lines have recently converged, the path of their progress differs. Historically, European countries had the highest life expectancy and have been enjoying continued steady increases. In 1955, as shown in Figure 4.6, the highest life expectancies occurred in Norway, Iceland, the Netherlands, Sweden, and Denmark. While the European countries were benefiting from gradual and consistent gains, Japan and the Asian Tigers—Singapore, Hong Kong, South Korea, and Taiwan—were achieving large and rapid gains. By 1985, Japan surpassed the Europeans to take the lead in life expectancy, and was closely followed by Hong Kong and

FIGURE 4.6 Spurred by rapid economic development, life expectancy in several East Asian countries surged past the high rates in the top-ranking European countries.

Life Expectancy at Birth, in Years

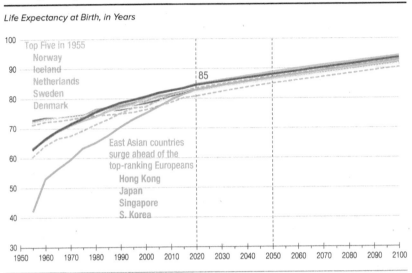

Data source: United Nations, *World Population Prospects 2019*, medium variant.

later by Singapore. South Korea recently surged past many others, and is projected to keep pace with Japan and Singapore—a noteworthy achievement considering its 1955 level of just 42 years.

The rapid pace of life expectancy gain in Asia is important for several reasons. It reflects enormous progress in health improvements, and it has contributed to significant population growth and rapid aging. In contrast, the slow but steady life expectancy gains in Europe have contributed to a much slower pace of aging. As you will see in Chapter 6, the Asian Tigers are projected to age much faster than the aging European societies, and three times faster than the United States.

As we learned from the map in Figure 4.1, the lowest-life-expectancy countries are all located in sub-Saharan Africa, with life expectancies ranging from 53 to 61 years. The lowest, as shown in Table 4.2, occurred in the Central African Republic, at 53 years, followed by Lesotho, Chad, and Sierra Leone. Surprisingly, Nigeria has the world's fifth-lowest life expectancy at just 54 years.

TABLE 4.2 The 20 countries with the lowest life expectancies are all located in sub-Saharan Africa.

Lowest 20 Life Expectancies (at Birth, in Years), 2020				
2020 Rank	Country	1955	2020	Change 1955–2020
1	Central African Rep.	32.7	52.7	19.9
2	Lesotho	45.0	53.5	8.5
3	Chad	36.1	53.8	17.7
4	Sierra Leone	28.8	54.1	25.3
5	Nigeria	33.8	54.2	20.4
6	Somalia	34.0	56.9	23.0
7	Côte d'Ivoire	30.2	57.2	27.1
8	South Sudan	27.9	57.4	29.5
9	Guinea-Bissau	35.6	57.8	22.2
10	Equatorial Guinea	34.0	58.2	24.3
11	Mali	27.0	58.7	31.7
12	Cameroon	38.5	58.8	20.2
13	Eswatini	40.4	59.3	19.0
14	Mozambique	35.0	60.1	25.1
15	DRC	39.1	60.2	21.2
16	Togo	35.3	60.5	25.2
17	Angola	35.9	60.5	24.7
18	Zimbabwe	49.7	60.8	11.2
19	Burkina Faso	30.9	60.9	30.0
20	Burundi	39.0	61.0	22.0
	Other			
	Niger	34.5	61.8	27.3
	Uganda	40.1	62.8	22.6
	South Africa	44.8	63.6	18.8
	Africa	37.5	62.7	25.2
	WORLD	*47.0*	*72.3*	*25.3*

Data source: United Nations, *World Population Prospects 2019,* medium variant.

Most of these are low-income countries and most are among the world's least developed. Many of them have had large gains in life expectancy, which, in turn, combine with their high fertility rates to create explosive population growth. As a result, despite their low life expectancy, many of these countries are among the fastest-growing populations.

Nigeria is the world's seventh-largest population and one of the fastest-growing, so its poor health status and fifth-lowest life expectancy are especially startling, and will have important implications for its economic growth and political stability. In addition to Nigeria, the list of 20 lowest life expectancies includes three other large countries with fast-growing populations—the DRC, Angola, and Mozambique.

LIFE EXPECTANCY IN THE LARGE ECONOMIES

Among the 15 largest economies, Japan ranks highest in life expectancy at 84 years, followed closely by Spain, Italy, and Australia. As shown in Table 4.3, nine of the 15 largest economies have life expectancies clustered between 81 and 84. The United States stands slightly apart, with a life expectancy of 79 years. These top 10 are all high-income countries.

The next group of countries includes five emerging economies. The first three, China, Brazil, and Mexico—with life expectancies ranging from 75 to 77—have experienced large gains in life expectancy. Next on the list is Russia, with a life expectancy of 72.3 years, just matching the global average, followed by India, with a 2020 life expectancy three years below the global average.

You can see in Figure 4.7 some important differences in how life expectancy has increased across these large economies. Over the past 65 years, the United States and many European economies have enjoyed slow but steady gains in life expectancy. Among the large economies, the US posted the smallest gain—only 10 years—since 1955, and as you can see, the US recently suffered a slight decline. While remaining relatively high, US life expectancy continues to lose ground to Europe.

TABLE 4.3   Among the large economies, Japan has the highest life expectancy, at 84 years. South Korea, China, and India had the largest gains.

Life Expectancy at Birth, in Years, 15 Largest Economies			
	1955	**2020**	**Change 1955–2020**	
Japan	62.8	84.4	**21.6**	
Spain	64.6	83.4	18.8	
Italy	66.5	83.3	16.8	
Australia	69.4	83.2	13.8	
South Korea	41.9	82.8	**40.8**	**High-Income Countries**
France	67.3	82.5	15.2	
Canada	69.1	82.2	13.2	
UK	69.4	81.2	11.7	
Germany	67.5	81.1	13.6	
US	68.7	78.8	10.1	
China	43.8	76.6	**32.8**	
Brazil	50.8	75.6	**24.7**	
Mexico	50.7	75.0	**24.3**	**Emerging Economies**
Russia	58.5	72.3	13.8	
India	37.0	69.3	**32.3**	
WORLD	*47.0*	*72.3*	*25.3*	

Data source: World Bank; and United Nations, *World Population Prospects 2019*, medium variant.

Japan's life expectancy surpassed both the cluster of European countries and the United States during the late 1960s. During this time, South Korea achieved one of the largest life expectancy gains of any country—nearly 41 years since 1955—and over the last decade surpassed the US, Germany, the UK, Canada, and France. While India and China also had large gains—more than 32 years since 1955—India's life expectancy grew more gradually, while China achieved a steep gain during the 1970s.

Although Russia's life expectancy has recently recovered from its dip during the 1990s, it has diverged from the advanced country trends since 1965. Russia's life expectancy stagnated after 1965 at around 68 years, then fell after the collapse of the Soviet Union to a

FIGURE 4.7   The US continues to lose ground in life expectancy, while South Korea surges past many European countries. Despite the recent gain, Russia remains an outlier.

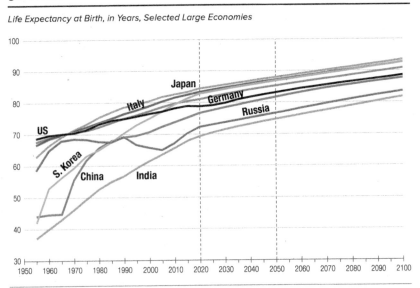

Life Expectancy at Birth, in Years, Selected Large Economies

Data source: United Nations, *World Population Prospects 2019*, medium variant.

low of 65 years in 2005. Following recent gains, Russia's life expectancy increased to 72.3 years, past the 1990 peak, and just reaching the global average.

LIFE EXPECTANCY BY AGE

The analysis of life expectancy by country and region reveals several patterns of life expectancy gains from 1955 to 2020, ranging from steep gains to slow and steady increases. Most dramatic and arguably most consequential for population growth are the large gains achieved by developing countries, such as those in South Korea, India, and China. Their large gains largely reflect reduced death rates among children due to improvements in basic sanitation and other public health measures. The role of reduced childhood mortality becomes clearer when you look at life expectancy by age for an individual country.

Using South Korea as an example, Figure 4.8 shows how life expectancy and the gains in life expectancy vary by age. The solid blue line indicates the large increase in life expectancy at birth. Most of this gain resulted from a dramatic reduction in childhood deaths, from 251 deaths per thousand in 1955 to just three in 2020. More than 80% of the decline in childhood mortality occurred from 1955 to 1975, as reflected in the steep increase in life expectancy. Gains in life expectancy in the upper ages have been much smaller than gains at birth. For example, life expectancy at age 65, shown in solid gray, increased by 13 years from 73 to 86, compared with an increase of 41 years for life expectancy at birth. The rate of increase in life expectancy is projected to slow, especially for life expectancy at birth, and the age gap will narrow as room for improvement at younger ages diminishes.

The figure shows several important trends that shed light on demographic changes and potential government policy responses. Given the low life expectancy at birth in developing countries during the 1950s, the life expectancy at age 65 seems surprisingly high.

FIGURE 4.8   Gains in life expectancy vary by age. The large gain in life expectancy at birth stems mainly from declining childhood death rates.

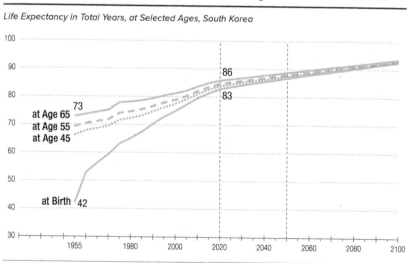

Life Expectancy in Total Years, at Selected Ages, South Korea

Data source: United Nations, *World Population Prospects 2019*, medium variant.

In South Korea, a person who had survived to age 65 in 1955 could be expected to live on average to age 73, and a person who reached age 45 could be expected to live to age 66. The probability of reaching older ages was much lower than it is today, and as a result, the number of people age 65 and older was small; but if you were lucky enough to reach the older ages, you were likely to survive even longer. The biggest challenge in the developing countries was surviving childhood and young adulthood.

The gap between life expectancy at older ages and life expectancy at birth mainly reflects the higher death rate for younger ages. Once the child mortality rate is reduced due to basic improvements in sanitation, nutrition, and medical care, the gap decreases. As living standards substantially improve, death rates decline, and it becomes more challenging to achieve further reductions, so the rate of increase in life expectancy typically slows. Conversely, for higher-income countries, more of the gains in life expectancy will occur in the older age brackets. Such gains stem largely from advances in medical care, including new pharmaceuticals and innovative surgeries.

The implications of continued increases in life expectancy are already important and will become even more consequential as populations age. Reliable projections of the number of old people will be critical for developing effective policies and practices, from social security to health care and housing. Also, the data on death rates at different ages could contribute to informed discussions about how best to channel resources for improving life expectancy at those ages. For example, better data could influence the choices about allocating funds to particular initiatives, such as reducing diseases of old age and improving highway safety, which could reduce death rates among young and old.

DECREASING LIFE EXPECTANCIES

There are important exceptions to the upward trend in life expectancy. Many countries have suffered from declines brought about by various economic, political, and social events, such as war, famine, epidemics, or poor medical care. You will see a few examples below.

HIV/AIDS Impact in Africa

The HIV/AIDS epidemic reduced life expectancy in many countries and produced an especially severe impact on many sub-Saharan African countries. Figure 4.9 shows life expectancy for several African countries, illustrating the differing impacts.

In South Africa, life expectancy declined by nine years from 63 years in 1995 to a low of 54 in 2005. The downturn reversed around 2010, and by 2020 life expectancy in South Africa slightly exceeded its previous peak. After decades of experiencing a 10-year advantage, South Africa's life expectancy is projected to just match the continent's average.

In contrast, life expectancy in Kenya, which had fallen by seven years, surpassed its pre–HIV/AIDS peak by 2010. By 2020 it

FIGURE 4.9   Even though life expectancies in Kenya and South Africa have recovered, they remain significantly behind the progress made in North Africa.

Life Expectancy at Birth, in Years

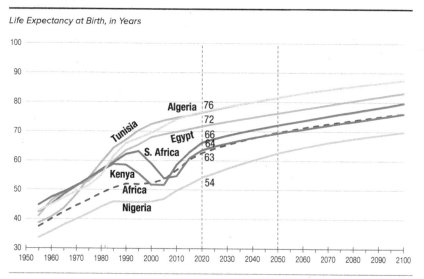

Data source: United Nations, *World Population Prospects 2019*, medium variant.

exceeded the previous peak by seven years, and now appears to be on a higher trajectory than South Africa's.

Nigeria, Africa's most populous country and the world's seventh largest, provides another example: life expectancy was stalled for 20 years during the AIDS crisis, but started increasing again after 2005. As of 2020, Nigeria's life expectancy of just 54 years ranked fifth lowest in the world, and nine years below the continent's average.

The incidence of AIDS was much lower in North Africa and generated little impact on life expectancy. Indeed, most countries in North Africa have achieved large gains in life expectancy, and three of them—Algeria, Tunisia, and Morocco—have posted the highest life expectancies in Africa, all above 76 years in 2020. What's interesting is that life expectancy in Kenya and South Africa had been closely tracking Egypt's and registering a few years above Algeria's until around 1985, when the AIDS crisis started to dampen both countries' life expectancies. Since then, the life expectancy trajectories have diverged. Even though Kenya and South Africa have reached their previous peaks, they remain significantly behind the progress made in North Africa. The gap has been narrowing, but both Kenya and South Africa appear to be on a much lower trajectory of increase. Perhaps continued pharmaceutical innovations will push these rates higher than currently projected. Of course, it remains to be determined how COVID-19 will influence life expectancy in these vulnerable countries.

Russia's Post-Soviet Decline in Life Expectancy

Life expectancy in Russia is another important exception to the global trend of increasing life expectancy. As you read above, Russia is the only large economy where life expectancy so starkly deviated from a steadily increasing trajectory.

While most countries have enjoyed continued gains in life expectancy, Russia's stagnated after 1960, following a post–World War II increase, and peaked at only 69 years. It then dropped after the collapse of the Soviet Union in 1991, as shown in Figure 4.10. By 2005, Russia's life expectancy had fallen by four years, to reach a low of 65 years. The decline is attributed to a combination of alcohol

FIGURE 4.10   Russia and Ukraine suffered declining life expectancy, while other Eastern European countries, including Poland and Hungary, achieved significant gains.

Life Expectancy at Birth, in Years

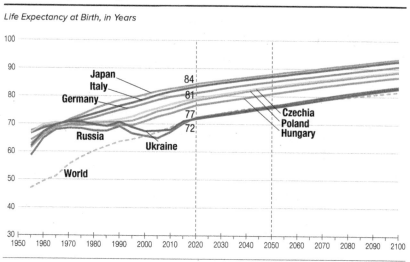

Data source: United Nations, *World Population Prospects 2019*, medium variant.

and tobacco abuse, auto fatalities, dangerous working conditions, and poor health care. While other former Soviet republics, including Kazakhstan, Belarus, and Ukraine, also saw life expectancy declines, Russia had one of the largest declines and one of the slowest recoveries.

Although the downturn was precipitated by the fall of the Soviet Union, Russia's life expectancy was already well below that of other European economies and had been deviating from the generally increasing trend since 1960. Russia's life expectancy has recovered past the peak achieved before the 1991 fall of the Soviet Union but remains well behind that of other European countries. As of 2020, life expectancy had increased to 72, the third-lowest life expectancy among the 40 European countries, ranking slightly ahead of Ukraine and Moldova. Russia's life expectancy is 11 years below those of top-ranking Switzerland, Spain, and Italy, and nine years below Germany's.

You can see in Figure 4.10 that other Eastern European countries have achieved higher life expectancies than Russia. In particular,

Czechia, Poland, and Hungary have had significant gains since 1990, following decades of stagnation. The steady increases in these three countries contrast sharply with the pattern that occurred in Russia. Although Russian life expectancy has recovered past the pre-1991 levels, the country's subpar health care and continued behavioral challenges have kept it from reaching the higher life expectancies seen elsewhere.

Iran and Iraq—Temporary War-Related Declines

Iran and Iraq, notable for their large gains in life expectancy since 1950, have also suffered periods of decline. As shown in Figure 4.11, both saw declines during the Iran–Iraq War, but their recoveries unfolded differently. Iran's life expectancy has been steadily increasing, except for a five-year drop during the war with Iraq. During the war, life expectancy for men fell by 11 years from 1980 to 1985, but quickly recovered. Within a decade, life expectancy for both men and women returned to its steady upward trajectory—an

FIGURE 4.11   Life expectancy in Iran and Iraq quickly recovered from their war-related downturns, but Iraq's continued political instability and civil war put it on a lower path.

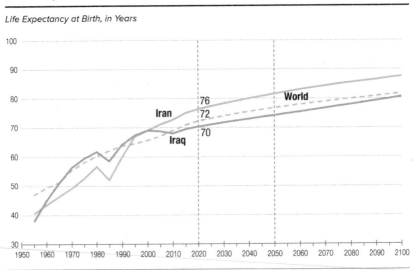

Life Expectancy at Birth, in Years

Data source: United Nations, *World Population Prospects 2019*, medium variant.

example of a temporary downturn associated with a discrete event. Iran's life expectancy surpassed the global average in 1990 and reached 76 by 2020.

Like Iran, Iraq recovered quickly from the life expectancy downturn during the Iran–Iraq War, with continued gains until around 2000. But life expectancy gains reversed during the US occupation, and continued to decline during the ensuing civil war. Since 2010, Iraq's life expectancy has increased to 70 years, but the political instability and civil war have dampened the recovery.

North Korea—Sustained Effects of Famine

In contrast to the temporary effects of war in Iran and Iraq, North Korea's famines and poor health care have had a sustained impact and moved the country's life expectancy to a much lower trajectory. The pattern is particularly stark both in light of its previous remarkable gain and as compared with South Korea's stunning and lasting gain.

Both North and South Korea enjoyed large boosts in life expectancy before World War II as the Japanese industrialization of the Korean peninsula produced significant health care improvements. However, life expectancy dropped in both countries during the Korean War due to war-related deaths, with North Korea suffering an 11-year decline from its previous peak of 49 in 1950, while South Korea's decline was much smaller. By 1955, as you can see in Figure 4.12, North Korea's life expectancy had fallen to 38 years— four years lower than in South Korea.

Both countries have had large gains since 1955, but their trajectories differed, reflecting the divergent economic and political forces affecting living standards. Fueled by its rapid economic development and industrialization, South Korea enjoyed one of the largest gains in life expectancy—a 41-year increase since 1955—and at 83 years in 2020, its life expectancy is now one of the world's highest. In contrast, North Korea's life expectancy, fueled by Soviet economic aid, reached 70 years in 1995, but dropped sharply after the fall of the Soviet Union and the concomitant end of this aid; life expectancy dropped by seven years as North Korea subsequently suffered from

FIGURE 4.12 North Korea's life expectancy continues to be constrained by the long-term effects of devastating famines and poor health care following the loss of Soviet aid.

Life Expectancy at Birth, in Years

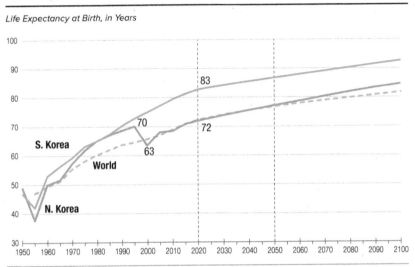

Data source: United Nations, *World Population Prospects 2019*, medium variant.

famines and poor medical care. Although life expectancy has slowly recovered to the previous peak, the sustained effects of poor living conditions have put the country on a lower trajectory, just matching the global average. In North Korea we see both the temporary effect of war-related deaths during the Korean War and the long-term effects of the poor health care associated with the loss of Soviet aid.

US and Mexico—Stalled Gains

Mexico and the United States are examples of stagnant and slightly declining life expectancies. The comparison in Figure 4.13 clearly shows Mexico's plateauing life expectancy. (Note that the comparison does not reflect any declines from the impact of COVID-19.) Like many developing countries, Mexico enjoyed a large increase in life expectancy due to declining child mortality. But Mexico's steep gain since 1955 stalled around 2005 due to increased violent crime and the growing incidence of chronic diseases, including heart disease, diabetes, and kidney disease. Both causes are worrisome, especially

FIGURE 4.13   Mexico's steep gain in life expectancy has stalled, largely due to increased violent crime and growing incidence of chronic diseases.

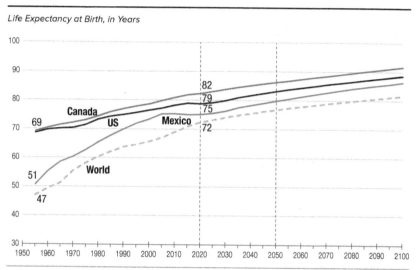

Life Expectancy at Birth, in Years

Note: These trend lines do not reflect the impact of COVID-19.

Data source: United Nations, *World Population Prospects 2019*, medium variant.

due to the difficulty of developing policies and behaviors to reduce these trends. Furthermore, because the non-communicable chronic diseases that have contributed to this leveling off are more prevalent in older people, the rising death toll from these diseases will be increasingly worrisome as the population ages.

While the United States has a growing incidence of chronic disease, the stalled and slightly declining life expectancy in the United States primarily reflects the opioid crisis and fatal drug overdoses among young and middle-aged adults. Other contributors include deaths from various chronic diseases, especially among the elderly. Another major health concern for the United States is the increasing obesity epidemic, which contributes to many causes of death, including heart disease, stroke, diabetes, and some cancers. These mortality statistics are worrisome in themselves, but they are also concerning as the US falls further behind other wealthy countries in life expectancy. (See Figure 4.7 for a comparison of large economies.)

In contrast to the slower gains and recent decline in US life expectancy, Canada's life expectancy has continued to increase. As of 2020, with a life expectancy of 82, Canada had the world's 15th-highest life expectancy, nearly matching France, Sweden, and Iceland.

GENDER DISPARITY IN LIFE EXPECTANCY

Women live longer than men everywhere. As a result, older populations everywhere will have more women than men. This is not just a global average phenomenon, but it is true in *every* country.

Globally, the female life expectancy advantage in 2020 was 4.8 years, ranging from an average of nine years in Eastern Europe to less than two in West Africa. Research to unlock the mystery of the female survival advantage continues, with scholars suggesting a combination of factors, including biological and behavioral; women are more physically resilient and can recover more quickly from disease and other hazards, and they are more likely than men to avoid risky behaviors, such as smoking, drinking, fast driving, and dangerous working conditions.

TOP 10

Hong Kong has the highest life expectancy for both males and females, with the other high-life-expectancy countries tightly clustered around the top value. The top 10 life expectancy lists shown in Table 4.4 include most of the same countries, with only a few differences. Iceland, Israel, and Sweden make the top 10 for males but not for females. Spain, South Korea, and France make the top 10 for females, but not for males.

The differences in these lists are interesting, but more telling about the female survival advantage is that in *all* 10 countries with the highest life expectancy for women, female life expectancies exceed the top male life expectancy of 81.8. Indeed, 37 countries post 2020 female life expectancy levels higher than the highest male life expectancy.

TABLE 4.4   In all 10 countries with the highest life expectancy for women, female life expectancies surpass the top male life expectancy of 81.8 found in Hong Kong.

Life Expectancy at Birth, in Years, by Gender						
Highest Male Life Expectancy				Highest Female Life Expectancy		
Rank	Country	2020		Rank	Country	2020
1	Hong Kong	81.8		1	Hong Kong	87.5
2	Switzerland	81.6		2	Japan	87.5
3	Japan	81.3		3	Macao	87.0
4	Singapore	81.3		4	Spain	86.1
5	Iceland	81.2		5	South Korea	85.7
6	Australia	81.2		6	Singapore	85.5
7	Macao	81.1		7	Switzerland	85.4
8	Italy	81.0		8	France	85.4
9	Israel	81.0		9	Italy	85.4
10	Sweden	80.8		10	Australia	85.2

Data source: United Nations, *World Population Prospects 2019,* medium variant.

Among these top-ranking countries, there are some especially large male-female disparities: the female advantage in 2020 was more than six years in Japan and South Korea, and reached 5.9 in France and 5.5 in Spain. Several other top-life-expectancy countries show smaller gender disparities of around four years, including Switzerland, Singapore, and Italy. In most countries, the disparity has persisted for decades and is not the result of short-term impacts, such as war-related casualties, which affect men more than women. In some countries, the disparity has widened as life expectancy for males grew more slowly than for females, and in some cases the disparity has narrowed when the male life expectancy gains exceeded female gains.

Outside of the top 10, the gender disparity is much wider. More than 25 countries have a female-survival advantage exceeding seven years, with about half of those in Eastern Europe. Besides Russia, where life expectancy for women in 2020 was 10.7 years higher than for men, the Eastern European countries with a large gender disparity in life expectancy include Belarus, Ukraine, Kazakhstan,

Poland, and Hungary. In Asia, the high disparity countries include Vietnam, the Philippines, and Thailand. Latin American countries with a high gender disparity in life expectancy include El Salvador, Venezuela, and Brazil.

Notably, the world's two most populous countries show relatively small gender disparities in life expectancy, with China's disparity reaching 4.5 years in 2020, and India reaching 2.4 years. In the United States, the disparity is five years, close to the global average of 4.8.

MORE OLDER WOMEN

Due to gender disparity in life expectancy, older populations will have more women than men. This is already true, but will become more evident as populations age and the number of older people increases. More importantly, with the increasing financial burdens of a growing number and share of old people, the larger share of women will become more obvious and concerning.

One key implication relates to the economic disadvantage that women may face. Though women live longer, in many countries they are less secure financially: their survival advantage is often accompanied by economic disadvantage. Frequently this economic disadvantage has several threads. First, women on average earn less than men during their working years, which accumulates into an economic disadvantage that worsens over time. Their lower lifetime earnings will usually result in lower savings and lower retirement benefits than what men accrue. Second, because women are more often the caregivers for children and parents, their professional growth and income may be delayed or curtailed. Third, women often become the unpaid caregivers for their aging spouses and partners and may use substantial financial resources for their care. Thus, although women live longer, they may bear financial consequences of economic disparities that affected them professionally, along with financial burdens that occurred later in life. Living and care arrangements in aging societies will attract increasing attention, and the issues will be especially important for older women.

Other implications relate to how societies might adapt to the disparities or seek to reduce them. As populations age, the economic well-being of women will become increasingly important. With increased global attention to girls' education and economic empowerment, perhaps the economic disadvantage will diminish. In many countries, probably most, women have a lower retirement age than men. Perhaps this should be adjusted upward to reflect their survival advantage or at least be equalized. Similarly, perhaps there could be incentives to raise the labor force participation of women. This will be increasingly important as growth in the overall working-age population slows and growth in the numbers of older workers accelerates.

CONCLUSION

The dramatic increase in life expectancy has been described as a remarkable success, and this chapter has shown you how the success story has unfolded differently around the world. Most notably, the largest gains have occurred in the developing countries, while small but steady gains continued in the advanced economies. More specifically, emerging economies, including China, South Korea, and Mexico, have seen large gains. In contrast, Russia has seen little overall progress beyond recovering from its downturn after 1991. Surprisingly, although life expectancy in the United States has been generally increasing, other advanced economies have seen larger gains. The US lost further ground over the last several years as the opioid epidemic caused a slight decline in life expectancy.

Increased life expectancy contributes to population gains at all ages, but one of the most important impacts is the increase in the number of people reaching old age. For advanced economies with already high life expectancy, population aging has been slowly unfolding for decades, while for emerging economies, it is occurring more rapidly. In addition, shrinking total populations are becoming more common as many countries with aging populations now have death rates exceeding birth rates, with only minimal growth from immigration. We can expect future population shifts to include the contrasting trends of increased population in developing countries and depopulation in advanced economies.

Most of us anticipate continued life expectancy gains throughout the world. But many uncertainties could affect how the success story of increasing life expectancy continues to unfold. On the plus side, scientific and medical advances could produce gains in life expectancy that would significantly increase population growth, especially in the older age brackets. In addition to scientific advances, basic advances in public health could lead to continued reductions in childhood mortality, especially in sub-Saharan Africa. On the negative side, besides the impact of COVID, some other known threats that might dampen the prospects for continued gains in life expectancy include increased resistance to antibiotics, increasing obesity, as well as increases in a host of unhealthy behaviors, such as drinking and drug use.

While life expectancy is a critical driver, more important is the way it combines with other drivers to paint the full picture of population change. Later chapters will show how changes in life expectancy combine with fertility declines and net migration to determine changes in age structure, including population aging and workforce growth.

5 | INCREASING INTERNATIONAL MIGRATION

"To Make the World Richer, Let People Move"
Economist.com, November 14, 2019

"In Refugees, Companies Find a Talent Pool—and Training Challenges"
Wall Street Journal, by Kelsey Gee, February 21, 2017

"How Russia Wins the Climate Crisis"
New York Times, by Abrahm Lustgarten, December 16, 2020

"Migration: Needed but Not Wanted"
The Economist, September 29, 2016

"How Migration Became a Weapon in a 'Hybrid War'"
Financial Times, by Ben Hall, Sam Fleming, and James Shotter, December 4, 2021

The news about migration over the past several years has been crowded with stories of the thousands of refugees and unaccompanied minors from the Northern Triangle of Central America seeking to cross into the United States, the million Syrian refugees pouring into Europe, the million Rohingya from failing Myanmar swamping Bangladesh, and the millions of Afghan refugees fleeing the Taliban, to give just a few examples. Soon you can expect news of accelerating climate-induced migration. In addition to the cross-border migration we hear so much about, you will continue to hear disturbing news about the internal displacement of refugees who remain in their own countries but are forced out of their homes because of drought, civil conflict, and violence.

Much of the recent press coverage about migration relates to disruptive events that require immediate attention because of humanitarian concerns and national security implications. In many ways these "urgent" developments distract attention from the positive role of migration, including the economic contributions that migrants make through remittances sent home and through boosting labor supply in their new countries. The contribution of immigrants to technological innovation in the United States is well established and extends far beyond just the numbers of migrants.

The policy debates continue regarding the desired number of immigrants, potential threats to national security, citizenship, refugee limits, national quotas, and desired assimilation. Some observers estimate that migrants take jobs and overuse services, while others acknowledge that we need migrants to do jobs that would otherwise go unfilled; still others suggest that perhaps migration could offset shrinking workforces and aging populations. Some say we have a moral obligation to welcome refugees into our countries. Some believe that the way countries handle migration will be the defining issue on the horizon.

Like the other key drivers, migration is both an agent of population change and a demographic outcome affected by political, economic, and social conditions around the world. For most countries, immigration plays a small role in population growth, but for some, international migration has not only contributed significantly to population growth, but has played a key role in shaping economic, political, and cultural developments. As with the other drivers, it is important to understand the historical context if we want to gain a thorough understanding of how migration trends have been changing.

In this chapter, you will see the big picture of migration and learn where it has occurred and how it has evolved in key countries. This global historical context will help you better understand how the various urgent challenges and disruptive events fit into the broader context of population growth. The premise you've seen throughout the book continues here: the better you understand the historical trends that led to the current situation, the better you will be able to evaluate and address future challenges.

It will help to open with several key questions: Where are international migrants living and where did they come from? What countries are most affected? What are the demographic characteristics of the migrants by age and gender? How has migration affected the populations of the countries involved?

BIG PICTURE: 270 MILLION

Migration is a global phenomenon. International migrants—people living outside their country of birth—have come from nearly all 200 countries and territories across the globe, and are hosted in just as many places. Over the last 60 years, global migration has more than tripled, with the number of international migrants reaching 272 million in 2019, up from 77 million in 1960. In Figure 5.1, you see an especially steep increase during the 1980s, with continued large increases in each decade since then. However, even though migration has been steadily on the rise, the immigrant share of world population remains quite small. It rose from 2.5% in 1960 to 3.5% in 2019.

FIGURE 5.1   Migration is increasing but accounts for only 3.5% of world population.

International Migrants in Millions and Percent of World Population

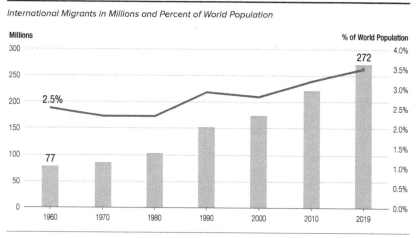

Note: International migrants are people living outside their country of origin.

Data source: United Nations, *International Migrant Stock 2019.*

You can see from these percentages that the global share is small, but judging from the news, the impacts in many countries are large.

REGIONAL PATTERN OF NET MIGRATION

Most of the migration has been from lower-income countries to higher-income countries and from developing regions to more developed regions. The key destinations are North America and Europe, while the major originating areas are Asia, Latin America, and Africa. Figure 5.2 shows the regional distribution of the migration over time. The movements generally reflect the search for opportunities in higher-income areas that would be both welcoming and offer better economic prospects.

This regional overview illustrates average annual net migration, and points to several key developments. First, you can see that the

FIGURE 5.2 The top migrant destinations have been North America and Europe; Asia, Latin America, and Africa have been the major originating regions.

Average Annual Net Migration by Region, by Decade, 1950–2030, Millions per Year

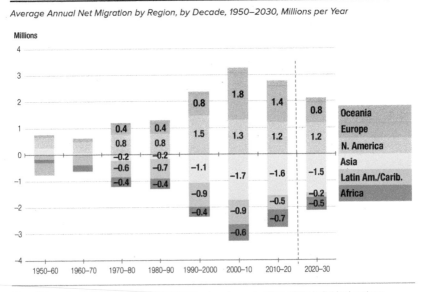

Note: This regional view of net migration does not capture migration within individual regions.

Data source: United Nations, *World Population Prospects 2019*, medium variant.

annual flows increased sharply during the 1990s, with especially large increases in out-migration from Asia, averaging 1.1 million per year during the 1990s and increasing to 1.7 million per year from 2000 to 2010. Due to this outflow, net in-migration doubled in North America and Europe. During the 1990s, the level of in-migration reached 1.5 million per year in North America and 0.8 million per year in Europe. Then, during the early 2000s, net migration to Europe more than doubled again, declining only slightly after 2010. The relatively small out-migration from Africa is notable because it remains such a small share of Africa's explosively growing and low-income population. We expect out-migration from Africa, or at least the desire for out-migration, to increase substantially as the growing working-age population faces weak economic prospects and the impact of climate change further threatens domestic economic growth.

OVERVIEW OF GLOBAL MIGRATION

As you can see on the map in Figure 5.3, most migrants live in a few key countries, with the United States being the top destination.

TOP 10 DESTINATIONS AS OF 2019

Although migrants live in nearly every country, most migrants are concentrated in a few well-known destinations. As shown in Figure 5.4, the United States is by far the largest host country; in 2019, it was home to 51 million foreign-born residents. The next-largest hosts are Germany and Saudi Arabia, each with 13 million residents born outside the country. The United States alone accounts for 19% of the world's migrant population, while the top 10 hosts together account for half of the total. The other half is more widely dispersed. As of 2019, two-thirds of all migrants live in the 20 largest destinations. The remaining one-third are widely dispersed around the world.

As noted above, one reason for migration is the pull of better economic prospects. Indeed, nine out of 10 of the host countries are high-income countries that offer opportunities by virtue of their

FIGURE 5.3 Migration is a global phenomenon, but most international migrants live in a few key countries. Half of all migrants live in the top 10 destinations.

Number of Foreign-Born Living in Each Country, in Millions, 2019

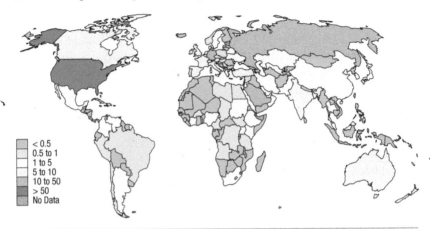

Legend:
- < 0.5
- 0.5 to 1
- 1 to 5
- 5 to 10
- 10 to 50
- > 50
- No Data

Data source: United Nations, *International Migrant Stock 2019.*

FIGURE 5.4 The 10 largest destination countries host half of all migrants.

Top 10 Destination Countries, Population in Millions, 2019

	Foreign-Born Population	% of Global Migrant Population	Total Population	Foreign-Born Share of Total Population
US	51	19%	329	15%
Germany	13	5%	84	16%
Saudi Arabia	13	5%	34	38%
Russia	12	4%	146	8%
UK	10	4%	68	14%
UAE	9	3%	10	88%
France	8	3%	65	13%
Canada	8	3%	37	21%
Australia	8	3%	25	30%
Italy	6	2%	61	10%
Top 10 total	137	50%	858	16%
World Total	272	100%	7,713	3.5%

Data source: United Nations, *International Migrant Stock 2019.*

economic wealth and growth. Russia, with its downgraded income status, is the only middle-income country on the list. Eight of the top destinations are among the world's largest economies, while two others—Saudi Arabia and the UAE—are growing, oil-rich economies in the Middle East. Four of the large destination countries are English-speaking, and three—the United States, Canada, and Australia—have long histories of immigration and are regarded as "traditional immigration countries."

It is revealing to see that the foreign-born shares differ greatly across the top destinations, as illustrated in the right-hand column of Figure 5.4. While the United States is by far the largest destination in millions, we see the highest share of foreign-born occurs in the oil-rich countries of the Middle East, due to their heavy reliance on foreign workers in their oil and construction industries. The US percentage of foreign-born recently returned to the prior peak of 15%, which occurred in 1910. Although this increase surprised and concerned many people, this share actually marks a return to the historical range of 10% to 15% that occurred from 1850 up until World War II. The decline to less than 5% in 1970 was more of a cultural anomaly, and rose after the 1965 Immigration Act to around 15%. Although the other traditional immigration countries are much smaller in total population, their shares of foreign-born are much higher: 21% in Canada and 30% in Australia. There is also diversity in foreign-born share across Europe. The shares in Germany, the UK, and France are close to the US share, but much higher than Italy's 10%.

Only a few countries in the world have a foreign-born share higher than the 21% in Canada. Those high-share countries are mostly small populations and include Qatar and Kuwait in the Middle East, Monaco and Liechtenstein in Europe, and Singapore and Hong Kong in Asia. The high shares in Saudi Arabia, Australia, and Canada look even more striking because they are the only populations over 25 million with such high shares of foreign-born.

In addition to being high-income countries, most of the large destination countries have older populations, characterized by high median ages as well as significant and growing shares of people age 65 and older. Saudi Arabia and the UAE are the exceptions. The other eight large destinations have seen decades of low fertility, declining levels of natural population increase, and median ages ranging from a low of 38 in the US and Australia to a high of 47 in Italy. Notably, Italy and Germany have the oldest populations among the top destinations, while Australia and the United States have the youngest. You will see later how migration can affect the age structure of the destination countries.

TOP 10 ORIGINS AS OF 2019

While the top migrant destinations are concentrated in a few rich and aging countries, the top origin countries are primarily middle-income countries with young populations. As shown in Figure 5.5, the largest country of origin in 2019 was India, which accounted for 18 million international migrants, 6% of the world's total. Three other large origin countries with more than 10 million migrants living outside their borders were Mexico, China, and Russia. Syria was the fifth-largest country of origin, with 8.2 million migrants.

FIGURE 5.5   The world's largest developing countries are also major migrant origin countries. India is the largest country of origin.

Top 10 Origin Countries, Population in Millions, 2019

	Diaspora Population		% of Global Migrant Population		Total Population	
India		17.5		6%		1,366
Mexico		11.8		4%		128
China		10.7		4%		1,458
Russia		10.5		4%		146
Syria		8.2		3%		17
Bangladesh		7.8		3%		163
Pakistan		6.3		2%		217
Ukraine		5.9		2%		44
Philippines		5.4		2%		108
Afghanistan		5.1		2%		38
Top 10 Total		89		33%		3,684
Total		272		100%		7,713

Data source: United Nations, *International Migrant Stock 2019.*

As you can see in the figure, the top 10 countries of origin together account for a third of the world's international migrants.

We know that most migrants seek better economic prospects, and in general, move from low- or middle-income countries in developing regions to higher-income countries. There are, however, some exceptions to this general pattern. Although most of the top 10 source countries are lower-middle-income or low-income countries, three exceptions—Mexico, China, and Russia—exceed those income thresholds and fall in the upper-middle-income range.

Geographically, the top source countries are located in three regions. Seven of the 10 largest source countries are Asian, including four countries from South Asia—India, Bangladesh, Pakistan, and Afghanistan. The top 10 list also includes two Eastern European countries—Russia and Ukraine, and one country from Latin America—Mexico.

The top 10 countries of origin all have several elements in common. Most are among the world's most populous countries, and the amount of out-migration represents only a small share of their total populations. In most of these countries the out-migration is primarily economic in character, and most benefit from remittances sent home to families. The exceptions include Syria, Ukraine, and Afghanistan, where out-migration has been driven more by political and security-based factors. The most notable of these is Syria, where migration stemmed from the decade of civil conflict; in 2019 the number of Syrians living outside the country was more than 8 million and the population living in Syria dropped to 17 million, including 6.5 million who were internally displaced, meaning they were uprooted from their homes, but still resident in the country.

Another commonality is that most of the top originating countries have young populations with median ages of less than 30. With its median age of 38 and its rapidly aging population, China is an exception to the youthful profile of the origin countries. The populations of Russia and Ukraine are also much older, with median ages of 40 and 41, respectively. Afghanistan and Pakistan have the youngest populations of this group. Although population growth will be slower than in the past, most of these countries will continue to see large population gains, which could in turn fuel increased out-migration. Most notably, Pakistan is projected to add nearly 159 million people over the next 30 years, and to nearly double in population by the end of the century. As you will see later, most of these top origin countries have consistently been among the top sources over the past few decades. Syria is the only newcomer to the list, with its recent surge of refugees fleeing the country.

INTERSECTION OF THE TOP SOURCES AND ORIGINS

Knowing the top 10 destinations and origins for international migrants provides a useful frame of reference, but gives us only a part of the whole picture. As you've seen, the top 10 destination countries host about half the world's total. And the top 10 originating countries account for about one-third of all migrants. Figure 5.6 puts these numbers in perspective and shows that the intersection of the top origins with the top destinations is surprisingly small.

FIGURE 5.6   Half of all migrants concentrate in the top 10 destinations, but they originate from dispersed locations.

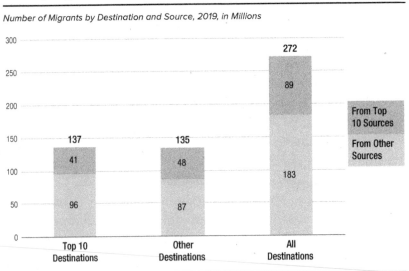

Number of Migrants by Destination and Source, 2019, in Millions

Data source: United Nations, *International Migrant Stock 2019.*

Looking at Figure 5.6 you can see the geographic distribution of migrants from different perspectives: Focusing on the first column, you see that 137 million migrants live in the top 10 destinations, and of these migrants, only 41 million have come from the top 10 originating countries. Then, by looking across the columns, you can see that of the 89 million migrants from the top 10 source countries, less than half (41 million) settled in one of the top 10 destinations.

Because the intersection of top destinations and top sources is small, we need to look beyond the top sources to better understand the global distribution and composition of the migrant populations. First, we will see the history and sources for the major destinations, and you will learn where migrants to the top destinations originate. Later you will learn further about the originating countries and where migrants from the largest sources now live.

TOP 10 DESTINATIONS IN MORE DETAIL

HISTORY OF MIGRANT FLOWS TO THE TOP DESTINATIONS

The 2019 overview chart showed you where international migrants now live. But to understand migration more fully, it will help to see how the current situation evolved and how the top host countries have grown or changed over the past three decades. Historically, most of the top 10 destination countries have been among the top 10 since 1990, but as you will see later, political and economic events have contributed to new patterns of migration that have changed the relative rankings and brought newcomers to the list.

As shown in Figure 5.7, the United States, consistently the largest host country, dominates the ranking of the top destinations. The number of international migrants living in the United States more than doubled over the past 30 years, from 23 million in 1990 to 51 million in 2019. This looks dramatic, but the migrant populations grew even faster in several other countries.

Figure 5.8 excludes the United States and captures an expanded view of historical trends for the other top host countries. You can

FIGURE 5.7   The number of international migrants living in the United States, by far the largest destination, more than doubled over the past 30 years.

Top Five Destination Countries, as of 2019
Number of Migrants in Each Destination, in Millions

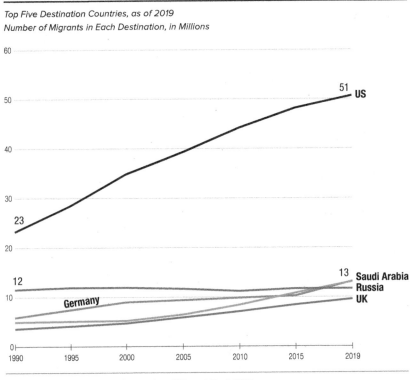

Data source: United Nations, *International Migrant Stock 2019.*

see from this chart that the number of immigrants more than doubled in Germany, Saudi Arabia, and the UK, and nearly doubled in Canada and Australia.

The expanded chart showing 15 countries looks complicated at first, but the chart offers a comparison of various large destinations, each with its own history and distinct features. Several important developments stand out: you can see stagnation of Russia as a destination; skyrocketing of two Middle Eastern countries as destinations; growth across the European destinations, with a recent surge in Germany but more sudden growth in Italy and Spain from relatively low levels 30 years ago; and finally, the well-reported surge in Turkey. You can also clearly see the declines in Ukraine and India.

FIGURE 5.8 Growth in migration across the largest host countries has been uneven, with some large hosts such as Germany more than doubling, and others, including India, declining.

Top 15 Destinations, as of 2019 (US not shown)
Number of Migrants in Each Destination, in Millions

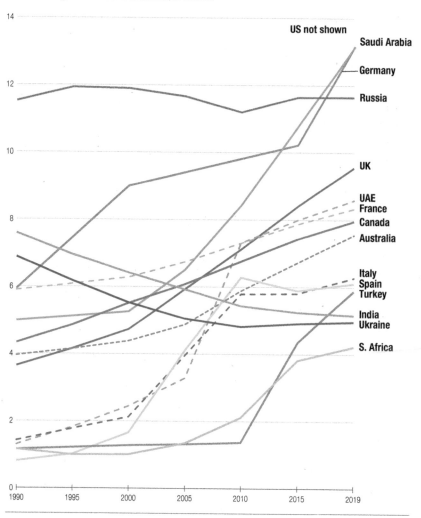

Data source: United Nations, *International Migrant Stock 2019.*

Looking at the chart you can understand particulars of the migrant boom in each country. The UAE's migrant population increased more than sixfold and Saudi Arabia's more than 2.5 times. The steep increases in Saudi Arabia and the UAE reflect growth of the oil-rich economies, while the growth in Germany's migrant population largely reflects policies to supplement its workforce in the face of an aging population, combined with the recent influx of Syrian refugees. Turkey, the 12th-largest destination on this graph, saw a steep increase in its migrant population as it became host to an increasing number of Syrian refugees after 2015.

Italy participated in the migrant boom as well, with a more than fourfold increase in migrants and an especially sharp increase during the 2000s. Over the past 30 years, Italy's share of foreign-born increased abruptly, from just 2.5% in 1990 to over 10% in 2019.

One exception to the pattern of strong growth is France, where the migrant population increased by only 40%, with just a small rise in the percentage of foreign-born. Another exception is Russia, where the migrant population has been stable for the last 30 years at around 12 million. Although some migration between Russia and the former Soviet republics continues, Russia remains among the top 10 hosts by virtue of the size of past migration. Finally, while most countries have seen an increase in their migrant populations, several previously large host countries have had declining migrant populations. India, Ukraine, Pakistan, and Iran were among the top 10 host countries in 1990, but have since experienced substantial drops in the number of foreign-born residents.

As noted above, the top 10 host countries in 2019 accounted for 50% of the world's international migrants. Migration has become increasingly concentrated in these countries since 1990, when their combined total was 43%.

Another important migration trend is that in most of the top 10 destination countries, the migrant population has been growing faster than the total population, which means that the share of foreign-born has been increasing, as you can see in Figure 5.9. Already among the highest, the shares in Saudi Arabia and Australia have steadily increased since 2000. Germany and the UK also

FIGURE 5.9 The migrant share has been steadily increasing in most host countries. Russia stands out as an exception.

Migrant Stock as a Share of Total Population, 1990–2019

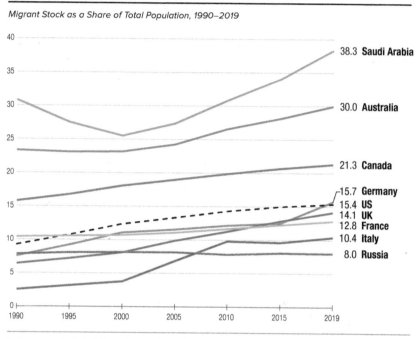

Data source: United Nations, *International Migrant Stock 2019.*

saw substantial increases in the foreign-born share, while in France the increase was smaller. Perhaps most startling is the steep rise in Italy; the 10% share is low compared with other European countries, but the growth from such a low base of 2.5% compounds the challenge of integrating migrants into the economy. The UAE (not shown in this chart), with a total population of 10 million, had the highest share of foreign-born, a number approaching 90%.

WHERE DO MIGRANTS TO THE TOP DESTINATIONS COME FROM?

To gain a fuller picture of where migrants come from, we can look beyond the top global sources and consider the top sources for each separate destination. When we do this, we see that no general patterns emerge. Instead, each host country appears to have its own distinct profile of international migrants, reflected in the variety of source countries and the numbers of migrants from each source. Figure 5.10 illustrates the different profiles by showing the top five origins for each top host. While there is some overlap of the sources, most of the host countries have distinct profiles, reflecting the separate economic and social history of migration for that country.

As you look at the chart, you will see that the 10 columns are in order of migrant population, with the US, the largest, on the left,

FIGURE 5.10 Each top destination has attracted migrants from a distinct combination of origin countries.

The Top 10 Destinations and the Top Five Origin Countries for Each, as of 2019

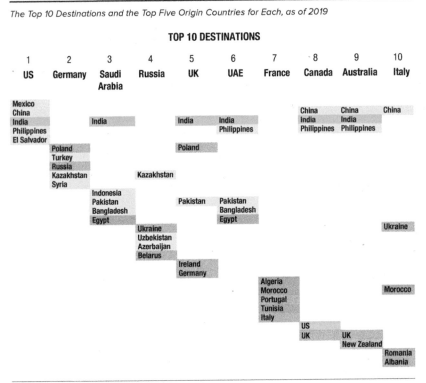

TOP 10 DESTINATIONS

1 US	2 Germany	3 Saudi Arabia	4 Russia	5 UK	6 UAE	7 France	8 Canada	9 Australia	10 Italy
Mexico China India Philippines El Salvador		India		India	India Philippines		China India Philippines	China India Philippines	China
	Poland Turkey Russia Kazakhstan Syria		Kazakhstan	Poland					
		Indonesia Pakistan Bangladesh Egypt		Pakistan	Pakistan Bangladesh Egypt				
			Ukraine Uzbekistan Azerbaijan Belarus						Ukraine
				Ireland Germany					
						Algeria Morocco Portugal Tunisia Italy			Morocco
							US UK	UK New Zealand	
									Romania Albania

Note on how to read this table: Read down each column to see the top five origin countries for each of the top destinations; for example, the top five origins for the US include Mexico, China, India, the Philippines, and El Salvador. Read across to see common origins: India is a common origin for the US, Saudi Arabia, UK, UAE, Canada, and Australia. Read diagonally to see notable additions to the list of origins: for example, Algeria and Morocco come into the picture as large origins for France, but not for larger destinations shown to the left.

Data source: United Nations, *International Migrant Stock 2019.*

and Italy, the 10th largest, on the right. Each row of the chart represents a different source country, so it is possible to read across and see which source countries are important for each host. To highlight the various profiles, the rows are ordered to show the top five origins for the largest destination, then the top five for the second-largest destination, and so on—unless the origin country is already listed for another host country. To further illustrate the major concentrations of migrants, the source blocks are color coded by region. For example, light blue represents Latin America, and orange and yellow represent Asia.

As you can see in Column 1, the top five origin countries for the United States are Mexico, China, India, the Philippines, and El Salvador. These five together account for 41% of the foreign-born in the US. You will see later that Mexico alone accounts for nearly a quarter of the total. As expected, Germany, shown in Column 2, has a completely different set of top source countries: Poland, Turkey, Russia, Kazakhstan, and Syria. Saudi Arabia, in Column 3, has yet another combination of sources, including four Asian countries— India, Indonesia, Pakistan, and Bangladesh.

Reading along the diagonal pattern appearing at the bottom of the columns reveals which countries have been added to the list as each destination is accounted for. For example, the list for Russia includes four additional source countries, all former Soviet republics; for the UK, Ireland and Germany were added; and for France, several North African countries, all former French colonies, were added.

Reading left to right along the rows and across the columns shows which host countries have similar origin countries. For example, you can see that India, in row 3, is one of the top sources for six of the 10 large destinations. China and the Philippines are top sources for four of the 10 destinations. In contrast, Mexico, the largest origin for the United States, is not a large source for any other country.

While India, China, and the Philippines are the source countries for several of the large hosts, most source countries on the list are top sources for only one or two of the top destinations. This further illustrates the distinct profiles of the host countries. Even the countries with a few common sources are still distinct by virtue of differences in the shares from these common sources and the contributions from other sources as well. For example, the three traditional immigrant countries—the US, Canada, and Australia—have three common source countries—China, India, and the Philippines—but the percentages from these countries differ, and each of these hosts also has other sources.

Similarly, Saudi Arabia and the UAE, which both have high percentages of foreign-born, have four source countries in common—India, Pakistan, Bangladesh, and Egypt—but the overall share of foreign-born and the composition of the foreign-born differ greatly from country to country. In the UAE, migrants account for 88% of the population, compared with 38% in Saudi Arabia. India, the top source for both, has sent a larger number and share of migrants to the UAE; for the UAE, Indian migrants account for 40% of the foreign-born, compared with 19% in Saudi Arabia.

For some of the 10 host countries, the foreign-born population comes largely from the top five origins, but for others the top five origins account for less than half of the total, suggesting a greater diversity of the migrant population. The UAE, at 81%, with high shares of migrants from South Asia, has the highest concentration of migrants coming from its top five sources. Russia, with 74% of its migrants coming from five former Soviet republics, has the second-highest concentration. In contrast, the United States has a much more diverse profile: the five largest sources account for 20 million migrants, just 41% of the total, and the remaining 30 million come from more than 140 other countries, showing that the US has attracted migrants worldwide.

These profiles of the 2019 composition reflect the cumulative impact of the economic and social history of international migration, and in turn, these distinct profiles point to divergent challenges faced by each country—some based on economic migration, some on religious conflict rooted in colonial heritage, and still others stemming from political disruptions and humanitarian concerns. The following analysis highlights the history of the migration trends for individual countries that led to these current profiles. To emphasize similarities and differences, the discussion presents the countries in groups, including the traditional immigration countries, Europe's large host countries, and the oil-rich destinations.

TRADITIONAL IMMIGRATION COUNTRIES

The traditional immigration countries, the United States, Canada, and Australia, together account for 66 million migrants, nearly one-quarter of the world's total. Their overall migration profiles differ, but as you read above, they share three common source countries: China, India, and the Philippines. The number of migrants from these three source countries has been steadily increasing, while other sources have decreased in importance. Figure 5.11 shows the migration to each of these countries from its top sources. Several common trends are clear: migration occurs from around the geographic neighborhood—for example, from Mexico to the United States, and New Zealand to Australia; also, some migration is linked to cultural and political roots, such as the UK to Canada and Australia; and finally, migration from Asia has increased, especially from China and India, which are among the top sources for all three destinations.

United States

As of 2019, the United States hosted 51 million international migrants, or 19% of the world's total. As a share of the US population, the total number of foreign-born has increased from 9% in 1990 to 15% in 2019, bringing the foreign-born share back to the 1910 high of 15%.

Mexico is by far the largest origin of the foreign-born population in the United States, with immigrants from Mexico totaling more than 11.5 million in 2019, or nearly one-quarter of all international migrants to the US. The next-largest origin countries for the US include three Asian sources—China, with 2.9 million migrants living in the US, India with 2.7 million, and the Philippines with 2 million. Together these three Asian sources account for 15% of the US total migrant population. The fifth-largest origin is El Salvador,

FIGURE 5.11 For all three traditional immigration countries, China and India are becoming more prominent sources.

Number of Migrants from each Origin Living in the Designated Destination, in Millions

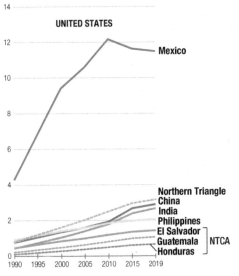

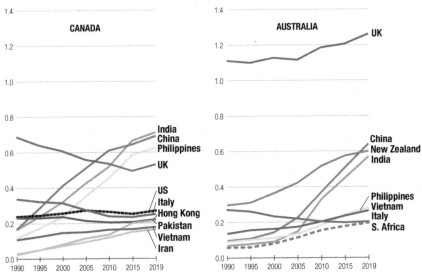

Note: Canada and Australia are shown on the same scale, which is 1/10 the scale for the United States. NTCA = the Northern Triangle countries of Central America.

Data source: United Nations, *International Migrant Stock 2019.*

with 1.4 million migrants, or 2.8% of the US total. The combined total from the three Northern Triangle countries of Central America— El Salvador, Honduras, and Guatemala—reached 3.2 million in 2019, just slightly larger than the total from China.

As you might expect, the economic and social characteristics of the migrant populations reflect the economic push-pull factors stimulating the migration. During the 1960s, Mexican immigrants were primarily farm workers and low-skilled manufacturing workers. As the US economy continued to shift from manufacturing to services, the Mexican immigrant occupations diversified into a variety of service industries, including accommodation and food services. Chinese and Indian migrants, the second- and third-largest groups, have included students and high-tech workers, attracted to the US by educational opportunities and growth in the high-tech sector. The Filipino community is known for its significant share of health care workers, while migrants from the Northern Triangle countries are primarily identified as refugees from drought and violence in their countries of origin.

The 2019 picture described above reflects the past trends and the cumulative history of migration to the US. A key feature of the past migration has been the role of Mexico as the largest source country. Note, however, that recent patterns of migration reflect a dramatic shift in the source countries. The migration from Mexico has not only slowed but actually reversed, with the number of Mexican migrants living in the US declining from a peak of 12.2 million in 2010 to 11.5 million in 2019.

This decline in the number of Mexican immigrants stems from several important developments, including demographic, economic, and political changes. The declining number of births in Mexico reduced the size of the working-age population and the pool of potential migrants seeking jobs in the US, a trend that will continue. At the same time as growth in the labor pool was slowing, Mexico's economic expansion and educational improvements created new job opportunities at home. On the US side, work possibilities were reduced for several reasons: the recession of 2007–08 dampened job growth, especially for construction and agriculture workers, and the

US strengthened its immigration enforcement. (Migration Policy Institute, May 21, 2015)

While Mexican migration has slowed, the numbers of Chinese and Indian migrants have increased. Growth in tech industries has attracted Asian immigrants for high-skill jobs as well as educational opportunities. China and India have been among the top countries of origin for many employment-based visa categories and are also the top countries of origin for international students in the US. As a result, China has now replaced Mexico as the largest source country for new migrants to the US, followed closely by India; and Asia has replaced Central America as the largest regional source of new migrants.

El Salvador is the fifth-largest origin of foreign-born individuals living in the United States. To put this in perspective, in 2019 the number of El Salvador–born migrants in the US, 1.4 million, was about equal to the number of migrants from Vietnam. As shown in Figure 5.11, the numbers of migrants from the Northern Triangle countries living in the United States have been steadily increasing over the past 30 years. Since 1990 the total has quadrupled, from 800,000 to 3.2 million in 2019, with the numbers from Guatemala and Honduras increasing the fastest.

As of 2019, nearly 90% of all migrants from the Northern Triangle countries live in the United States. Although out-migration from these countries peaked in 2000, the border crossings into the United States attracted more attention in recent years as border enforcement policies changed. The separation of children from their parents has drawn notice from all over the world and contributed to the refugee crisis on the southern border. The humanitarian and political disruptions associated with this refugee flow may well be a harbinger of future migration trends as the forces driving these migrants out of their own countries show little signs of abating.

Overall, the US hosts migrants from 150 countries, making its foreign-born population quite diverse compared with that of other destination countries. Although Mexico is by far the largest source country for US migrants, accounting for nearly one-quarter of the US total, the top five source countries combined account for only

41% of the total. Only 11 of the 150 source countries have each sent more than 1 million migrants, and 60 countries have each sent fewer than 50,000 migrants.

Canada

Canada is the eighth-largest host country. Its 8 million migrants in 2019 accounted for one-fifth of its total population, 37 million. The top three source countries are India, with 715,000 migrants in Canada; China, with 691,000; and the Philippines, with 627,000. With a combined total of 2 million, these three Asian sources together account for one-quarter of Canada's migrant population. As shown in Figure 5.11, these three Asian source countries are also large source countries for the US and Australia. Although the US has a larger total from these three countries—7.6 million—due to its large total population, the share from these three is 15% in the US, much smaller than Canada's 26%. The share in Australia is 20%.

The migrant populations from India, China, and the Philippines have been steadily increasing, with India recently overtaking China to become the largest source country for Canada. All three surpassed the migrant population from the UK, which before 2005 had been the largest source, but has been steadily declining. The shift toward Asian sources has moved the UK from Canada's top source to its fourth largest. The US remains the fifth-largest source, with its 270,000 accounting for 3% of Canada's total migrant population in 2019. In Figure 5.11 you can see the declining number of Italian migrants and the large increase in Pakistani migrants.

With a long history as a migrant-friendly country, Canada has a population that includes migrants from all over the world, with at least a small number from nearly every country. The share from Asia has recently been increasing, but the origin countries remain diverse.

Australia

Australia, home to 7.5 million foreign-born, is the world's ninth-largest host. Among the large economies, Australia has the highest share of international migrants, its 7.5 million foreign-born accounting for 30% of the total population. The UK is by far the largest source country, with 1.3 million migrants living in Australia in 2019. With its steep increase since 2000, China, with 642,000 migrants, has replaced New Zealand as the second-largest source country. India has become the fourth-largest source, with 569,000 migrants, and the Philippines, though closer geographically, is a much smaller source, with 281,000 migrants.

Since 2005, Australia has seen large inflows from both China and India. These "parallel" increases are especially notable, because similar, parallel increases occurred in Canada and the United States. In all three countries, China and India have recently been the fastest-growing sources of migrant populations. Migration from other Asian countries in the geographic neighborhood has also been increasing.

EUROPE'S LARGEST HOST COUNTRIES

The four large European destination countries as of 2019 hosted a combined total of 37 million migrants, or 14% of the world's total. The total has more than doubled since 1990, and all four have seen large increases both in the number of migrants and in the share of foreign-born in their populations. The migrant populations in Germany and the UK more than doubled, while France saw a much smaller 40% increase. Italy, starting from the smallest base, had the largest increase, with its migrant population more than quadrupling, and the foreign-born share increasing from 2% to 10%. In contrast, the foreign-born share in 2019 in France, UK, and Germany ranged from 13% to 16%, close to the 15% share in the United States.

All four of these host countries have seen significant changes in their migrant population mix, with the changes reflecting economic and political developments. They have few large source countries in common, with a few exceptions. Germany and the UK have both seen large increases in the number of migrants from Poland, while Germany and Italy have had large increases from Romania. France and Italy have both had continued increases from Morocco, while the

UK, France, and Italy have all seen small increases from Germany. Other changes occurring in individual countries include the influx of Syrians to Germany, the increase in Indians and Pakistanis to the UK, and the large rise in Algerians arriving in France after 2000.

Because they point to divergent challenges, it is useful to consider the unique migration histories of these countries. Figure 5.12 shows the changing composition of migrants from the largest origins for each country as of 2019. You can see stark differences in the sources and timing of migration to these large European destinations.

Germany

Germany is the world's second-largest host country, with 13 million foreign-born residents as of 2019. This foreign-born population accounts for 15.7% of Germany's total population, just slightly higher than the 15.4% for the US. While the shares are similar, Germany's foreign-born population is about one-quarter as large as the US foreign-born population.

It is interesting to note that Germany's top five origin countries include Poland, Turkey, Russia, Kazakhstan, and Syria. As of 2019, Poland was the largest source country, with 1.8 million migrants, or 14% of the total. Next is Turkey, with 1.5 million or 12% of the total, followed by Russia and Kazakhstan, with about 1 million each. The fifth-largest source, Syria, is a newcomer to the list of top sources. Although a small number of Syrians had previously been living in Germany, the number suddenly swelled to 590,000 after 2015, as Syrian refugees fled to Germany. The sudden rise differs from the generally slower steady increases from other countries.

Figure 5.12 shows the changing composition of Germany's migrant population, with notable increases in numbers from Russia, Poland, and most recently from Syria. Germany had an especially large increase in international migrants during the 1990s; the total number grew from 6 million in 1990 to 9 million in 2000, with large numbers from Eastern European countries, including Russia, Kazakhstan, and Poland. Since then, the number from Poland has continued to rise substantially. These relatively large increases

FIGURE 5.12 The origin profiles for the large European destinations differ dramatically, reflecting cultural history and labor markets.

Number of Migrants from Each Origin, in Millions

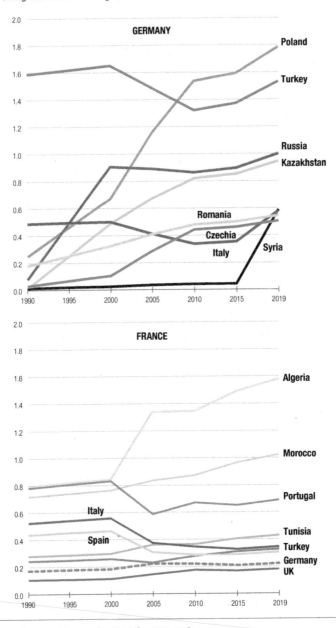

Note: These four countries are shown on the same scale.

Data source: United Nations, *International Migrant Stock 2019.*

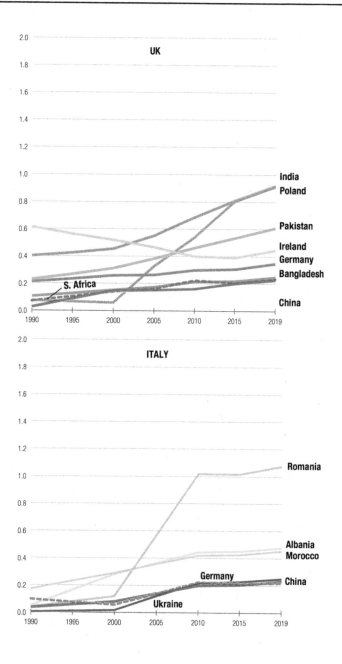

occurred as Germany was modifying its immigration policies to offset the demography of its slow population growth and decreasing native-born population.

The composition of the foreign-born population in Germany shifted again over the four years from 2015 to 2019, following the Syrian refugee crisis. With the addition of half a million refugees, Syria became the fifth-largest origin for migrants to Germany. As of 2019, Syrian immigrants numbered 590,000, accounting for 4% of the total number of Germany's foreign-born population. The number of migrants from Italy also increased during this time, surpassing the numbers from Romania and Czechia. While there are many other source countries, no others account for more than a half million migrants.

United Kingdom

The UK is the world's fifth-largest destination country, with 9.6 million international migrants. In 2019 international migrants accounted for 14% of the total population, close to the share in the US. As in the US, the foreign-born population of the UK is diverse. The top five origin countries account for only about a third of the total. These include India and Poland, with 10% each; Pakistan, with 6%; Ireland, with 5%; and Germany, at 4%.

Figure 5.12 shows the eight largest origins to the UK, and illustrates how the composition has shifted over the past 30 years. Three changes are particularly interesting: the steady increase from India and Pakistan, the sharp rise from Poland, and the decline from Ireland.

India, the largest source country in 2019, with 900,000 migrants, or 10% of the total, replaced Ireland as the largest source around 2000, as Irish migration continued to decline. Migration from Poland increased substantially after 2000, and by 2019 nearly matched the total from India. Pakistan has remained the third-largest source to the UK, accounting for 6% of the total. Bangladesh, the sixth-largest source country, accounts for 3% of the total foreign-born. The increases from India, Pakistan, and Bangladesh bring the combined total from South Asia to 1.8 million, or 19% of the UK total.

Both South Africa, with 232,000, and China, with 225,000, have growing migrant populations in the UK, and account for about 2% of the total foreign-born. The next-largest source countries are the US and Nigeria, each with 200,000 migrants, or 2% of the total.

France

France's migration story is a bit different. With 8.3 million international migrants, France is the world's seventh-largest host country. The share of foreign-born reached 13% in 2019, up from 10% in 1990. More than a third of the migrants to France originate in former French colonies in North Africa, which gives France a distinct profile. As of 2019, Algeria, the largest source, accounted for 1.6 million migrants, or 19% of the French total. Algerians thus make up about 2.5% of the total population. In addition, Morocco is the source for 1 million migrants to France, and Tunisia is the source for another 400,000. The largest European sources are Portugal, with 700,000, and Italy, with 300,000.

While Algeria has long been the top source of migrants to France, the total number of migrants from Algeria nearly doubled over the past 20 years, from 800,000 in 2000 to 1.6 million in 2019. During these last 20 years, migration from Morocco and Tunisia increased gradually, while the numbers from Portugal, Italy, and Spain dropped sharply.

There is a long history of travel back and forth between the North African source countries and France. But over the recent past, the work rules and anti-Muslim sentiments have led to increased tension, political disruption, and protest.

Italy

Italy, the 10th-largest destination country, was host to 6.3 million migrants in 2019. Unlike other large destinations, Italy has not been known as a migrant destination until recently. As a newcomer to the top 10 destinations, it has just recently exceeded Spain's foreign-born population.

Italy's foreign-born population more than quadrupled over the past 30 years, from 1.4 million in 1990 to 6.3 million in 2019. As a result, the share of foreign-born increased sharply from 2.5% in 1990 to 10.4% in 2019, about the same as the European average, but much lower than the foreign-born share for other top European destinations, such as Germany at 16%, and the UK at 14%.

Along with these increases in number and share came a shift in the source countries. Morocco and Albania had been the top sources until 2005, when there was a large increase in migrants from Romania. After Romania joined the European Union in 2006, the number of Romanian migrants increased even more sharply.

As of 2019, by far the top source country for migrants to Italy was Romania, with 1.1 million migrants, or 17% of the total. Second-largest was Albania, with 475,000, followed closely by Morocco, with 451,000. The number of migrants from Asia has also been rapidly increasing. While China remains the largest Asian source country, the combined total from South Asia, including India, Pakistan, Bangladesh, and Sri Lanka, increased from 36,000 in 1990 to 493,000 in 2019, a 13-fold increase. At the same time, the combined total from East Asia, including China and the Philippines, rose from 98,000 in 1990 to 382,000 in 2019.

The changing demographics of Italy, including the aging population and shrinking workforce, created a demand for foreign workers at the same time as global economic and political events increased the numbers of economic migrants and asylum seekers. Because of its geography, Italy became a "logical passage" for maritime arrivals following the Arab uprisings, and it will likely attract migrants from Africa as climate-induced migration accelerates.

OIL-RICH DESTINATIONS

Two of the top 10 destinations are oil-rich countries in the Middle East, which are heavily dependent on foreign oil-field and construction workers. India is the largest source country for each, but the migrant population profiles differ, as described below and shown in Figure 5.13.

Number of Migrants from Each Origin, in Millions

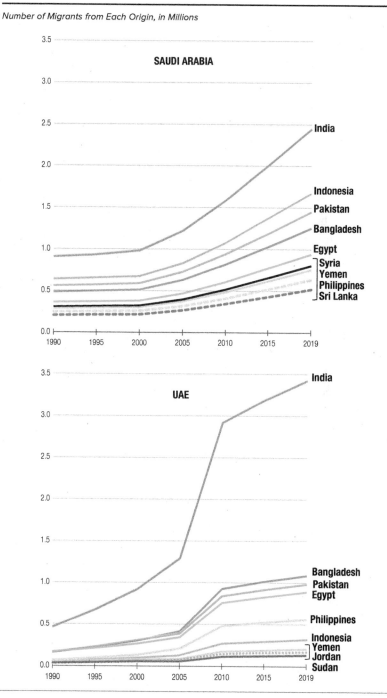

Data source: United Nations, *International Migrant Stock 2019.*

Saudi Arabia

Saudi Arabia, the world's third-largest destination country for international migrants, hosted 13.1 million migrants as of 2019, almost as many as Germany, but with a completely different profile. Like many Middle Eastern countries, Saudi Arabia has a high share of immigrants, and as of 2019, the share of foreign-born had increased to 38%. The share had dipped to 25% in 2000, but since then, the migrant population has more than doubled, from 5.3 to 13.1 million, growing much faster than the total population.

India is the largest source country for Saudi Arabia, accounting for 19% of the migrants, followed by Indonesia with 13%, Pakistan with 11%, Bangladesh with 9%, and Egypt with 7%. Together these top five origins account for almost 60% of all migrants to Saudi Arabia. More than half of all the immigrants came from South Asia, another 17% from East Asia, and about 15% from other Middle Eastern countries. Only 12% came from North Africa, with Egypt being the largest, followed distantly by Sudan.

The Saudi migrants, primarily oil-field and construction workers, are 69% male—one of the highest ratios in the world. The presence of these immigrant workers dramatically changes the population composition. You can see the impact by looking at the age histogram in Figure 5.14. This frequency distribution, sometimes called an age pyramid, shows the number of people by age and sex. Each bar represents a five-year age bracket, with males on the left and females on the right. The bulge on the left around ages 25 to 45 reflects the relatively large number of male workers, and is a common feature of the oil-rich countries that rely on foreign-born labor. The histogram on the right shows a similar situation in the UAE.

United Arab Emirates

As of 2019, the UAE became the world's sixth-largest destination country, with its nearly 9 million immigrants accounting for 88% of its total population of only 10 million. The number of migrants more than doubled over the five years from 2005 to 2010, and has continued to increase. The high immigrant share is not new for the

FIGURE 5.14   The migrants to these oil-rich countries are predominantly young males.

Population by Sex and Age, in Millions, 2020

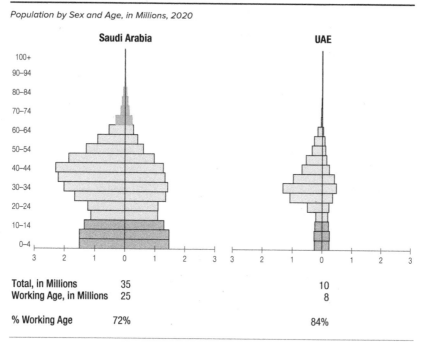

Total, in Millions	35	10
Working Age, in Millions	25	8
% Working Age	72%	84%

Note: Population in millions by five-year age bracket; 0–4 on the bottom, 100+ at the top; males at left, females at right.

Data source: United Nations, *World Population Prospects 2019,* medium variant.

UAE, as its share of foreign-born was already 72% by 1990, and the continued inflow pushed the share up to 88%.

As in Saudi Arabia, most of the immigrants are working-age male oil-field and construction workers, and most originate in Asia. While the UAE and Saudi Arabia pull from a similar set of source countries, there are some differences in the overall migrant profiles. The UAE has a much higher share of foreign-born than Saudi Arabia, 88% compared with 38%. India is by far the largest source country, accounting for 40% of the total foreign-born in the UAE, followed by smaller contributions from Bangladesh and Pakistan, which together make up one-quarter of the total foreign-born. Egypt, with 10%, is the fourth-largest source, followed by the Philippines. Compared with many other countries, including Saudi Arabia, the origins are highly concentrated, with these five countries accounting for 81% of all migrants to the UAE. The 3.4 million Indian migrants account for 40% of all migrants and 35% of the UAE's total population.

In the UAE, 74% of all the migrants are male, one of the highest ratios in the world, even higher than the 69% seen in Saudi Arabia. The bulge of working-age males in the UAE histogram in Figure 5.14 shows the dramatic effect of the migrant population on the total age distribution.

Many other Persian Gulf countries have high shares of international migrants brought in to work in the oil industry. These include Qatar, 79% foreign-born; Kuwait, 72%; Oman, 46%; and Bahrain, 45%. The high shares of international migrants in these small populations—all less than 5 million—point to how dependent their economies are on foreign labor. For all these countries, India is by far the largest source, followed by Bangladesh and Pakistan.

RUSSIA

With 11.6 million migrants, Russia is the fourth-largest host country for international migrants. Russia has drawn from a distinct combination of source countries, one unlike any other large destination. As you can see in Figure 5.15, nearly all the migrants come from former Soviet republics, with Ukraine and Kazakhstan the largest source countries by far, together accounting for half of all the foreign-born living in Russia. The other large source countries include Uzbekistan, Azerbaijan, and Belarus. Just 2% of the migrants were born in other European countries, primarily Germany (142,000), and just 1% originated in Asia, with most from East Asia. China was the largest Asian source, with 56,000 migrants, followed by Mongolia (21,000), Vietnam (14,000), and North Korea (11,000).

Another distinctive feature of Russia's migrant profile is that the number of foreign-born has been almost unchanged since 1990, hovering around 12 million. While other large-destination countries have seen increased numbers of immigrants, Russia's foreign-born

FIGURE 5.15 Russia's total migrant population consists almost entirely of people from former Soviet republics.

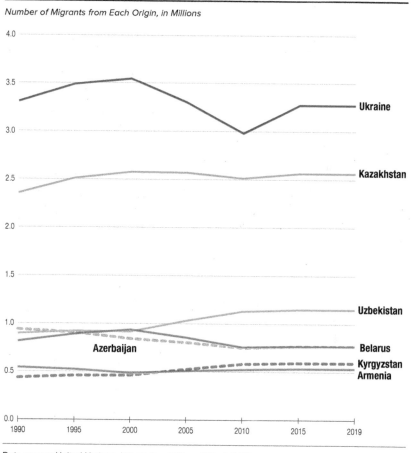

Number of Migrants from Each Origin, in Millions

Data source: United Nations, *International Migrant Stock 2019.*

population has not increased. It ranks as the fourth-largest host country, largely because of the migrants who arrived from former Soviet republics in the 1990s—not because it continued to attract new migrants. From 2000 to 2010, the total dropped by a half million, mostly due to a decline in the number of Ukrainians, but the number rebounded slightly by 2015.

The relative composition by source country has also not changed much; Ukraine and Kazakhstan are still by far the largest source countries, accounting for 28% and 22% respectively. The number of migrants from Uzbekistan has increased slightly, now accounting for 10% of the total foreign-born.

Unlike elsewhere, Russia's share of foreign-born has been stable, around 8% of its total, reflecting stagnation in both total population and migrant flows.

TOP ORIGIN COUNTRIES IN MORE DETAIL

HISTORY OF MIGRANT FLOWS FROM THE TOP SOURCES

Now that you have looked closely at the top destinations and their distinct combinations of sources, we turn to looking in more detail at the top origins. You saw that only a third of migrants from the top sources live in the top destinations, so now you will learn where else they settle. While there is some overlap with what we learned in the destination section, looking at migration from the perspective of the originating countries helps frame what we might see in the future: Will migration from these large source countries increase? Will other originating countries become more prominent as populations grow and economic and environmental pressures mount?

In Figure 5.16 you can see how emigration from the large source countries has changed. Most of these top origin countries have consistently been among the most common sources over the past few decades, even as the total number of migrants has increased. Syria is the only newcomer to the list, with its recent surge of refugees fleeing the country.

Although the overall ranking of source countries hasn't changed much in recent decades, several source countries have seen especially rapid growth in the number of emigrants. As shown in Figure 5.16, India has had the largest absolute increase, to become by far the top source. Other countries with notable increases include China and the Philippines from East Asia and Bangladesh and Pakistan from South Asia. The decline from Russia reflects that migration from

FIGURE 5.16   As of 2019, the top 10 sources accounted for 89 million migrants, one-third of the world's total, with India surpassing Mexico to become the world's largest source of international migrants.

Number of Migrants from Each Top 10 Origin Country, in Millions

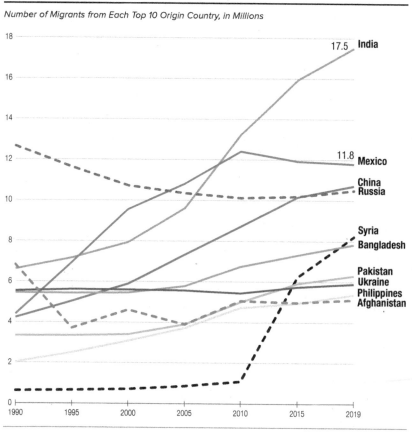

Data source: United Nations, *International Migrant Stock 2019.*

Russia to the former Soviet republics has been slowing. The decline from Mexico is also striking, especially after the long upward trend that peaked in 2010.

While no African countries currently rank among the top 10 origins, several African countries have had recent increases in out-migration, including Egypt, Morocco, and South Sudan, with between 2.5 and 3.5 million migrants as of 2019. As population growth accelerates across Africa and as many countries face weak economic prospects, we can expect to see rising pressure for migration. The expected upswing in climate-induced migration will exacerbate the outflow.

Although not among the top 10, two other large origins are also important. Indonesia and Poland, which rank 11th and 12th, have seen their out-migration nearly triple since 1990, reaching 4.5 million in 2019. As you saw above, Indonesia has become a top source for Saudi Arabia, and Poland the number one source for Germany.

GEOGRAPHIC OVERVIEW OF MIGRATION FROM THE TOP SOURCES

Now that you've learned about the numbers of migrants from the top sources, it will be revealing to consider differences and similarities in where they settle. Figure 5.17 provides a broad geographic perspective on the migrant flows from the top sources to key geographic regions.

The first thing you may notice is that the regional similarities in the outflows reflect cultural and historical connections. As you can see in the top three bars of the chart, more than half of the migrants from South Asia have gone westward to the oil-rich Middle Eastern countries; and a large share has settled in other Asian countries, mostly in East and Southeast Asia. North America accounts for most of the migration to destinations outside the region. About 20% of India's migrants now live in the United States and Canada.

Similarly, China's out-migration has generally occurred within its regional neighborhood; more than half of Chinese migrants have stayed in the area, going to nearby countries in East and Southeast Asia, including Hong Kong. About a third have journeyed to North America.

Several other important migration patterns stand out as well. You have already seen that nearly all Mexican migrants have relocated to the United States and most Russian migrants have gravitated to former Soviet republics. As expected, most of the migrants from the political hot spots of Syria and Afghanistan have stayed within their home regions—most Syrian refugees have remained

FIGURE 5.17 While half of all migrants from South Asia have gone to the Middle East, half of all migrants from China stay within the region.

Number of Migrants from Each Top Origin Going to Each Region, in Millions, as of 2019

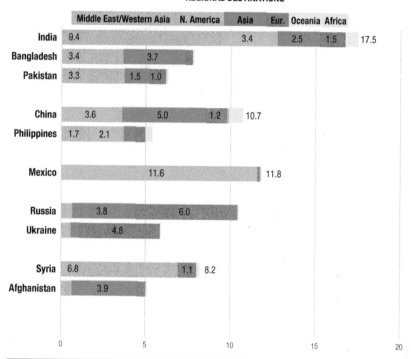

Note: As indicated elsewhere, Western Asia, according to the UN's definition, includes many countries we generally think of as part of the Middle East. Asia in this figure excludes countries in Western Asia and represents the rest of Asia.

Data source: United Nations, *International Migrant Stock 2019.*

within Western Asia, and most Afghan refugees have remained in other parts of Asia.

HISTORICAL CHANGES IN OUT-MIGRATION FROM ASIA

Because migration is expected to be an increasingly important issue affecting national security and economic prospects, it is important to understand how migrant flows can change and adapt to economic incentives and political and cultural pressures. The next section discusses how the historical patterns of out-migration have changed in the five largest Asian source countries.

India

India is by far the world's largest originating country, even though it accounts for only 6% of the world's migrants in 2019. The total number of Indians living outside the country more than doubled over the past 20 years, from 8 million in 2000 to 17.5 million in 2019. More than half, a total of 9.4 million, have migrated to the Middle East, nearly all to Persian Gulf countries; another 19% have migrated to North America; and another 12% left India but remained in the region.

The top destination for Indians as of 2019 was the UAE, which hosts 3.4 million Indian migrants, or 20% of the total; this is followed by the US, with 2.7 million, and Saudi Arabia, with 2.4 million. The migration patterns have shifted over the past 30 years. The number of Indians living in Pakistan has been steadily declining, while the numbers going to the United States and to Persian Gulf countries have steadily increased, with an especially sharp rise in migration to the UAE after 2005. As noted above, migration to the Persian Gulf reflects a regional pattern, as Persian Gulf countries have attracted working-age men from several South Asian sources, including India, Pakistan, and Bangladesh. As oil production declines, the number of migrants might also decline or shift to other industries.

China

China, the third-largest origin, has two main destination countries. The US is the largest, accounting for 2.9 million, or 27% of the total, followed by Hong Kong, which in 2019 had 2.3 million Chinese-born people, or 21% of the total. The inflow to Hong Kong over time, which has recently stabilized, contributed to Hong Kong's having a 40% share of foreign-born population. Another 25% or 2.7 million Chinese have migrated to other Asian countries, with the largest numbers in Japan, with 785,000, and South Korea, with 620,000. Australia hosts 640,000 or 6% of the total—slightly more than South Korea. The number of Chinese living in Singapore has recently declined slightly, while the number in Australia has been steadily increasing. The Chinese-born population living in Europe totals 1.2 million, with Italy the largest destination at 228,000. The total living in Africa is reportedly less than 1%.

Bangladesh

Bangladesh is the world's sixth-largest source country, with 7.8 million migrants living outside its borders. Interestingly, this diaspora includes more than 3 million Bangladeshi-born people in India, reflecting the historical pattern of Bangladeshis seeking political refuge and work in neighboring India. The number has declined sharply, from 4.4 million in 1990 to 3.1 million in 2019. While the number living in India has decreased, the number going to Saudi Arabia, the UAE, and other Middle Eastern countries has increased, and by 2019 accounted for 43% of the migrants. The number migrating to Malaysia has also increased and now accounts for 5% of the total.

Aside from its political history, Bangladesh is an especially interesting source country because its steep fertility decline has led to a bulge in working-age population. While local industries benefited from the expansion in labor supply, many workers sought jobs outside the country. Further, because of its topography and the presence of many lakes, Bangladesh is already heavily affected by the rising sea level, so we can expect to see increasing out-migration. The diversification of Bangladeshi migration patterns bears watching as migration intensifies and occupational demands change.

Pakistan

Pakistan, the seventh-largest source of migrants, accounted for 6.3 million in 2019. If we compare Pakistan with Bangladesh, we can see several important features. As with Bangladesh, the top destination countries for Pakistan are the Middle Eastern oil countries, with Saudi Arabia the largest. As with Bangladesh, the number of Pakistanis living in India has been declining. A key difference compared with Bangladesh is the large share and number of Pakistani migrants now living in the UK. In 2019 the UK hosted over

600,000 Pakistani migrants, or 10% of the total, while the US hosted 400,000, or 6% of the total.

Pakistan is worth monitoring as a growing source of migrants. With its lower-middle-income population projected to double from 200 million to 400 million by 2050, and its youthful population facing low economic prospects at home, many more Pakistanis will likely be prompted to migrate.

Philippines

The Philippines is another example of an Asian country with substantial out-migration to the Middle East, with Saudi Arabia and the UAE being the most common Middle East destinations. More striking is that the US remains by far the largest host for Filipino migrants, hosting 2 million migrants, or 38% of the total, as of 2019, with a large share being trained health care workers seeking jobs in the US. It is easy to see how these major migrant flows reflect economic trends and occupational needs elsewhere in the world.

OTHER LARGE ORIGIN COUNTRIES

Russia

After declining by about 2 million during the 1990s, the Russian diaspora has stabilized at around 10 million. Not surprisingly, the former Soviet republics together accounted for nearly 80% of all Russian migrants as of 2019. Despite a decline in the 1990s, Ukraine remains the top destination, with 3.3 million, or 32% of the total, in 2019. Kazakhstan was the destination for another 23%. While most Russian emigrants live in former Soviet republics, the remaining 20% is widely dispersed across many countries. Migration to Germany increased during the 1990s and reached 1 million in 2019, making Germany the third-largest destination for Russian migrants, accounting for 10% of the total. The United States hosts 411,000 Russian migrants or 4% of the total. And Israel has 111,000, making it the 10th-largest destination for Russian emigrants.

Russia is one of the few countries that is both a top origin and a top destination as of 2019. It is the source for 10.5 million emigrants and the host destination for 11.6 million immigrants from other countries. Ukraine and Kazakhstan have been the largest destination countries for emigrants from Russia, and conversely, the same two countries have been the largest source countries for migrants going to Russia. This situation reflects the cumulative effect of the ongoing cultural and economic ties across the former Soviet republics. Over the past 30 years since the fall of the Soviet Union, net migration has totaled 11.7 million, an average of 390,000 per year, which has only partially offset the natural population decline of 440,000 per year.

Syria

Due to its sudden and significant out-migration, Syria is a newcomer to the list of top origins. Unlike the economic migrants that relocate from many other top origins, migrants from Syria were primarily political refugees seeking asylum. The numbers are staggering, and the impact of the huge refugee movement became a humanitarian crisis punctuated with deaths and major displacements both internally and externally.

The climate-induced origins of the Syrian Civil War deserve some attention because they portend what we might expect in many other countries and regions. The Syrian drought prompted a wave of rural migration into the cities, and the resulting civil conflict eventually evolved into an international conflict involving Russia and the United States. The huge international refugee movement has become a humanitarian crisis with a high death toll and displacement of millions of Syrians. The impact on the refugee destinations throughout the region and in Europe has also been enormous.

Syria's prewar population registered around 22 million. As of 2019, the total population living in Syria had dropped to 17 million, with an estimated 8.2 million Syrians living outside the country. Another 6 million, forced to leave their homes, have become internally displaced. Most of the Syrians who crossed the border are now living in nearby countries in the Middle East. All of a sudden, Turkey became home to 3.7 million Syrian refugees, nearly half the total. Lebanon, the second-largest host, had 1.2 million, or 14%, followed by Saudi Arabia with 802,000 (10%), and Jordan with 725,000. Germany became the largest European host country, with 590,000 Syrians, or 7% of the total. As of 2019, the US hosted 92,000, or 1% of the total.

The implications for the various host countries differ greatly. Turkey, the largest host for Syrian migrants, historically had only a small percentage of immigrants, but with the Syrian refugee crisis, the foreign-born share increased from 2% of the country's total population to 7% by 2019. While this is small compared with other countries in the Middle East, the social and economic disruption brought on by abruptly adding nearly 4 million people posed enormous challenges, starting with how best to shelter the unexpected influx.

For Germany, the sudden influx of nearly 600,000 Syrian refugees threatened the political future of Angela Merkel. Even though Syrian refugees to Germany represented less than 5% of Germany's foreign-born population, and less than 1% of the total population, the disruption and political turmoil was huge as anti-immigrant protests escalated across Europe.

IMPACT ON OVERALL POPULATION GROWTH AND COMPOSITION

For most countries, the impact of migration on total population growth is small; but for some, migration contributes significantly to population growth. In these cases, we can expect to see changes in the overall age mix, especially as countries seek to bring in working-age migrants or people with particular skills. In many countries, even where the numerical impact on population levels is small, the social and political impact might be large, especially where the influx of migrants has been sudden and unexpected. It is difficult to forecast such changes, but we can generally expect that migration will be substantially on the rise around the world in the coming decades as economic, political, and environmental factors spur increasing numbers to seek improved and more stable prospects outside of their countries of origin. The following discussion will show you how migration contributes to total population and how it might affect the age mix of the destination.

COMPONENTS OF POPULATION CHANGE: NET MIGRATION AND NATURAL INCREASE

To understand the overall impact of migration on total population it is useful to segment the two components of population change. First, we have the natural increase, defined as births minus deaths. The second factor to influence total population is net migration, the number of people arriving from across borders minus the number of people leaving. Most of the top destinations have older populations with declining birth rates and increasing death rates. Thus, for most of these large destinations, the natural increase from births minus deaths is slowing, and in some cases is already negative. Whether migration can offset the decline has important policy implications, both for managing aging populations and migration itself. Figure 5.18 focuses on the large economies and illustrates several patterns of growth for the two components of population change over the past 30 years. The chart shows the relative impact of migration compared with natural population growth.

First Pattern: Net Migration Adds to a Positive Natural Increase

In the first pattern of population growth, net migration adds to a positive natural increase. Countries in this category include the traditional immigration countries—the US, Canada, and Australia—plus the United Kingdom and France. For these countries, net migration accounts for a significant share of total population change.

The United States benefits from both a continued natural increase as well as a large net migration. Over the past 30 years, net migration of nearly 34 million was less than the natural increase, 45 million, and accounted for 43% of total population change. Over the next 30 years, the natural increase is projected to decline owing to fewer births and more deaths, but will remain positive. If net migration remains near the historical average of 1 million per

FIGURE 5.18 Over the past 30 years, population in most large economies would have grown even without migrant inflows.

Population Change by Component, in Millions, 1990–2020

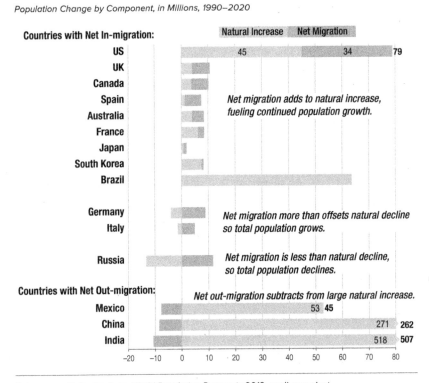

Data source: United Nations, *World Population Prospects 2019*, medium variant.

year, we can expect migration to account for an increasing share of population change. According to the UN projection, net migration in the United States would increase from 43% of total population growth to nearly two-thirds of total population change over the next 30 years. Migration is difficult to project, so these estimates could vary substantially.

While the US has the highest number of immigrants, the role of net migration is much larger in several other large economies. In the UK and Canada, net migration has accounted for more than 60% of total population change over the past 30 years. In Australia, the components have been about equal, with net migration contributing 51% of the total population change. As in the United States, the contribution of migration to total population growth is projected to increase dramatically over the next 30 years. In Canada, due to its rapidly growing natural decline, net migration will account for nearly all the projected population growth. Similarly, the migration share is projected to increase to nearly 60% in Australia and 80% in the United Kingdom.

France offers a stark contrast; over the past 30 years, net migration accounted for only 27% of total population change. Comparing France with the UK illustrates how the components of change contribute differently to total population. In 1990, France and the UK had about the same total population, 57 million. Over the 30 years from 1990 to 2020, the UK grew faster, adding 11 million people, while France added about 9 million. However, net migration accounted for 61% of the increase in the UK, compared with only 27% in France. The relatively large natural increase in France reflects its higher birth rate compared to other European countries.

Several other countries fit the pattern of this group, though with some differences. In Spain, a particularly large influx of migrants over the past 30 years boosted the migration share to 81% of total population growth, but immigration has recently dropped. With a projected natural decline, and less migration, total population is projected to fall.

It is a bit of surprise to see Japan on the list with positive net migration since we generally think of Japan as restricting immigration. The net migration was small, only 1.1 million, and the natural increase was smaller. Over the next 30 years Japan is projected to experience a dramatic natural decline of 22 million, with in-migration of only 1.5 million.

Although South Korea's population had been fueled primarily by natural increase and little immigration over the past 30 years, in the future it will likely follow a pattern similar to Japan's—a large natural decline with little offsetting net migration.

Finally, Brazil stands out because of the size of its natural increase. It has had little net migration, but unlike most other large economies, it has a young and growing population, and its natural increase is projected to continue until around 2050.

Second Pattern: Migration More Than Offsets Natural Decline

In this second group, natural population growth is negative, as the number of deaths exceeds births, but migration offsets this loss. We know that Germany and Italy are among the world's older populations, so it isn't surprising to see the natural population decline. For both countries, net migration in the past was large enough to more than offset this decrease. In Germany net migration was more than twice the size of its natural decline, while Italy's was more than three times the natural decline. However, over the next 30 years, net migration is projected to be smaller and will no longer offset the growing natural decline. Even with continued immigration, Italy is projected to see a total population decrease of 10% by 2050. Germany will see a smaller decline of 4%.

Third Pattern: Net Migration Not Enough to Offset Natural Decline

With this pattern, the natural population has declined but is not fully offset by migration. For example, in Russia, even the high level of net migration, nearly 12 million, was not enough to offset the large natural population decline of more than 13 million. Continued population decline is projected.

Among the large economies Russia is the only country currently in this category. As you read above, Germany and Italy will soon fall into this category, with net migration insufficient to offset increasing natural decline. Other countries that will soon find themselves in this category include Spain, Japan, and South Korea.

Fourth Pattern: Out-migration Subtracts from Natural Increase

Finally, three large economies experienced sizable out-migration, each with different circumstances. In Mexico, out-migration over the past 30 years totaled nearly 8 million, subtracting 15% from its natural increase of 53 million. Over the next 30 years, the impact will be much smaller. The natural increase is projected to halve, and out-migration is projected to fall significantly; as a result, projected out-migration of less than 2 million will subtract about 5% from the natural increase.

For China and India, the two most populous countries, out-migration in the past subtracted only small shares from the total population. However, their future population trajectories diverge, with India's population continuing to grow and China's starting to fall. Because of its continued strong natural population increase, projected at 270 million over the next 30 years, India's out-migration is projected to remain only a small share of its population.

China faces more of a surprising turn because its natural population growth in the past has already started to reverse. This is a startling development in the world's most populous country. Over the next 30 years China is projected to see a population decline of 37 million, including a natural decline of 27 million and continued out-migration of 10 million. The percentage change is small, but as you can see, the direction is significant.

PROJECTED POPULATION GROWTH—WITH AND WITHOUT MIGRATION

Another way to look at the impact of migration is to compare the population projections for the scenarios with and without migration. Figure 5.19 shows the comparison for the large economies, illustrating the dramatic effects of a zero-migration scenario.

As expected, for the traditional immigration countries, total population growth is heavily dependent on migration and will be much smaller in the zero-migration scenario. Assuming continued immigration, the United States population is projected to grow 15% by mid-century, but without migration, growth would be only 2%. In absolute terms, population growth would be 48 million with migration and less than 8 million without. As you read above, Canada depends more heavily on migration than the US, and without migration Canada's population would decline by 4%. For Australia, the least populous

FIGURE 5.19 In the future, countries' openness to migrants will substantially affect their population growth.

Projected Population Change, with and without Migration, 2020–50.

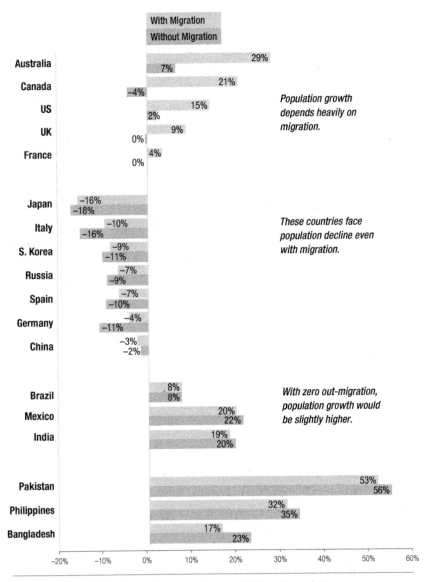

Data source: United Nations, *World Population Prospects 2019*, medium variant.

of the traditional immigration countries, the zero-migration scenario reduces population growth to 7%, compared with 29% with migration.

Two European countries stand out from the pack of mostly shrinking populations. The UK and France have been among the top migrant destinations, and with continued migration, their populations are projected to grow by 9% and 4% respectively by midcentury. Population growth in both would slow to zero without migration.

Seven of the largest economies, shown in the middle of Figure 5.19, including China and Japan, were already facing population decline, even with immigration. Without migration, the declines would be larger.

The largest impact of migration occurs for Italy and Germany. Over the past 30 years migration was large enough to offset their natural declines, but the equation won't hold in the future as the natural decline expands. Without migration, the total population declines would be even larger, reaching 16% in Italy and 11% in Germany.

All three large Asian economies face declining populations even with migration. For Japan and South Korea, the declines are somewhat greater in the zero-migration scenario. For China, the opposite is true because China is a large source country. With zero out-migration—no people leaving—China's population decline would be slightly smaller, at 2% rather than 3%.

Brazil, the world's sixth most populous country, is another special case: migration has been almost zero, so there is no difference between the two scenarios.

A zero-migration scenario would increase population growth in the large origin countries, except for China as discussed above. For Mexico, zero migration would increase the 30-year growth from 20% to 22%, an increase of 2 million people. For India, zero out-migration would increase growth from 19% to 20%.

While the zero-migration scenario may be unlikely, the comparison shows you a likely range of possibilities. The medium variant scenario, reflecting the UN's most likely projection, assumes migration will continue at levels similar to the recent past, while the zero-migration scenario assumes migration will stop as of 2020.

The actual amount of migration is likely to lie somewhere in between, so these two population scenarios can be viewed as bracketing the uncertainty about the impact of migration on total population growth.

IMPACT ON AGE STRUCTURE

In addition to adding to or subtracting from total population, migration can affect the age mix of the population and lead to changes in the relative size of the working-age and elderly populations. The initial impact might be an influx of working-age people seeking better economic prospects, but the cumulative impact is more complicated. Some migrants bring family members, including children and elderly, and some remain and have families later. There are also age differences by gender, with some countries attracting more working-age men, say for construction work, and others attracting more working-age women, typically for hospitality or nursing. The impact on age structure is especially important in the countries with aging populations and potentially declining numbers of workers. Indeed, one of the big economic policy questions is whether migration can offset long-term declines in the workforce. Understanding the potential changes in age structure will shed light on that question.

The comparison of the United States and Germany in Figure 5.20 shows how the migrant populations have supplemented the native-born populations; in both countries the migrant population has increased the working-age share of the total population. The three 2019 histograms for each country show the native-born population on the left, the foreign-born in the middle, and the total on the right. Each bar reflects the population in that five-year age bracket, with males on the left and females on the right. The total histogram on the right shows the sum of the two segments.

Looking at the age profile of the US native-born population on the left, we can see the baby boomer bulge around age 60, and the echo boom around age 25; the indentation in the middle reflects the baby bust. While the native-born population is concentrated in two places—the older and younger brackets—the migrant population is

FIGURE 5.20 The migrant populations have supplemented the working-age populations of the native-born in both the United States and Germany.

Population in Millions by Five-Year Age Bracket, 2019; Native-Born, Foreign-Born, and Total Population

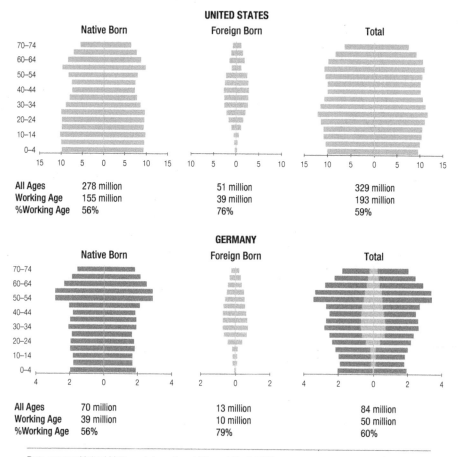

Data source: United Nations, *International Migrant Stock 2019.*

heavily concentrated in the working-age brackets. As you can see at the bottom of the histograms, the working-age brackets account for 56% of the native-born population and 76% of the migrant population. When combined, the pendulum shape of the migrant population partially offsets the indentation in the hourglass shape of the native-born population, supplementing the working-age population and increasing the total share of working-age people to 59% of the total population.

Though the age structure situation looks completely different in Germany, the overall impact is similar. While the US population has a more even age distribution, Germany's population is top-heavy with older people, with the prominent bulge occurring from ages 50 to 65, at the top of the working-age segments. As in the US, the working-age brackets account for 56% of Germany's native-born population. You can see that the migrant population is more heavily concentrated in the younger working-age brackets than in the United States, with 79% of the migrant population falling in the working-age brackets. The combined histogram for Germany shows that the migrant population boosted the overall working-age population to 60% of the total, slightly higher than in the US.

While Figure 5.20 compares the population segments in the two countries, Figure 5.21 shows the impact of migration on the total

FIGURE 5.21 In the United States and Germany, migrants account for about one-fifth of the total working-age populations, though the shares differ across age brackets.

Migrant Share of Population in Each Five-Year Age Bracket, United States and Germany, 2019

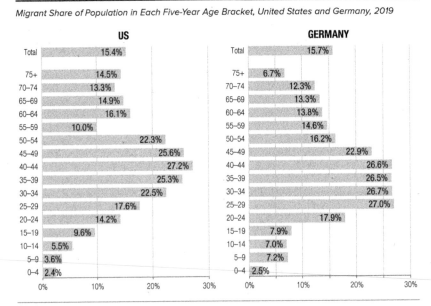

Data source: United Nations, *International Migrant Stock 2019.*

age structure by illustrating the migrant-population share of each bracket. Overall, in the United States, migrants of all ages account for 15.4% of the total population, but the share varies by age. The highest shares occur in the three age brackets from 35 to 49. Overall, the migrant working-age population accounts for about 20% of the total working-age population, or 39 million out of 193 million.

In Germany, the distribution is different, but the overall share is similar. As you can see in the figure, the migrant working-age population in Germany accounts for 21% of the total working-age population compared with 20% in the US. For Germany, the highest shares occur from ages 20 to 44.

CONCLUSION

We've seen that migration is a global phenomenon affecting all areas of the world. And we have seen that the large host countries generally have specific migrant profiles reflecting the social, political, and cultural history that connects the host and source countries. Examples include the long history of migration from Mexico to the United States, migration from former colonies to France and the United Kingdom, and migration among the former Soviet republics.

We have also seen that although migration represents a small share of global population, just 3.5%, for many countries it can have significant demographic as well as social and economic implications. The measurable demographic impacts include adding to or subtracting from total population and influencing the age structure of the population as migrants are concentrated in the working-age brackets.

In the future, we can expect international migration to accelerate. We will see that the push-pull factors are similar to what they have been in the past, but in the future, they will have much more force, owing to the major demographic transitions under way globally and to the changing economic and political context. Economic migration, as workers seek better prospects in the advanced economies, will accelerate, especially as explosive population growth continues in parts of the developing world, particularly in places with weak economic prospects. At the same time, many advanced economies will likely become more open to in-migration as a possible avenue for offsetting slower-growing or even shrinking workforces. We also expect climate-induced migration to increase. And finally, mounting civil and international conflicts spurred by political instability will fuel migration as well.

Given this array of factors driving migration, we know that the level of migration to any particular country is difficult to forecast. The migrant flows will depend on how each country chooses to manage its migration and refugee policies. In many countries, these policies are currently being revised as countries seek to adapt to political and economic pressures at home and abroad. For example, in 2020 Germany enacted new rules to admit qualified skilled immigrants from outside the European Union. And under former President Trump, the US greatly restricted the total number of migrants allowed into the country.

What seems clear is that each country's story is different, and there will be differences in how countries manage the levels of migration, whether it be long-term economic migration rooted in historical connections or disruptive refugee movements. Ideally, each country would adapt to its own changing demography and develop migration policies that leverage existing strengths and address current and projected weaknesses, with particular attention to industry and occupational labor supply issues.

Understanding how partners and adversaries address their demography will be important for economic growth and international security. It will be increasingly essential to keep in mind that countries face different demographic challenges, have different social and economic priorities, and will therefore need diverse policies. No one set of policies will fit all countries.

KEY DEMOGRAPHIC CHALLENGES

6 POPULATION AGING

"Lousy Demographics Will Not Stop China's Rise"
Financial Times, by Gideon Rachman, May 3, 2021

"Iran's Aging Population Raises Red Flags for the Islamic Republic"
Inside Arabia, by Maysam Bizaer, March 18, 2020

"This Economy Is Not Aging Gracefully"
New York Times, by Eduardo Porter, June 15, 2019

"Slower Growth in Aging Economies Is Not Inevitable, But Avoiding It Means Tough Policy Choices"
The Economist, March 30, 2019

The proportion of old people is sharply on the rise. And the pace is accelerating. By midcentury 16% of the world's population, or one in six people, will be age 65 and over (65+). In Europe, nearly 20% of the population is already age 65+, and by midcentury the share will increase to 28%. The share in Southern Europe will reach 35% making Western Europe look young with its 29%. Japan's share of 65+ will increase to nearly 38% but will be slightly outranked by the rapidly aging South Korea.

These trends are astonishing and alarming—and almost totally predictable. What is not predictable is how societies will anticipate and adapt to the changes already under way. These changes may lead to many politically challenging policy issues, stirring up debate about raising retirement ages, adjusting entitlements, improving educational outcomes, boosting immigration, encouraging larger families, and improving childcare and senior care, to name just a few issues with implications for aging populations.

For sure, we are experiencing unprecedented developments. As we celebrate the slowdown in explosive population growth, we should recognize that this slowdown leads directly to a slower-growing labor supply. This challenges some of our conventional thinking that has been based on ever-growing populations. Our social models based on traditional family structures are outmoded as well. To address the changes, we need to think differently about the future, and essential to this new thinking, we need to understand the dynamics of the dramatic population shifts.

We should first understand that population aging isn't just about the growing *number* of old people, it's about the shift in the whole age structure that has occurred as more people are reaching older ages and as people are having fewer and fewer children. As a result, both the *number* and *share* of old people are increasing. Further, population aging is not just about aging baby boomers and graying European countries. Aging is a global trend—it is happening everywhere. The consequences are enormous, especially for economic and social well-being, but also for national security. As you've already read, because of differences in the timing and pace of changes in fertility and life expectancy, the pace of aging is unfolding differently around the world. Understanding these differences will be helpful in assessing the priorities and practices of our allies and adversaries. We can clearly see that aging is about to take off with a vengeance in many middle-income countries, while it is more slowly accelerating in more advanced economies.

One of the challenges in analyzing demographic change is deciding on a time frame, as you've read earlier. In the business world, the focus is generally short and often driven by quarterly returns or annual shareholder reports. But for understanding important demographic shifts, we need a different time horizon. It turns out if you don't use a long perspective, you will miss seeing critical inflection points in important drivers and outcomes. Consequently, you will miss the chance to prepare for the coming changes. For example, if in 2000, you had set a five-year horizon or even a 20-year horizon, you would have missed seeing the drama of aging about to unfold throughout the world. To fully anticipate important future demographic developments, this book focuses on changes expected over the next 30 years, and in addition shows how the trends will continue to unfold over the rest of the century.

The most often used indicator of population aging is change in the proportion of old people—more precisely, change in the percentage of the population that is age 65 and older. Few people like the term "old" and even fewer agree on what chronological age is old. Nonetheless, we will stick with the conventional age of 65 as the benchmark for old people. And we will call them retirees to distinguish them from working-age folks, even though many people age 65 and over continue to work, and conversely, many working-age individuals are not actually working. Using the conventional age ranges will allow us to make global comparisons even though they may not fully reflect labor market choices.

POPULATION AGE 65 AND OLDER IN 2020

Globally, the number of people age 65 and older will more than double over the next 30 years, increasing from 728 million in 2020 to 1.5 billion by 2050. This age group is the fastest-growing segment of the population, and its share of world population will increase from 9% to 16% by midcentury; by century's end, people age 65 and over will account for nearly one-quarter of the world's total population. Figure 6.1 shows the regional distribution.

It's not surprising that Asia dominates growth in the population age 65+, but the scale is startling, especially for China. In 2020 China already had 172 million people in the 65-and-over bracket, and that number is projected to more than double over the next 30 years. The especially rapid pace of aging has already given China a disproportionate share of the world's older population. In 2020, China accounted for 24% of the world's older people, much larger than its 18% share of total population. By 2050, with 366 million people age 65 and up, China will still account for nearly a quarter of the world's 65+ even though its total population will have declined to 14% of world total.

FIGURE 6.1 Global population age 65 and over is projected to double to 1.5 billion by 2050. China accounts for one-quarter of the total.

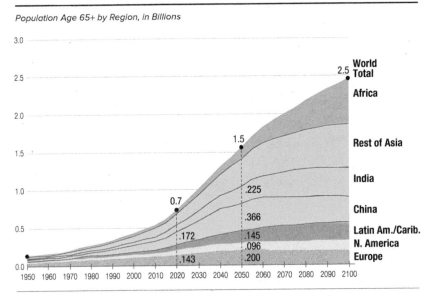

Population Age 65+ by Region, in Billions

Data source: United Nations, *World Population Prospects 2019,* medium variant.

GLOBAL POPULATION AGING, 2020 TO 2050

The most often used indicator of aging is the change in share of people age 65 and over. The increasing proportion of old people stems from the interaction of the two key drivers: increasing life expectancy raises the number of people who reach older ages, and declining fertility reduces the number of children and slows growth in the total population. Another way to think of this is through the math of disproportionate growth rates. The population age 65 and over is growing faster than the other age groups, so its share of the population is increasing.

Today, most countries are still relatively young, as you can see by the broad swath of red and orange on the 2020 map in Figure 6.2. In these countries, less than 10% of the population is age 65 and over. The group includes all of Africa, most of South America, and

FIGURE 6.2   By 2050, all advanced economies will be old. Only Africa remains young.

Percentage of Population Age 65+, 2020 and 2050

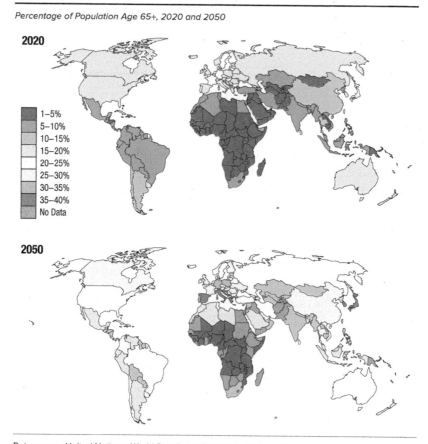

Data source: United Nations, *World Population Prospects 2019,* medium variant.

most of Asia. China, at 12%, is already an outlier in Asia. Another group, shown in beige, includes the United States, Canada, and Australia, where 16% to 18% of the population is age 65+. Japan is the oldest country with 28% of its population age 65 and over. Italy is the second oldest at 23% with many other European countries close behind. The life expectancy and fertility trends already under way will significantly change this map.

Over the next 30 years divergent patterns of aging will emerge, so that by 2050, many more countries will have old populations, including China and South Korea—and many fewer countries will remain young. As depicted in the 2050 map, the large youthful band across the Southern Hemisphere has diminished. By 2050, most young countries will be located in Africa with only a few in the Middle East. Afghanistan and Pakistan stand out as the youngest populations in Asia.

To show how population aging unfolds differently, Figure 6.3 compares selected countries. The pace of aging differs across countries depending on the timing and pace of their life expectancy gains and fertility declines. Japan is currently the oldest country, with 28% of its population age 65 and over. By 2050, the share is projected to rise to an astonishing 38%. One of the most striking features about Japan's aging trajectory is how far and fast it has already moved: Japan has

FIGURE 6.3 The pace of aging will accelerate over the next 30 years.

Percentage of Population Age 65+, Selected Countries

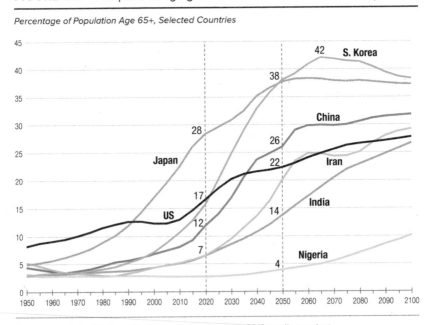

Data source: United Nations, *World Population Prospects 2019*, medium variant.

evolved from being a relatively young country in 1950 to being the oldest, as its share of people age 65 and older increased from 5% to 28% by 2020. This gave Japan the label of having the fastest-aging population. But based on its steeper line, it looks like South Korea will overtake that speed record. More startling than the speed is that South Korea's share is projected to reach 42% by 2065.

In contrast, the pace of aging is much slower in the US, which will remain relatively young, despite concerns about the huge impact of aging baby boomers. The sudden but short 20-year rise in the older population started around 2010, as the first baby boomers turned 65. But the percentage age 65 and over—17% in 2020—is much smaller and growing more gradually than in many other countries. The share will increase to just 22% by midcentury. This relative youth makes the US an exception and offers a competitive advantage.

China will pass the US by 2040 as the number and share of its old people swell. By 2050, China's proportion of older people will be 26%, up from just 12% in 2020. The sharp increase stems largely from the steep fertility decline, which policy makers are now desperately working to reverse or at least slow. The huge increase in life expectancy also contributed to the increase in the number of old people.

Iran is another example of a country with a steep fertility decline—similar to China's, but occurring about 20 years later. In 1990, Iran had a young and growing population; but with fewer and fewer children, the share of older people has been steadily on the rise. As the impacts of lower fertility set in, the pace of aging is projected to accelerate, pushing the share of older people from 7% in 2020 to 20% by 2050.

In contrast to China, India will remain relatively young and will age much more gradually, with its share of 65+ reaching only 14% in 2050, compared with 26% in China. Even as India's population reaches 1.6 billion around 2060, it will remain a relatively young country. These divergent aging patterns have important consequences for the labor supply. China's rapid aging has resulted in a shrinking workforce, while India, with much slower aging, is projected to see continued workforce growth through midcentury.

POPULATION AGING BY REGION

Regional comparisons provide a useful context for understanding the key differences between countries. Europe, with its decades-long history of low fertility and high life expectancy, has the oldest population. Its share of people age 65 and up is projected to increase from 19% in 2020 to 28% by 2050, and then level off, as shown in Figure 6.4. This acceleration in aging reflects both that more people are reaching older ages and that the rest of the population is growing more slowly. For Europe overall, the number of children has been declining since 1965, and the working-age population has been declining since around 2010. Over the next 30 years, the continent's total population is projected to decline by 37 million, but the population age 65 and up will increase by 57 million, bringing the share of old people to 28% by 2050.

FIGURE 6.4   Over the next 30 years, Asia and Latin America will see the steepest increases in the proportion of old people.

Percentage of Population Age 65+, by Region

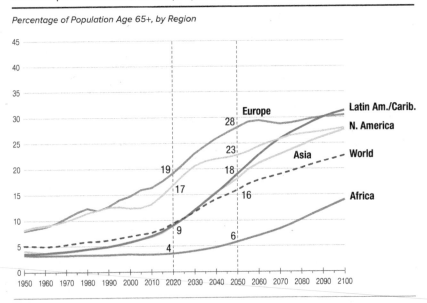

Data source: United Nations, *World Population Prospects 2019,* medium variant.

North America, the second-oldest region, has a completely different trajectory than Europe. The pace of aging started to accelerate as the first baby boomers turned 65 around 2010, and will continue to rise until around 2030, when the last of the boomers reaches 65; after that milestone, the pace of aging slows and the curve starts to flatten.

As reflected in the overlapping lines in Figure 6.4, Asia and Latin America follow similar trajectories until midcentury. The percentage of the population age 65 and over in both regions started to climb around 2010 as the impact of declining fertility began to take hold, and it will continue rising quite steeply over the next 30 years, doubling from 9% to 18% for Asia and to 19% for Latin America. After midcentury, the patterns diverge: aging in Latin America accelerates while the pace in Asia tapers off.

Africa remains the youngest region, but thanks to gains in life expectancy, the number of people who reach older ages will start to increase. Africa's population age 65 and over is projected to triple over the next 30 years, from 47 million in 2020 to 143 million by 2050, and quadruple after that. Unlike in other regions, even though the number of Africa's old people is rapidly growing, their proportion in the total population will remain low, as continued high fertility rates fuel growth, and keep the population relatively young. The share age 65 and over is projected to increase more quickly after midcentury. Despite the low shares, many African countries will experience enormous impacts of population aging as their absolute numbers of old people rise.

POPULATION AGING BY INCOME

As you will see, aging is a challenge not just for high-income countries. In fact, the pace of aging is much faster in many middle-income countries, especially those that had steep fertility declines. The lens of income is particularly revealing because income is so correlated with increasing life expectancy and declining fertility—both of which contribute to increasing shares of people age 65 and over.

Indeed, as shown in Figure 6.5, the pace of aging for the upper-middle-income countries stands out, with the steep increase stemming from particularly large gains in life expectancy and especially sharp declines in fertility. The upper-middle-income group of countries, currently young, is projected to see the fastest pace of aging, as the share of individuals 65 and over more than doubles from 11% to 23% over the next 30 years. China heavily influences the pattern, but many other countries will also experience steep increases in the percentage of people 65 and up, as you will see below.

High-income countries have the oldest populations, with the population age 65 and over accounting for 18% of the total. They have generally had the highest life expectancy coupled with decades of low fertility, and as a result have been gradually aging. But there was an inflection point around 2010 as the post–World War II baby boomers started to turn 65. The pace of aging is projected to accelerate, but then slow after most of the baby boomers pass age 65. Among the high-income countries, the United States is a relative

FIGURE 6.5   Due to their steep fertility declines, upper-middle-income countries face especially rapid aging.

Percentage of Population Age 65+, by Income

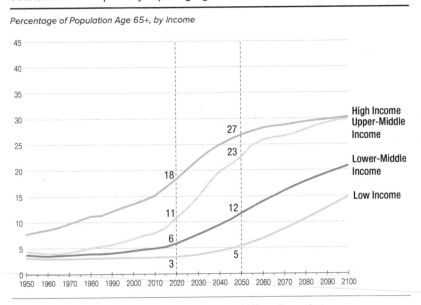

Data source: United Nations, *World Population Prospects 2019,* medium variant.

youngster with its share of 65+ well below other high-income countries, such as Japan, Italy, and Germany.

SELECTED COUNTRIES BY REGION

To give you a more complete view of aging patterns, this section highlights individual countries in each region. To make the visual comparisons easier to understand, the figures in this section include Japan, currently the oldest country and one of the most rapidly aging, and the United States, one of the youngest advanced economies and definitely the slowest-aging large economy. These reference lines will help you gauge the level and speed of aging relative to two well-known examples.

Europe is home to most of the world's oldest countries. As of 2020, except for Japan, the world's 25 oldest countries were European. All of these had 2020 shares exceeding the European average of 19%, and five had shares of 22% or greater, including Italy, Germany, Portugal, Greece, and Finland. As shown in Figure 6.6, Italy overtook Germany around 2000 and reached 23% in 2020; along with Spain, Italy is projected to be among the fastest-aging countries in Europe. By midcentury, their shares of older people will exceed one-third, and they will nearly match Japan's 38%. In contrast, thanks partly to immigration, Germany will see a slower pace of aging, but will still reach 30% by midcentury. These three countries—Italy, Spain, and Germany—already have more old people than children, but it is nonetheless startling to imagine that one-third of their populations will be over 65 within the next 30 years. As you can see in Figure 6.6, France and the UK are relatively younger and are aging much more slowly than their European neighbors.

Most European countries, already grappling with the challenges of population aging, will face even greater economic, social, and political threats as the dramatic age shift continues to unfold over the coming decades. Their shrinking shares of workers to support a growing number of older people will worsen the current challenges, including the growing fiscal burdens of social security and pensions, as well as

FIGURE 6.6 Italy, already the oldest large economy in Europe, is projected to be among the fastest-aging, surpassing the pace of Germany, France, and the UK.

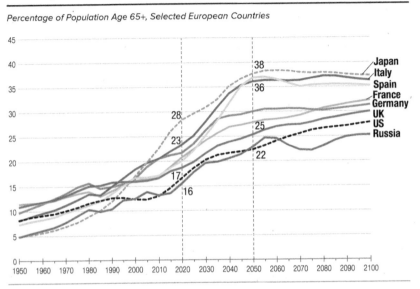

Percentage of Population Age 65+, Selected European Countries

Note: Japan and the US are shown for reference.

Data source: United Nations, *World Population Prospects 2019,* medium variant.

the need for increasing social services and housing. It will be increasingly important—and necessary—to adapt to the shift in age composition through some combination of technology, immigration, and labor policies. The sooner such strategies are in place, the better.

Unlike in Europe, where most countries have been "old" for decades, in Asia the current picture is much different. Until recently only Japan had a high share of 65+, while the rest of the region was much younger. The Asian Tigers—South Korea, Taiwan, Hong Kong, and Singapore—started aging around 1990, and are now aging even faster than Japan. You can see this in Figure 6.7 by comparing the slopes of the lines; those for South Korea and Taiwan are steeper than Japan's. The reason for this early and rapid aging is explained by the demographic drivers. The Asian Tigers were among the first developing countries to see sharp fertility declines. Such declines were associated with their rapid industrialization,

FIGURE 6.7   The Asian Tigers are the fastest-aging countries in Asia, followed closely by China. All are aging faster than Japan.

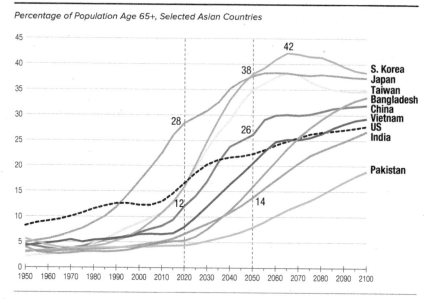

Percentage of Population Age 65+, Selected Asian Countries

Note: Japan and the US are shown for reference.

Data source: United Nations, *World Population Prospects 2019*, medium variant.

and as of 2020 their fertility rates were among the world's lowest, ranging from 1.1 births per woman in South Korea to 1.3 in Hong Kong. Contributing to this accelerated aging, these countries also have some of the world's highest life expectancies. Given these two drivers, this speed of aging is not at all unexpected, even if the projections are startling.

The Asian Tigers may represent the extremes in population aging, but many other Asian countries, including China, are not far behind. We can see in Figure 6.7 that China's aging starts a little later than South Korea and Taiwan's, and although quite rapid, it unfolds a bit more slowly. Indeed, the successive age waves in Asia are directly tied to the timing and pace of the fertility declines. Steep drops in fertility occurred first in the Asian Tigers, then in Thailand and China, then Vietnam, then Bangladesh. India's much slower aging reflects that its fertility decline has been much more gradual than China's, and as of 2020 was still above replacement rate. Even so,

India's population age 65+ is projected to increase to 14% by 2050, making the country slightly older than China was in 2020.

Although China's aging situation may attract a lot of attention, looking at China in the context of other Asian economies helps you see that the situation is not unique to China, but is connected to the fertility declines that occurred throughout the region. As in Europe, these rapidly aging countries will need to develop strategies to address their shifting age structures. China's three-child policy is one attempt and South Korea's housing incentives are another. It is important for countries to adapt to their own aging patterns, but it is also important for their allies and adversaries to monitor and understand that fiscal and social priorities in these countries may change.

Turning to Latin America in Figure 6.8, we see patterns of aging similar to what we saw in Asia—further evidence that aging is a

FIGURE 6.8 The pace of aging will accelerate throughout Latin America, with Chile and Brazil surpassing the US level by 2050, while Mexico remains much younger.

Percentage of Population Age 65+, Selected Latin American Countries

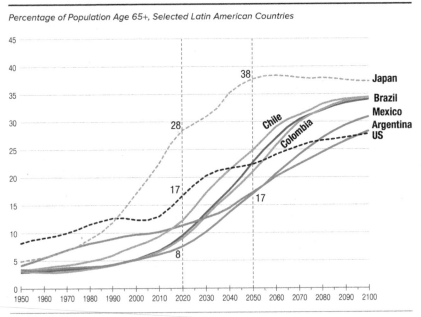

Note: Japan and the US are shown for reference.

Data source: United Nations, *World Population Prospects 2019,* medium variant.

global phenomenon even though it is unfolding in stages. As elsewhere, the rate of aging in Latin America is projected to pick up speed, with successive age waves reflecting the divergent fertility declines occurring across countries. Chile, Brazil, and Colombia will see rapid aging due to their steep fertility declines, and they will age faster than Mexico. By 2050, Chile and Brazil will have populations older than the United States, with Colombia close behind. Mexico's share of older people is projected to more than double from 8% in 2020 to 17% by 2050, but even so, Mexico will remain younger than the US for many more decades.

The Middle East's picture of aging is completely different from the other regions. Most of the countries will age later than other developing countries. As shown in Figure 6.9, some countries, such as Egypt and Yemen, are still relatively young with rapidly growing populations; others, including Turkey, Iran, and Saudi Arabia,

FIGURE 6.9   Due to steep fertility declines, Turkey, Iran, and Saudi Arabia will face rapidly aging populations over the next 30 years.

Percentage of Population Age 65+, Selected Middle Eastern Countries

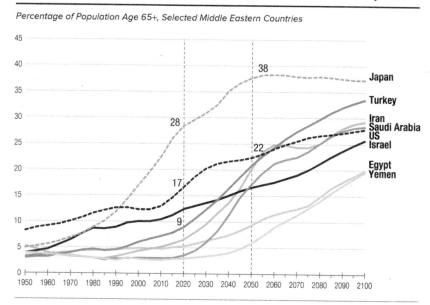

Note: Japan and the US are shown for reference.

Data source: United Nations, *World Population Prospects 2019,* medium variant.

while still young, have had steep fertility declines and will soon see aging start to accelerate. Probably more concerning than aging is that these steep fertility declines will result in slower-growing work-forces, as we will see in the next chapter.

TIMELINE OF AGING

You have seen that aging is a global phenomenon, no longer just occurring in the advanced economies. You've also seen from the line charts that aging is unfolding differently around the world and that today's countries with younger populations will age much faster than the advanced economies have aged. The series of line charts in the previous section compared the increases in aging across countries showing how the timing and pace of aging differs; the slope and level of the lines were the key indicators to compare.

The timeline in Figure 6.10 presents a different perspective on how aging will unfold around the world and further shows how the younger countries will see their populations age more quickly than the advanced economies have. The figure takes the lines from the previous charts and lays them out horizontally on a timeline so you can see just when countries start to age and how fast they age.

Each line in the chart reflects the number of years it will take that country to transition from 7% to 14% age 65 and over. The World Bank benchmarks help you to compare countries: At 7% a country would be considered "aging" and at 14% it would be "aged." At 20%, a country would be considered "super-aged." These cutoffs are somewhat arbitrary, but they have become benchmarks, and they help when making comparisons.

As shown in the top bar of the chart, it took France 125 years for its population to increase from 7% to 14% age 65+. The same aging transition started later in the United Kingdom but took much less time—only 45 years. The transition began even later in the youthful United States and has taken 69 years, from 1944 to 2013—faster than in France, but slower than in the UK. The key point is that this

FIGURE 6.10 Developing countries will age much faster than most advanced economies did, giving them less time to prepare. China has aged three times faster than the US; South Korea, even faster.

Number of Years to Transition from 7% to 14% of Population Age 65+

Data source: United Nations, *World Population Prospects 2019*, medium variant.

transition in these advanced economies occurred over several generations, in sharp contrast to the pace in Japan.

Japan, now the oldest country, with 28% of its population age 65+ as of 2020, is often called the fastest-aging country. Indeed, Japan's increase from 5% age 65+ in 1950 to 28% in 2020—past the United States and all the aging European countries—has been startling. The transition from 7% to 14% took just 27 years and was completed by 1995, well before aging took off in the US. While Japan's pace seemed alarming, we now see that many other countries will likely match this speed. South Korea has already exceeded Japan's pace, completing the transition from 7% to 14% in 19 years, in just a little more than two-thirds the time it took record-setting Japan. Like South Korea, the other Asian Tiger countries are also rapidly aging. Taiwan matched Japan's 27-year pace, and Singapore is on track to age even faster.

This chart puts China in the context of the Asian Tigers—all had steep fertility declines that led to rapid aging. According to the UN projections, China is on course to match Japan's pace of aging, reaching 14% by 2024. This will depend largely on whether China's new three-child program will work to promote an increase in the number of children and thereby slow the pace of aging.

Aside from the thinking about which country is aging faster, it is quite alarming to consider that the young developing countries are aging so fast. Many emerging economies are projected to age as quickly, or nearly as quickly, as China. A common description applied to the Chinese situation was that the country was getting old before getting rich. This applies to many developing countries, especially those that had steep fertility declines. They are getting old before they have sufficient resources to manage the potential fiscal and social burdens of an aging society. More important, these transitions are happening so soon, and so fast, that there is little time left to prepare, especially when the countries are focused on economic development and allocating resources for education and housing.

You can see from the chart that the aging transition in many developing countries will occur within a generation, and once it starts, it accelerates. It will be completely unlike the much slower population aging that has occurred in the United States and Europe, and more like the rapid aging that occurred in Japan, except in most cases, their economies may not keep pace.

CHANGING COMPOSITION OF THE OLDER POPULATION

So far you have been reading about the population that is age 65 and older. But the composition of this group of older people is changing in ways that pose additional challenges. These include rapid growth in the oldest-old population, a significant gender gap in the older population, and declining support ratios.

RAPID GROWTH IN THE OLDEST-OLD POPULATION

We have talked about how increasing life expectancy results in more people reaching the older brackets. And this has contributed to the rapid growth in the population age 65 and older. In 2020, the global population age 65+ equaled 728 million or 9% of the total. Only a small number of these older people had reached the top age brackets: globally, only 64 million people had reached age 85 by 2020. In 2020, what is known as the "oldest-old" segment represented less than 1% of the world's population. Even though this is the fastest-growing age group, projected to more than triple over the next 30 years, by 2050, it will represent just 2% of the world's total population.

The shares of the oldest-old differ dramatically across countries, depending on life expectancy. In countries with the highest life expectancies, more people will reach the top age brackets. In many of these high-life-expectancy countries, the fertility rate has been below replacement for decades, so while the population is rapidly aging, the total population may already be shrinking. For example, in Japan, the population age 85+ reached 6 million in 2020 and is projected to increase to 10 million by 2050. The 85+ shares of total population will rise from 4.8% in 2020 to a projected 9.3% in 2050. While the older brackets are projected to increase rapidly, the working-age population and the number of children are expected to decrease, leading to an overall population decline. This upward shift leads to an age structure top-heavy with old people.

Many other countries will also see their age structures change dramatically as the numbers and shares of older people increase. Due to its increasing life expectancy, South Korea might be the most extreme example; its population age 85+ will increase from 1.5% in 2020 to 8.5% by 2050. The other Asian Tigers will follow similar trajectories.

Many European countries will see similar increases in the shares of oldest-old. By 2050, Italy, Greece, Spain, Portugal, and Germany will all have shares of 85+ greater than 7%. The United Kingdom and the United States will look comparatively young with shares around 5%.

Why is this important? The increasing share of 85+ has several important implications. It is not surprising that more and more people are reaching the oldest ages. Indeed, we often see news about the growing number of centenarians. The main implication is that the oldest-old have different health, financial, and social needs than younger people. In addition, the incidence of certain diseases increases in older ages and pushes up health care costs. The increased prevalence and associated costs of dementia, especially Alzheimer's, among older people is particularly worrisome. At the same time, personal financial security may be diminished as these additional expenses accrue. We already know that many people have not saved enough for retirement, and this financial insecurity might be worsened if people haven't anticipated long lives. Public resources will also be challenged as governments' pension and health care obligations rise. Use of government resources for housing and health care is already subject to debate, and provision for a growing segment of the older population will increase the challenge of allocating scarce resources.

In thinking about the numbers of the oldest-old, we know that their percentage of the total population is likely to remain small, even though we recognize that their shares are fast approaching 10% in many European and Asian countries. There is another perspective that emphasizes how dramatic the age shift is. While it may be common practice, due to convenience and data availability, to lump all old people together in the 65+ category, we know this isn't representative in terms of labor force participation or medical needs and costs. As the older population grows, it will be increasingly important to consider the subgroups of age 65+. As outlined above, the shares of oldest-old are increasing throughout the developed world, and in most places this group is the fastest-growing segment. Consequently, this oldest-old segment is growing as a share of the 65+ population. For example, in Japan, by 2050, the oldest-old will account for one-quarter of the population age 65+. Even in the United States, which has a smaller overall share of older people, the oldest-old will account for just 5% of total population by 2050, but nearly one-quarter of the older population. Understanding the needs and characteristics of the distinct age groups will be helpful in planning necessary changes in social practices and public policies.

The charts in Figure 6.11 show how the age mix of the older population is projected to change in the United States and Japan. The

FIGURE 6.11 The population age 85+ will be an increasing share of the older population.

Population Age 65+ by Subbracket, in Millions

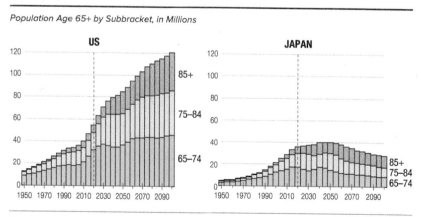

Data source: United Nations, *World Population Prospects 2019,* medium variant.

population age 85+ was quite small before 2020 but is projected to rapidly increase. These figures illustrate that the future age mix is completely different from what we have experienced so far.

GENDER GAP—MORE OLDER WOMEN THAN MEN

Another consequential change in the population composition is that there are many more older women than men. Because women live longer, this is logical, but the large disparity in many countries is still surprising as well as concerning. In 2020, among the world's population age 65+, there were 123 women for every 100 men. The ratio is even higher for the oldest-old: globally among the population age 85+ in 2020, there were 185 women for every 100 men.

The gender gap in the older population may be decreasing, but it persists and should be understood. Figure 6.12 shows how the population gap between older men and women in the US has changed. In

FIGURE 6.12 The US gender gap in the older population has been declining, especially in the oldest population.

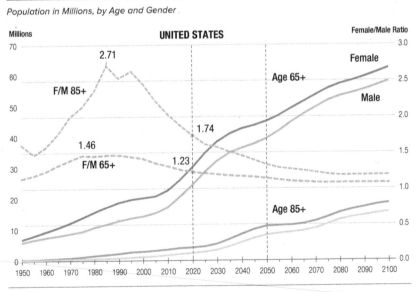

Population in Millions, by Age and Gender

Data source: United Nations, *World Population Prospects 2019*, medium variant.

2020, the US population age 65+ totaled 55 million, including 30 million women and 25 million men, or 123 women per 100 men, matching the global average. You can see the inflection point after 2010, when the first baby boomers began turning 65. The chart also shows the ratio of women to men. From the 1960s to around 1990, the population of women age 65+ was growing faster than the corresponding population of men, reflecting higher female life expectancy due to improved female health. This trend incorporates the higher death rate among men from greater incidence of various diseases, especially heart disease. During these three decades, the ratio of women to men continued to increase, peaking at 147 women per 100 men in 1985. Then, after 1990, the male population, while still lagging the female population, started to increase at a faster rate. As a result, the gap began to diminish, with the ratio declining to 123 women per 100 men by 2020. There are several threads to this 70-year development. In the early decades, women enjoyed larger gains in life expectancy than men. With advances in cardiac care and male health care in general, around 1990 the gains in life expectancy for men started to exceed those for women, producing relatively faster growth in the male population. There are still gender gaps in life expectancy and population, but the differences have been decreasing.

Although the population of the oldest-old is much smaller, the story is similar. The population gap in this age segment in the United States peaked in 1985, at 271 women per 100 men, when the total population of people age 85+ was just 2.6 million. By 2020, the population age 85+ had increased to nearly 7 million, with 4.2 million women and 2.4 million men. The faster population growth of men brought the ratio down significantly to 174 women per 100 men.

Many other countries show much greater gender disparities than the United States. Figure 6.13 compares the historical development of the female-to-male population ratios for several countries. The lines for the individual countries reflect differential changes in life expectancy for men and women. The numbers are startling and worrisome especially because of differences in financial and retirement security of women in various countries. You might have been concerned that the disparities would increase, putting the population of

FIGURE 6.13   Gender disparities in aging differ across countries but have been declining.

Ratio of Female to Male Population Age 65+, Selected Countries

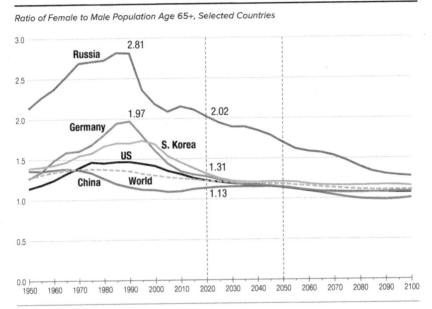

Data source: United Nations, *World Population Prospects 2019*, medium variant.

older women at a greater disadvantage in the future. However, this comparison demonstrates that the population disparities have been rapidly declining. The absolute population levels are much larger everywhere, but the ratio of women to men has been declining.

A comparison of the 15 largest economies reveals that except for Russia, the large economies show similar ratios, ranging from 110 to 130 women per 100 men in 2020. However, a look backward shows that the gender gaps unfolded very differently, peaking at different times, and then diminishing at different rates. These differences reflected differential gains in life expectancy over the years. The common thread is that the gaps have generally been decreasing from their peaks. The United States appears in the middle of the chart, while Russia and China represent the extremes.

Russia is particularly interesting for several reasons. Russian life expectancy has consistently been lower than in most advanced economies, and Russia also has one of the largest gender disparities.

In 2020, life expectancy at birth was 78 for women, nearly 11 years higher than for men. This is an improvement from 2000, when the gap was 13 years. By 2020, as shown in Figure 6.14, there were twice as many women age 65+ as men—15 million women compared with 7.5 million men. The 2020 ratio had decreased to 2.0 from its peak of 2.8 in 1985, when the life expectancy gap was even greater. As the gender gap in life expectancy decreased, the population gap also decreased, but remains astonishingly high. Among the oldest-old, the total 2020 population was small, just 2.2 million, but there were nearly four times as many women as men; this means that in 2020, nearly 80% of Russia's oldest-old population were women. This is down from 85% in 1990.

China's pattern differs markedly from Russia's. The life expectancy gap there has been relatively small, resulting in a much smaller population gap. Interestingly, the population gap has recently inched up, stabilizing at 113 women per 100 men. As you

FIGURE 6.14   In Russia in 2020, there were twice as many older women than men, but the gap has been decreasing since 1990.

Population Age 65+ in Millions, by Gender

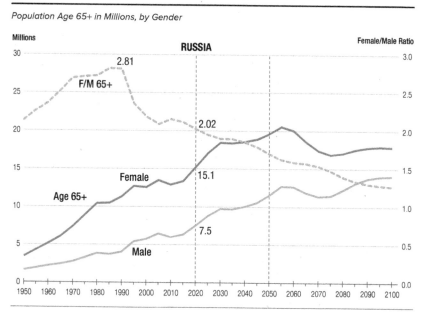

Data source: United Nations, *World Population Prospects 2019,* medium variant.

can see in Figure 6.15, the gap is projected to remain stable, even as the population age 65+ more than doubles, from 173 million to 366 million over the next 30 years.

You may be asking why this gender disparity is important. Many of the same issues affect both older men and women, but health and financial security disparities are especially concerning. We know that older people generally have greater health care needs, and we know that health care costs increase with age. We also know that the incidence of certain diseases is greater in older women, especially Alzheimer's and other dementias. Financial insecurity further threatens well-being in old age. Women are already disadvantaged because they still typically earn less, have caregiving responsibility, and often take time off for caregiving. As a result, they are likely to have lower lifetime incomes, lower pensions, and lower savings. Their longer lives intensify the economic disadvantage.

FIGURE 6.15 China has a relatively small gender gap in its older population, with 113 women per 100 men.

Population Age 65+, in Millions, by Gender

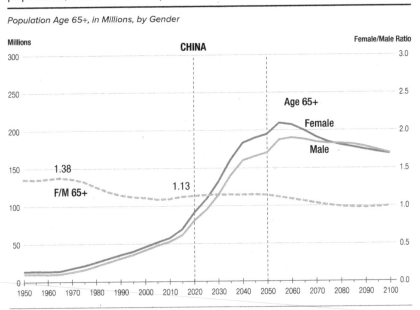

Data source: United Nations, *World Population Prospects 2019*, medium variant.

In an ideal world, improvements in health for both men and women, as well as improvements in financial equity would reduce health care costs and gender disparities. Absent those improvements, it will be important to consider the impact of the changing composition of the older population and what the changes mean for the kinds of services that will be needed and how they can be provided.

DECLINING SUPPORT RATIOS—FEWER WORKERS PER RETIREE

With that background on what population aging is and how it differs across countries, we come to questions about why it matters. One of the most widely discussed economic impacts of aging populations is the increased fiscal burden from old-age entitlements, such as pensions and health care, as well as the costs of other government-supplied services. The shifting age structure presents a twofold challenge: the total financial burden increases as more people reach retirement age, and that increasing burden falls on fewer workers. The key indicator for this burden is the declining ratio of workers to retirees.

We know that one of the drivers behind the upward shift in age structure is the drop in the number of children due to declining fertility rates. This soon leads to fewer workers. And all this is occurring while the number of older people is rapidly increasing. The result is that the ratio of workers to retirees will decline. Globally, the number of workers per retiree (W/R) will fall precipitously over the next 30 years from seven to four. It is especially interesting that this will occur while the number of workers continues to increase. This is simply because the working-age population (the numerator) is growing more slowly than the number of retirees (the denominator): over the next 30 years the working-age population is projected to increase by only about 20%, while the number of people age 65 and over will more than double.

The declining ratio of potential workers per retiree is one of the most important features of an aging population. It means fewer workers will be contributing to the financial support of each retiree. This decline in workers per retiree will increasingly strain national budgets as fewer workers fund the pension, health care, and other costs of an increasing number of retirees. The fiscal challenge of a decreasing worker-retiree ratio will be particularly burdensome for young but rapidly aging developing countries that face continuing steep declines in the ratio, as shown in Figure 6.16.

From what we know about population aging in Japan, it is not surprising that Japan has the lowest worker-retiree ratio, just

FIGURE 6.16 Rapidly declining worker-retiree ratios pose huge fiscal challenges.

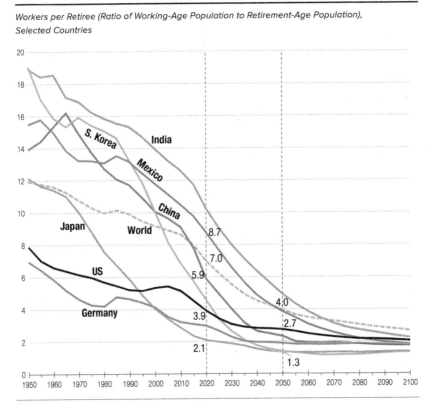

Workers per Retiree (Ratio of Working-Age Population to Retirement-Age Population), Selected Countries

Note: Working age=15–64; retirement age=65+.

Data source: United Nations, *World Population Prospects 2019*, medium variant.

2.1 in 2020 and projected to drop to 1.3 over the next 30 years. Rapidly aging South Korea will have an even steeper decline in its worker-retiree ratio, falling from 4.5 in 2020 to 1.4 by 2050. And China follows a similar pattern. In contrast, the picture for the United States appears less dire because growth in our working-age population is projected to continue, assuming it will be fueled by immigration. Also, even though the decline since 1950 has been large, it has been more gradual than what is projected for many developing countries.

It is helpful to think of the worker-retiree ratio as the "potential support ratio," based on the number of working-age people and the number of people at retirement age. It is also important to understand the limitations of this approximation. First, we know that not everyone within the working-age bracket actually works. Some are students, stay-at-home spouses, or early retirees. Similarly, not all people age 65 and older are retired. Many are still working productively and continuing to pay taxes. Furthermore, the ratio does not account for different rates of labor force participation at different ages. Nonetheless, changes in the worker-retiree ratio can offer guidance about the timing and magnitude of the aging burden. To make global comparisons, the ratios in Figure 6.16 use the conventional definitions of working age (15 to 64) and retirement age (65 and over).

The most striking conclusion from the comparison is that the support ratio declines are steepest for the young and growing economies. More importantly, the declining ratio offers a simple framework for thinking about policy changes: it is possible to improve the ratio through policies aimed at changing the individual variables. For example, it is possible to improve the ratio by boosting the number of workers via increased labor force participation or immigration. Similarly, it would be possible to improve the ratio by decreasing the number of retirees through instituting a later retirement age. In addition to improving the simple ratio, countries can seek to increase the actual support by enhancing the value of the work that gets done, through technology and education, for example.

CONCLUSION

We've seen how young developing countries are on track to age much faster than countries did 30 or 40 years ago. Beside the rapid pace, a key difference is that these developing countries will age before they get rich. They may have a greater incentive to adopt policies that reduce the burden of an aging society, including raising retirement ages, increasing labor force participation at all ages—and for women in particular—and enhancing productivity through education and technology.

7 | SHRINKING WORKFORCES

"Labor Force Participation Is Static, a Conundrum for the Fed"
New York Times, by Jeanna Smialek, November 5, 2021

"Regime Change in the Global Economy"
Project Syndicate, Michael Spence, January 14, 2022

"Middle East Needs to Close Gender Gap to Spur Growth"
Financial Times, by Mouayed Makhlouf, May 11, 2016

"The Era of Massive Low-Skilled Immigration May Already Be Over"
Wall Street Journal, by Ben Leubsdorf, March 23, 2017

As you may have heard, the factory floor of the world is shrinking! That's the tagline from many news stories about the decline in China's working-age population. Indeed, China's working-age numbers peaked around 2015, then began what is projected to be a steady decline. Looking at this development in context, we can see that over the past four decades China enjoyed a steep increase in its workforce, and it is this burgeoning workforce combined with economic reforms that fueled its economic boom. But now, after several decades of below-replacement fertility, and fewer and fewer children being born, China faces a continued decline in its working-age population. You can see the whole picture in Figure 7.1. Specifically, over the past three decades, the working-age population in China rose by 31%, adding more than 200 million people. Looking forward, the picture is quite different. Over the next three decades, the working-age population is projected to shrink by 17%, reaching midcentury with about 200 million fewer workers than in 2020. The steep increase resulted from high population growth, even

FIGURE 7.1   China's working-age population peaked in 2015. The projected decline mirrors the steep increase.

Population by Age, in Millions

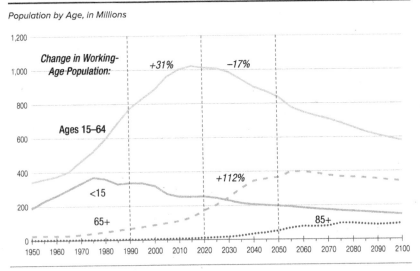

Data source: United Nations, *World Population Prospects 2019,* medium variant.

while the number of children was declining, but this falling number of children eventually reduces the supply of future workers. The slowdown and then decline in working-age population stem from the fertility decline followed by decades of low fertility, which decreased the number of future workers. With such a large decline in working-age population, the Chinese will have to change how work gets done, if the country's economic growth and well-being are to be sustained.

China's changing age mix presents quite a dramatic picture, but China is not unique. This arc of workforce growth illustrated in Figure 7.1—with a steady increase followed by a slowdown, and then decline—is a global phenomenon. The process is already unfolding in many countries and on the horizon almost everywhere else. You'll see later in this chapter, in Figures 7.9 and 7.10, that the illustrations of workforce growth resemble the successive arcs of landscape paintings, with some peaks taller and steeper than others, but most showing an arc of growth followed by decline. Of course, the patterns are not identical everywhere. As you've learned from reading about the demographic drivers, the countries each have their own trajectories of growth, with different sizes of working-age population, different growth rates, and different peak years. Understanding the divergent patterns will help us understand the implications for economic growth and national security, and this understanding should inform our strategic relationships as well as our investment strategies. Though shrinking workforces can threaten economic growth, the good news is that the arcs are generally predictable: we can see in advance when a country is likely to become vulnerable to its own declining workforce. And there should be time to adopt appropriate strategies to mitigate the consequences.

THE GDP EQUATION: LABOR SUPPLY PLUS PRODUCTIVITY

The equation for economic growth makes it easy to see the implications of workforce change: GDP growth is a function of labor supply growth and productivity growth. With a slower-growing or shrinking labor supply, there will need to be greater reliance on compensating gains in labor productivity. It is helpful to think of working-age population as an indicator of "potential" labor supply: people older than this conventional range may be working, while not everyone in the age range of 15 to 64 actually works. How this potential is managed will determine the actual labor supply. Most countries have policy options for improving labor supply, such as boosting the labor force participation at all ages, especially among women, and raising the age of participation to include older workers as well. Increased immigration is another policy option for enhancing the labor supply. On the productivity side, education at all ages and technology innovations are two critical options for improving the productivity of the existing labor supply.

The main driver of workforce change is a country's fertility rate. The impact is straightforward: a declining number of births per woman and the consequent declining number of children eventually results in a shrinking pipeline of future workers. That's why understanding how fertility trends unfold is critical for understanding workforce change. But fertility trends are not the only factors influencing workforce size. Increased life expectancy also affects workforce growth by creating additional labor supply, as more people reach working age and as older people become or remain economically active. Finally, migration plays an important role in supplementing the labor supply in many countries.

The equation for economic growth put forth above uses the conventional definition of GDP. Although some researchers suggest broadening the definition of economic well-being, the role of workers and growth of the workforce will be important in any definition; understanding the growth or decline in the working-age population may well be even more important for alternative models of economic well-being.

GLOBAL SLOWDOWN IN WORKING-AGE POPULATION GROWTH

As we look at differences across the world, we can see that the global picture is of course more dynamic than simple growth followed by decline. Globally, the working-age population will continue to rise, but the pace is projected to slow dramatically and the distribution across regions will markedly shift. As you can see in Figure 7.2, total worldwide working-age population has increased sharply since 1950. It more than tripled from 1.5 billion in 1950 to 5.1 billion in 2020. Half of this increase occurred over the 30 years from 1990 to 2020, when the global working-age population rose by 1.8 billion, registering an average growth of 1.5% per year. This pace will weaken over the coming decades as the effects of low fertility take hold. According to the UN's medium variant scenario, over the next 30 years, the rate of growth is projected to slow by more than half, falling to an average of just 0.6% per year. Then, after midcentury, global growth is projected to slow even further, stagnating by century's end.

You can see in the figure that the regional distribution of the working-age population is projected to shift dramatically. As you

FIGURE 7.2   Global workforce growth will slow dramatically over the next 30 years.

Working-Age Population (Ages 15–64), by Region, in Billions

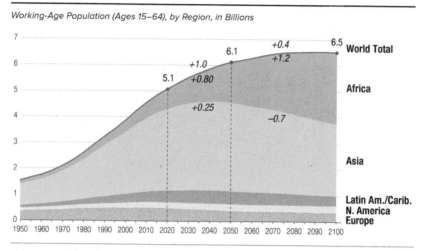

Data source: United Nations, *World Population Prospects 2019,* medium variant.

might expect, fueled by high fertility rates, Africa is projected to have the world's fastest-growing working-age population. Over the next 30 years, it is projected to account for three-quarters of the global working-age population growth, with its share of the world's workforce increasing from 15% in 2020 to 25% by midcentury. Although its growth will slow after midcentury, Africa's share of the global working-age population will continue to rise as those of the other regions.

In contrast to the explosive growth in Africa, Asia's arc of growth and decline is startling. Asia's working-age population is projected to peak around 2045 and then decline through the century. As we've seen, this slowdown will occur following many years of rapid workforce growth. Yet even with this slower growth, Asia's workforce will increase by more than 250 million over the next 30 years. Still, over these three decades, Asia will account for just one quarter of the global workforce growth, compared to Africa's 75%.

Like Asia, only much smaller, Latin America's working-age population is projected to see continued growth until 2045, when it will begin to shrink. In contrast, in North America, the arc of growth is projected to extend through the century. Fueled by immigration, the working-age population is projected to continue growing through the rest of the century, albeit more slowly.

Finally, Europe has the distinction of being the region with the earliest peak in working-age population. Due to its long history of low fertility rates, Europe's working-age population has been declining since 2010 and is projected to shrink by 78 million or 16% by midcentury.

From this brief comparison, you can see how the different patterns of working-age growth, especially the slowdown in Asia, have contributed to the dramatic overall shift to Africa. You can imagine that these different patterns point to different priorities and challenges. For example, Africa faces the challenges of educating, housing, and creating economic opportunities for its growing workforce. Successfully addressing these challenges is necessary for economic development and improved well-being. In contrast, workforce declines occurring elsewhere threaten well-being in a different way. The regions facing slower workforce growth or shrinking populations will need to alter labor policies and business practices to leverage their existing labor supply. Expanding labor supply through greater labor force participation or immigration and adopting productivity-enhancing innovations are two general options these countries have for adapting to anticipated workforce changes.

WORKING-AGE POPULATION BY INCOME

Looking at workforce growth by income level underscores the divergent patterns of growth you saw in the regional patterns. As shown in Figure 7.3, the two highest-income groups will see their workforces decline. The working-age population in the high-income group peaked in 2020 and is projected to slowly decline. The group of upper-middle-income countries has had a steep run-up in working-age population over the past few decades and is projected to experience a corresponding but less steep decline after peaking in 2020. China is by far the largest country in this group, so it's no

FIGURE 7.3   The two middle-income groups started to diverge when the impacts of their different fertility-rate declines took hold.

Working-Age Population (Ages 15–64), by Income, in Billions

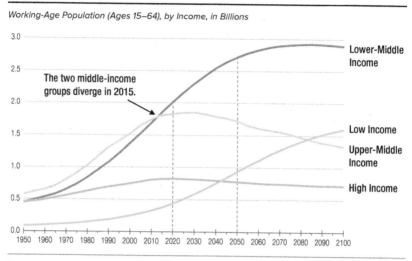

Data source: United Nations, *World Population Prospects 2019,* medium variant.

surprise that the upper-middle-income trajectory looks like the arc of growth for China.

In contrast to the two higher-income groups, which will be shrinking, the two lowest-income groups are projected to see continued workforce expansion until near the century's end. The low-income group, shown in yellow, approaching 500 million in 2020, is projected to have the fastest growth. Fueled by high fertility rates, its working-age population will double over the next 30 years, increasing to nearly 1 billion by midcentury. Growth will continue through the century. Similarly, the lower-middle-income group, shown in orange at the top of the chart, continues to be fueled by high fertility rates. It will see an increase to 2.7 billion by midcentury, but its growth will then taper off as the effects of falling fertility take hold.

The middle-income countries—both lower- and upper-middle— are often analyzed together as one large group, but segmenting the group reveals critical demographic changes that will shape the future. One of the most interesting observations from using this income lens is to see how the two middle-income groups diverged from each other after 2015. The two middle-income groups moved together until around 2015. But after that, the groups began reflecting distinct patterns of fertility decline. Of the two groups of countries, the upper-middle-income group, including China and Brazil, experienced earlier and steeper fertility declines. You can see in the figure that this group overall will soon experience a shrinking working-age population. For sure, there will be differences across countries in this group, and we will look at those in detail in the next section of this chapter. The key point here is that by understanding the underlying drivers, you can better identify how the demographic outcomes will differ across these groups. We can no longer assume they will follow similar paths.

THE LARGEST ECONOMIES

Workforce growth is already slowing in all the large economies, and several have already seen absolute declines. As illustrated in Figure 7.4, eight of the world's 15 largest economies face shrinking workforces. Seven of these will confront large and continued declines. The top bar for each country shows the percentage change over the next 20 years (2020–40), and the bottom bar shows the change over the subsequent 20 years (2040–60). The chart shows the countries in order of projected growth from 2020 to 2040, with the largest decliners at the top.

You should note several things about these projections. South Korea faces the largest percentage decline over the next 20 years, 23%, followed by Japan, Italy, and Spain, where declines range from 16% to 19%. The next-largest percentage declines occur in Germany, China, and Russia, with a much smaller decline in France. The declines in several countries, notably South Korea, China, and Russia, will accelerate as the impact of sinking fertility rates and slower growth in the number of children sets in. For example, South Korea's decline of 23% from 2020 to 2040 will accelerate to 26%, while China's decline of 11% over the coming 20 years will accelerate to 17%. For China and South Korea, the coming losses in the working-age

FIGURE 7.4 Eight of the 15 largest economies face shrinking workforces. The US is an exception.

Projected Change in Working-Age Population (Ages 15–64), 2020–60
The 15 Largest Economies in Order of Projected Growth

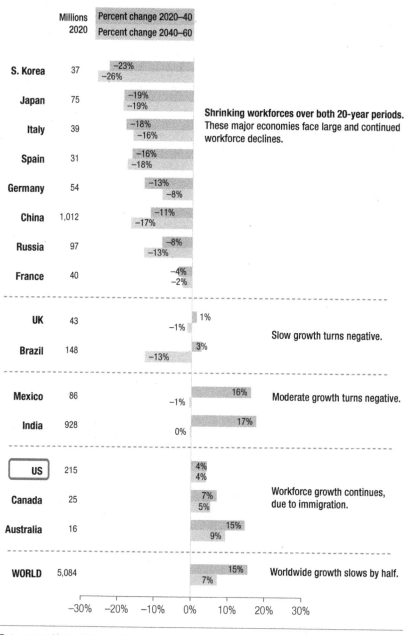

	Millions 2020	Percent change 2020–40 / Percent change 2040–60	
S. Korea	37	−23% / −26%	
Japan	75	−19% / −19%	Shrinking workforces over both 20-year periods. These major economies face large and continued workforce declines.
Italy	39	−18% / −16%	
Spain	31	−16% / −18%	
Germany	54	−13% / −8%	
China	1,012	−11% / −17%	
Russia	97	−8% / −13%	
France	40	−4% / −2%	
UK	43	1% / −1%	Slow growth turns negative.
Brazil	148	3% / −13%	
Mexico	86	16% / −1%	Moderate growth turns negative.
India	928	17% / 0%	
US	215	4% / 4%	Workforce growth continues, due to immigration.
Canada	25	7% / 5%	
Australia	16	15% / 9%	
WORLD	5,084	15% / 7%	Worldwide growth slows by half.

Data source: United Nations, *World Population Prospects 2019*, medium variant.

population will be especially abrupt because these downturns follow years of rapid growth that fueled their booming economies.

The next two countries on the chart are projected to see slow growth that turns negative. Workforce growth in the United Kingdom, which registered 13% over the past 20 years (not shown in the chart), is projected to slow to just 1% over the next two decades, and then decline slightly. Similarly, Brazil faces a dramatic slowdown, from 31% over the last 20 years to just 3% over the next 20, followed by a significant decline of 13% after that.

Among the large economies, the most rapid workforce gains over the next 20 years are projected to occur in two emerging economies: Mexico and India. Both are projected to see moderate workforce growth over the next two decades, followed by stagnation, before decline sets in.

Finally, there are several exceptions to the global pattern of workforce decline. As you have seen above, largely due to immigration, the United States, Canada, and Australia will see continued, albeit slower, workforce growth over both 20-year periods.

Comparing the six large economies over a longer period reveals key differences in how workforce growth will unfold. Figure 7.5 shows the relative differences by indexing working-age population to the 2020 level. The chart illustrates several important conclusions about workforce changes. Even though its growth is quite slow, the United States is projected to have the fastest-growing workforce among the world's six largest economies. Over the next 20 years, the US workforce is projected to increase by 4%, while China, Japan, and Germany all face significant losses. China's working-age population peaked in 2015, and by 2050 is projected to drop to 83% of its 2020 level, a loss of 174 million. As shown in the figure, this is about the same level China had reached in the mid-1990s, just as its economy was starting to boom. The workforce skills and education have since changed dramatically, as has the use of technology. A key challenge facing China and many other countries is how to keep their economies thriving in the face of declining labor supply.

Japan stands out in this figure because of its early peak in the mid-1990s, when the working-age population was nearly 20% larger

FIGURE 7.5 China, Japan, and Germany face steep workforce declines, while the US can expect slow, steady growth.

Working-Age Population (Ages 15–64) Indexed to 2020, Selected Large Economies

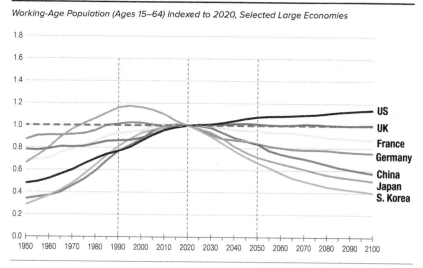

Note: The line for each country shows its working-age population relative to the level in 2020.

Data source: United Nations, *World Population Prospects 2019*, medium variant.

than in 2020. Japan is also notable because its decline is projected to be steeper than China's. Like Japan, Germany's workforce peaked in the mid-1990s, but in contrast to the steep declines in China and Japan, Germany's workforce decline is projected to be much slower. Nonetheless, Germany's workforce decline of nearly 9 million people by 2050 poses challenges. Although immigration has fueled past growth, continued reliance on immigration faces mounting political barriers. With its stable workforce, the UK is an exception to the overall European decline.

CHINA AND INDIA DIVERGE

Even though we know that India's total population will soon surpass China's, the idea that India's workforce will surge past China's is startling. Figure 7.6 shows that while China's workforce is shrinking, India's is projected to enjoy continued growth, exceeding the

FIGURE 7.6 India's higher fertility will fuel continued workforce growth well beyond China's peak.

Working-Age Population (Ages 15–64), in Millions, China and India

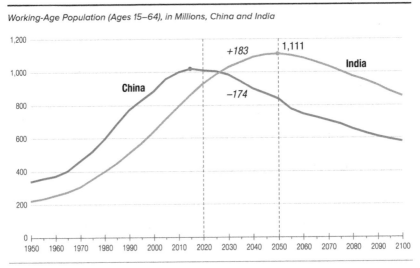

Data source: United Nations, *World Population Prospects 2019*, medium variant.

peak size of China's. The contrast between the two countries is quite startling. By 2050, China's workforce will have declined by around 174 million, and India's will have grown by 183 million. To put this in perspective, we can see that the projected 2050 peak for India, 1.1 billion, will be 100 million higher than China's peak. A key question facing India is whether and to what extent it can continue to capitalize on its workforce growth over the coming decades.

Some important differences shed light on the comparison between the two countries. First, the divergent patterns of growth largely reflect the underlying fertility differences. China had a relatively early and steep fertility decline, from 6.3 births per woman in 1970 to 1.8 by 1995. Thus, by 2020, China had already had more than 25 years of below-replacement fertility. This resulted in slower growth in the number of children and, in turn, slower workforce growth. In contrast, India had a later and more gradual fertility decline. This higher fertility will continue to fuel workforce growth over the coming decades, even though at a slower pace than in the past.

EMERGING ECONOMIES

You have seen several different patterns of workforce growth among the large economies. Most are projected to experience significant slowdowns over the coming decades. As noted above, India and Mexico are the only two large economies projected to see significant workforce growth. In both countries, the arc of growth peaks shortly after midcentury, then declines. Figure 7.7 shows workforce trajectories for several other emerging economies. As shown in the figure, the arcs of growth differ across the countries and the peaks

FIGURE 7.7   The young countries will see large workforce gains—at least for a while.

Working-Age Population (Ages 15–64) Indexed to 2020

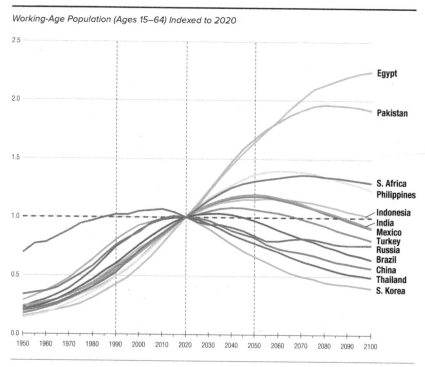

Note: The line for each country shows its working-age population relative to the level in 2020.

Data source: United Nations, *World Population Prospects 2019,* medium variant.

are varied in timing and height. Some of these countries are already facing workforce declines, while others are projected to peak and then decline starting around midcentury.

At the top we see explosive growth in Egypt and Pakistan. By midcentury, their workforces are projected to be 60% larger than in 2020. The Philippines, which had a much earlier fertility decline than Pakistan, is on a slow growth trajectory, with its workforce projected to peak around 2060, well before Pakistan's. Indonesia's workforce trajectory is even lower, with its peak coming earlier, due to its earlier fertility decline. These successively lower arcs of growth—Egypt, Pakistan, the Philippines, then Indonesia—reflect the timing of these countries' fertility declines.

The next four countries on the graph—India, Mexico, Turkey, and Brazil—also show successively lower trajectories. India and Mexico are projected to see continued growth until peaking in 2050, while Turkey's decline starts earlier. Notably, Brazil's workforce, by far the largest in Latin America, is near its peak and is projected to start declining by 2035.

Three additional countries—Russia, China, and Thailand—already face shrinking workforces and will have substantially smaller workforces by midcentury. South Korea, shown at the bottom, puts these declines in perspective. Due to its steep fertility drop, South Korea faces one of the world's starkest workforce declines. Over the 20 years from 2020 to 2040, South Korea's workforce is projected to decline by 23%, compared with 19% in Japan and 11% in China. These decreases are projected to accelerate. (See Figure 7.5 above for comparison of the large economies.)

LANDSCAPES OF WORKFORCE GROWTH

As shown in the previous charts of workforce growth, we can expect to see successive arcs of growth, or more importantly, we can expect successive declines, as workforces around the world start to shrink at different times. Because we know that fertility is a key driver of workforce change, it makes sense to look in more detail at the patterns of fertility decline to see what we can learn about the associated patterns of workforce change.

Figure 7.8 categorizes selected countries according to their patterns of fertility decline, and Figure 7.9 shows the workforce trends for each group. First, focusing on Figure 7.8, you'll see that the fertility data (from the line charts in Chapter 3) are presented as horizontal bars. Reading from left to right, the gray bars show the fertility transition from 1965 at the left to the 2020 level at the right. Thus, each bar reflects 55 years, with the length and horizontal placement of the bar indicating the timing and pace of change. The black tick mark on each bar indicates the 1995 level. The description at the right identifies the two key dimensions for each group: the pace of decline and the time period when fertility fell or is projected to fall below replacement rate. Within each group, the countries are arrayed in order of their 2020 fertility rate.

At the top of the chart, you see the First Movers. These advanced economies already had relatively low fertility rates in 1965, and all had fallen below replacement rate by 1980.

Next you see two groups of countries with steep fertility declines. The countries in the first group, including China and the Asian Tigers, had fallen below replacement-rate fertility by 1995. Their fertility declines continued, and these countries now have the world's lowest fertility rates. The second group of steep decliners had higher starting fertility rates, and as of 2020, most had not yet fallen below replacement-rate fertility.

The next two groups both experienced gradual fertility declines but fell or are projected to fall to replacement-rate fertility at different times. The first group of gradual decliners registered at or below replacement-rate fertility by 2020, while the second group is not expected to reach replacement rate until a few years later, by around 2025.

The last group of countries has had persistently high fertility rates, and most have seen only small declines. These countries are projected to reach replacement-rate fertility only after midcentury.

FIGURE 7.8 Several patterns emerge from grouping countries according to the timing and pace of their fertility declines.

Fertility Rates (Births per Woman), 1965–2020, Selected Countries
Legend: Each bar shows the fertility transition from 1965 at the left to 2020 at the right. The tick mark indicates the 1995 level. For example, the US fertility rate, shown in blue, fell from 3.2 in 1965 to 2.0 by 1995 and 1.8 by 2020.

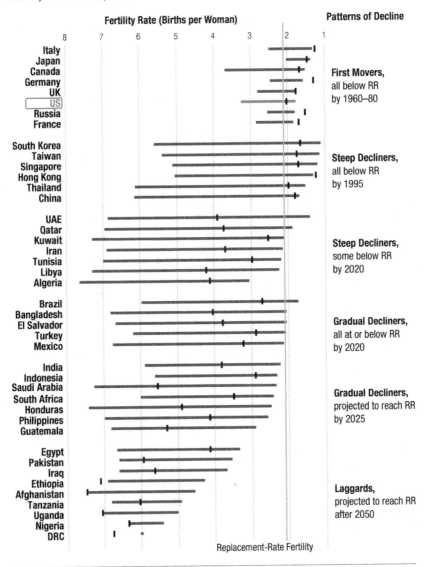

Note: Replacement-Rate Fertility (RR) = 2.1 births per woman

Data source: United Nations, *World Population Prospects 2019*, medium variant.

FIGURE 7.9   The four landscapes reveal successive peaks across the demographic groups.

Working-Age Population (Ages 20–64), 1950–2100, in Millions, by Demographic Group

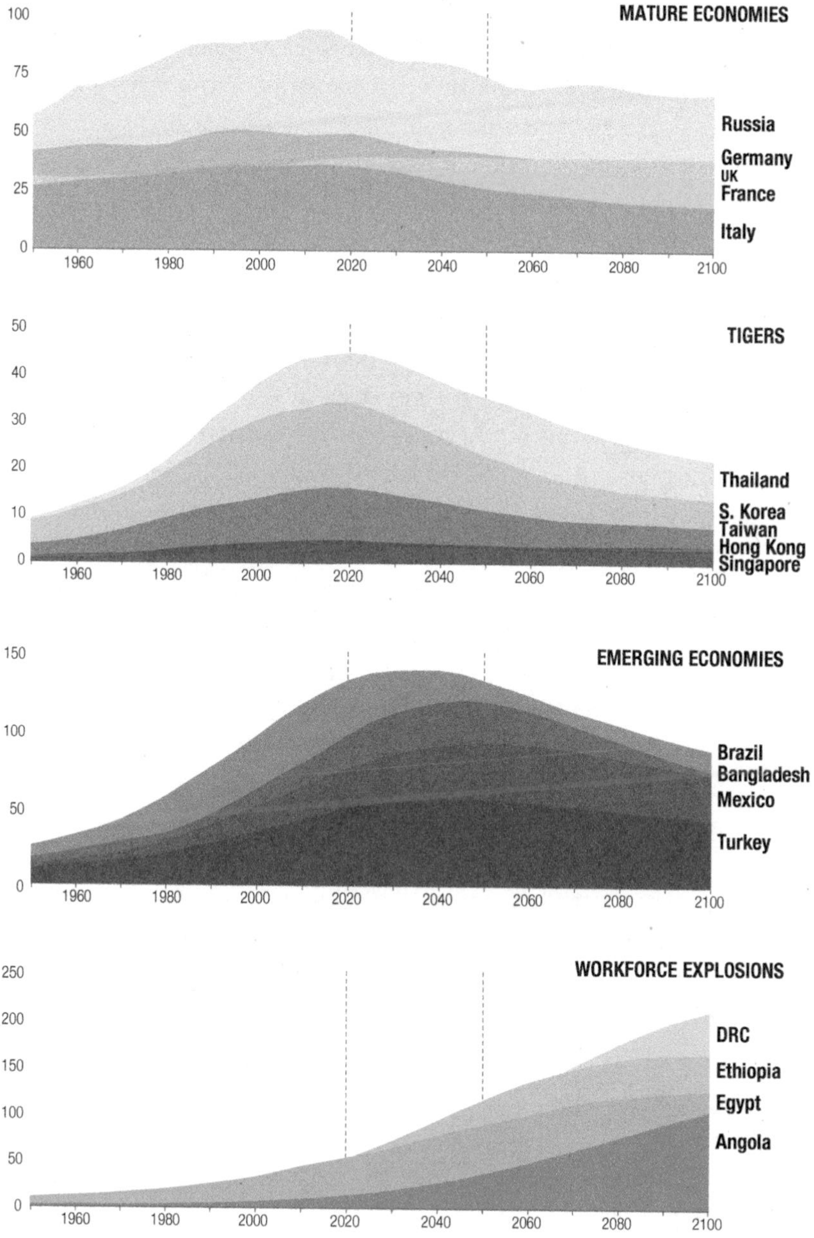

Note: The countries are layered, one behind the other, not stacked.

Data source: United Nations, *World Population Prospects 2019,* medium variant.

Building on this grouping of countries defined by their fertility patterns, the landscapes in Figure 7.9 illustrate the divergent workforce trends of each group. These four figures show working-age population in millions. The countries are layered one behind the other, so you can see the distinct pattern for each country. At the top you see selected Mature Economies. These countries had decades of low fertility and face slower or declining workforce growth. Most saw workforce peaks before 2020.

Next, we see the Asian Tigers, where the working-age populations peaked around 2020. Thailand, though not considered an Asian Tiger, followed a pattern similar to South Korea and Taiwan, with a steep run-up in working-age population. Significant declines are projected by midcentury. Countries in the third group experienced a more gradual increase in workforce, with their peaks projected to occur closer to midcentury. Finally, at the bottom we see the countries that will see explosive workforce growth.

This figure confirms several ideas that can help us anticipate the coming workforce changes. Within each group, you can see successive arcs of growth. Across the groups, reading the whole chart from top to bottom, you see successive peaks, with the high-income mature economies peaking early, followed by the Asian Tigers, which had some of the steepest fertility declines. Then you see the gradual peaking of the emerging economies, followed by the explosive workforce growth of many African countries.

The key point is the pattern of fertility decline can be a powerful indicator of the workforce shifts that will likely unfold. This perspective helps us anticipate future transitions while we still have time to adapt. In some countries, technology innovations and labor policy changes are already being adopted to address slower workforce growth. But despite some adaptations, countries and businesses should pay much more attention to the implications of workforce decline. It is especially important to recognize that many countries will experience not just slower workforce growth but may soon see absolute declines.

The tall landscape in Figure 7.10, scaled to fit China and India, shows differences across the world's largest workforces as well as

FIGURE 7.10 The landscape of workforce growth shows successive peaks and declines. Due to projections of continued growth, the US is an exception.

Working-Age Population (Ages 20–64), Selected Countries, in Millions

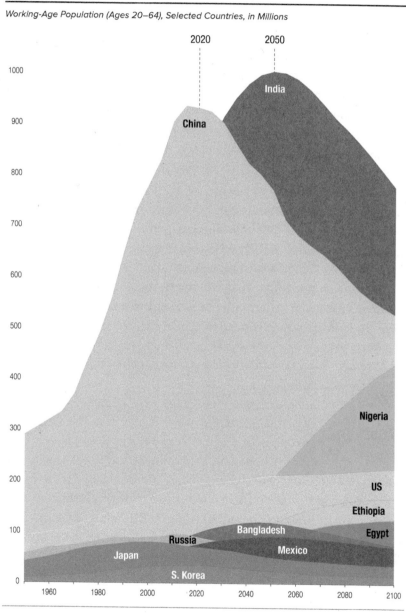

Note: The countries are layered, one behind the other, not stacked.

Data source: United Nations, *World Population Prospects 2019,* medium variant.

across selected other countries, including the United States. The peaks of China and India, of course, dominate the chart. China's immediate workforce decline already poses enormous challenges, and it will be important to watch how China addresses these threats. It will also be interesting to see what changes India might pursue to capitalize on its stronger growth over the next 30 years.

Several other parts of this landscape deserve your attention. First is the rapid growth in Nigeria, as its working-age population is projected to more than double by 2050, then double again by century's end. At the bottom, you see once more that many promising middle-income countries face slower workforce growth over the coming years and will need to adapt. Finally, you can see that the United States is projected to experience a slow but steady increase in its working-age population. This is a competitive advantage relative not just to other advanced economies, but also compared with other countries facing declining workforces. How the US leverages this advantage will have enormous economic, social, and political implications.

These various landscapes illustrate the successive peaks and declines of workforces around the world. From these comparisons, you can identify which countries are on the upward, more promising parts of the workforce arc, and which are on the downward side. That information should inform long-term policy choices as well as investment decisions.

While the landscapes give us a long-term perspective, the map in Figure 7.11, which summarizes key results from the UN's 2050 projection, focuses on projected growth over the next 30 years. Europe and East Asia, shown in dark blue, are projected to see the largest percentage declines, while countries in sub-Saharan Africa, in red and orange, are projected to have explosive growth. Many of these fast-growing countries, including Nigeria, Ethiopia, Egypt, and the DRC, are among Africa's most populous, so the near-doubling of their working-age populations contributes significantly to Africa's projected total. In the Western Hemisphere, Brazil and Chile are outliers with shrinking workforces, while most of Latin America will see moderate gains.

FIGURE 7.11   Most advanced economies face shrinking workforces, in contrast to explosive growth in Africa.

Growth in Working-Age Population (Ages 20–64), 2020–50

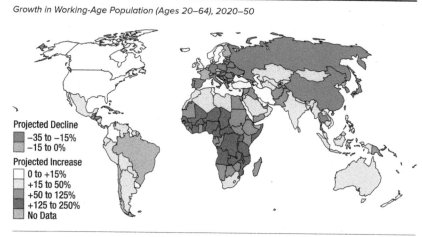

Projected Decline
- −35 to −15%
- −15 to 0%

Projected Increase
- 0 to +15%
- +15 to 50%
- +50 to 125%
- +125 to 250%
- No Data

Data source: United Nations, *World Population Prospects 2019,* medium variant.

LABOR FORCE PARTICIPATION

Returning to the GDP equation, there are two general policy avenues for adapting to slower-growing workforces while maintaining economic growth; the first is to increase the labor supply, and the second is to increase labor productivity. Countries and businesses can augment labor supply, or total hours worked, in several ways: increase hours worked by current workers; boost labor force participation within the traditional working-age brackets, especially among women; extend the definition of working age by raising the retirement age; and finally, allow increased immigration of workers. Each of these options has been met with varying degrees of public opposition. Proposals to raise the retirement age have prompted vocal demonstrations globally, including in China and Russia. Anti-immigration sentiment has also been on the rise throughout the world. Nonetheless, many countries have already adopted strategies to boost labor force participation, and we can see some success by looking at labor force participation rates in selected countries.

Using Germany as an example, the double histograms in Figure 7.12 illustrate some of the possibilities for increasing labor supply. The outside histogram (in shades of blue) shows the total population, while the inside histogram (in orange) represents the population in the labor force. Looking at the 1990 histogram on the left, it appears that there is plenty of room to expand the labor supply through higher labor force participation. First, the participation rate at each age could grow, which would increase the width of the orange bars. Second, the definition of working age could be extended, which would raise the height of the orange area. Two changes stand out from 1990 to 2020. The overall age structure has shifted upward, and female labor force participation has expanded: the orange bars on the female side of the histogram have widened and the total female labor force participation has increased from 45% in 1990 to 55% in 2020. In contrast, total male labor force participation declined from 72% to 66%.

Labor force participation rates vary dramatically across countries by age and gender, reflecting labor policies, economic incentives, and social norms specific to each country. However, two patterns hold across many economies. First, women are less likely to participate in the labor force at all ages. While some countries have reduced the gender gap, there is still plenty of room to increase employment of women. As education disparities diminish, the female labor supply will be increasingly valuable and can contribute more and more to labor productivity. Second, we see that labor force participation generally drops for older workers. As life expectancy rises and people remain healthier longer, more of them will be physically able to continue working—and more will need to continue working. This rapidly growing segment of the population offers increasing room to expand the labor supply.

In Figure 7.13 you can see the 30-year history of labor force participation in the four largest economies. Three of these countries—China, Japan, Germany—already have shrinking working-age populations, so it will be important to see how they seek to adapt their labor force participation rates to increase labor supply. The US is the only one of the four that can expect continued workforce

Population and Labor Force by Sex and Age, by Five-Year Age Bracket, 1990 and 2020, in Millions

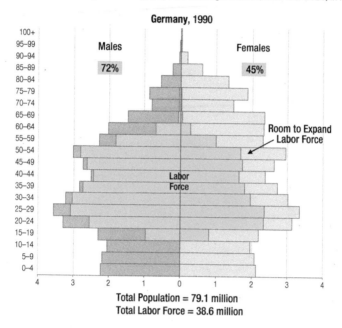

Germany, 1990

Total Population = 79.1 million
Total Labor Force = 38.6 million

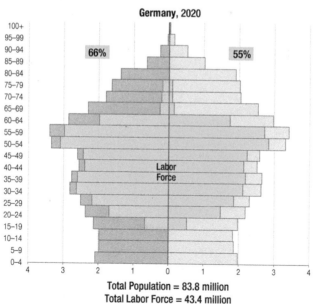

Germany, 2020

Total Population = 83.8 million
Total Labor Force = 43.4 million

Note: The labor force is the population that is working or seeking work. The labor force participation rate is the percentage of the population that is working or seeking work. The labor force participation rate for age 65+ is applied to the population ages 65–79.

Data sources: International Labour Organization, ILOSTAT; United Nations, *World Population Prospects 2019*, medium variant.

FIGURE 7.13 There is room to increase labor force participation, especially among women and older workers.

Labor Force Participation by Sex and Age, 1990–2020, Four Largest Economies

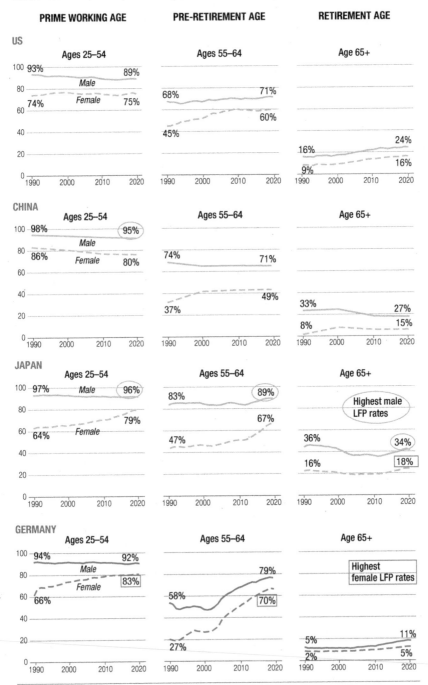

Data source: International Labour Organization, ILOSTAT.

growth. As you will see later in this chapter, that expectation depends on immigration to fuel the working-age population. From the figure, it looks like there is room for all four countries to boost their labor supply, especially through greater labor force participation among women and the older age groups.

In comparing these economies, you should note several general trends. Japan has the highest labor force participation among men, but despite recent improvements, it still registers a large gender gap. Germany has the highest labor force participation among women in the prime and pre-retirement ages, but not in the population age 65+. You can see that these countries diverge sharply on labor force participation of older workers. Much of this stems from retirement incentives, with Germany in the lead on this dimension. Notably, labor force participation among the population age 65+ has been increasing in Germany, Japan, and the US. Among these large economies, Japan has the highest labor force participation rates among its older population—34% among men and 18% among women.

While Germany has low labor force participation among the 65+ population, the country has seen large gains in labor force participation among the pre-retirement age group, especially among women. Both Japan and Germany had substantial gains in female labor force participation in the prime working-age group. For the US, the big increase in female labor force participation occurred in the 1970s and 1980s. Largely fueled by baby boomer females entering the labor force, female labor force participation increased from 55% in the mid-1970s to 74% by 1990, the starting point for these figures. As social norms evolved, labor force participation of older women also increased.

The data for the pre-retirement and retirement age groups suggests there is room to improve. Because these are the fastest-growing population segments, increased labor force participation could bode well for boosting the labor supply. However, this is not to say there will be a match between the types of jobs available and the skills of these older workers. Developing and maintaining the required skills is yet another challenge facing these aging populations.

IMPACT OF MIGRATION
ON GROWTH IN WORKING-AGE POPULATION

You have seen that increased labor force participation is one way to boost labor supply. Increased migration is also discussed as another option for increasing labor supply, as well as for meeting specific industry needs. Because migration depends on so many varied economic, political, environmental, and social factors, it is difficult to make accurate projections. However, by comparing alternative projections—with and without migration—we can get a general idea of how international migration contributes to working-age population.

For most countries, migration is a small component of population growth, but as discussed earlier in the book, for some countries, migration has had a substantial impact. Figure 7.14 focuses on the largest economies and compares the working-age population projections with and without migration. The medium variant projection, used throughout this book, assumes that recent levels of net international migration will continue until midcentury. The zero-migration alternative variant sets international migration at zero, starting in 2020.

For the traditional immigration countries, shown at the top—the US, Canada, Australia, and the UK—the impact of zero migration is startling. You can see that projected workforce growth depends entirely on migration. With zero migration, these workforces would be declining, or in the case of Australia, stagnant. Of these four countries, Australia would take the biggest percentage hit if migration stopped, with workforce growth registering zero, compared with 15% in the medium variant scenario. Because the United States is the largest migration destination, it would take the biggest numerical hit. With migration continuing, the workforce is projected to grow by 4%, adding 9.2 million over the 20 years from 2020 to 2040. The picture is quite the opposite without migration. In that scenario, the US workforce is projected to decline by almost 9 million over those 20 years.

FIGURE 7.14 Migration can substantially affect workforce growth in the large economies.

Projected Change in Working-Age Population (Ages 15–64), with and without Migration, 2020–40, Largest Economies

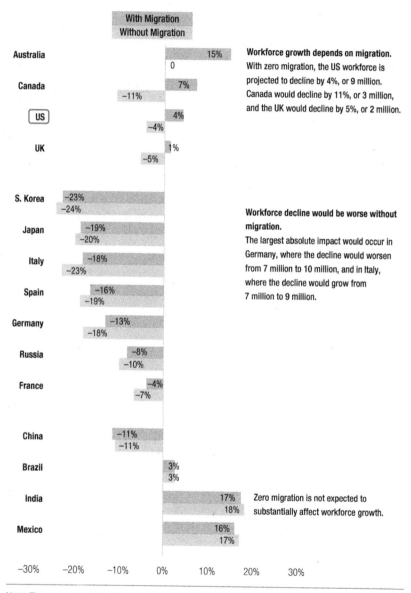

With Migration
Without Migration

Australia — 15% / 0

Canada — 7% / −11%

US — 4% / −4%

UK — 1% / −5%

S. Korea — −23% / −24%

Japan — −19% / −20%

Italy — −18% / −23%

Spain — −16% / −19%

Germany — −13% / −18%

Russia — −8% / −10%

France — −4% / −7%

China — −11% / −11%

Brazil — 3% / 3%

India — 17% / 18%

Mexico — 16% / 17%

Workforce growth depends on migration.
With zero migration, the US workforce is projected to decline by 4%, or 9 million. Canada would decline by 11%, or 3 million, and the UK would decline by 5%, or 2 million.

Workforce decline would be worse without migration.
The largest absolute impact would occur in Germany, where the decline would worsen from 7 million to 10 million, and in Italy, where the decline would grow from 7 million to 9 million.

Zero migration is not expected to substantially affect workforce growth.

Note: The projection "With Migration" (the medium variant) assumes that recent levels of net international migration will continue until midcentury. The projection "Without Migration" (the zero-migration variant) sets international migration at zero, starting in 2020.

Data source: United Nations, *World Population Prospects 2019.*

For the countries projected to have shrinking workforces even with migration, the workforce declines would be worse by a few percentage points without migration. The largest absolute impacts would occur in Germany, where the decline would increase from 7 million (-13%) to 10 million (-18%); and in Italy, where the decline would increase from 7 million (-18%) to 9 million (-23%).

For the large origin countries shown at the bottom, zero migration is not expected to substantially affect workforce growth.

Overall, the impact of the zero-migration scenario looks small. But keep in mind that these projections assume a continuation of current levels of migration; and based on those levels, migration doesn't look like a strong lever for increasing the size of the workforce in most places. Some countries may, however, choose to confront the anti-immigrant sentiment in the interest of fueling their workforce growth. Alternatively, or in combination with efforts to expand the workforce, countries will adopt technologies to improve the productivity of the existing workforce.

THE CHANGING SHARE OF WORKERS IN THE TOTAL POPULATION

So far in this chapter we have focused on growth in the working-age population itself. Now we turn to considering the size of a country's working-age population relative to the rest of its population. This age shift is captured in the support ratio of working-age population to dependent-age population, with dependents including children and older people. The support ratio is thus defined as workers per dependent, where dependents include children (ages 0 to 14) and older people (age 65+).

Changes in this support ratio of workers per dependent provide a useful indicator of workforce change and economic potential. Tracking this ratio is a helpful way to compare countries and to gain insights into the different economic challenges and opportunities they face. Specifically, a comparison of changes in the ratios can help us understand which countries might get a boost from the decline in fertility, with its resulting increase in the share of workers, and which countries face a potential drag from slow growth or declines in the ratio.

Economists call the boost in economic output stemming from growth in the share of working-age population a "demographic dividend." As a country's fertility rate declines and the number of children declines, the share of working-age people will increase, and this increase is potential fuel for economic growth. Not only will there be more potential workers, but there will be fewer young dependents to care for. The share of working-age population will continue to increase as long as growth in working-age population exceeds growth in the number of dependents, including children and older people. However, as the number of old people steadily rises and the working-age population levels off or falls, the share of working-age people will eventually decrease.

We know that China and the Asian Tigers benefited from steep increases in workers per dependent, but those ratios are now sharply declining as the numbers of older people increase. As shown in Figure 7.15, China benefited from the steep increase in workers per dependent that began around 1975. This increase continued until around 2010, when growth in dependent-age population exceeded growth in the working-age population, causing the ratio to decline. (If you go back to Figure 7.1 at the beginning of this chapter, you can see the overall age mix shifting, with the continued decline in the number of children, the rapid increase in the 65+, and the 2010 peaking of the working-age population.) The run-up in the support ratio and potential economic boost started even earlier in South Korea and peaked a little later, giving South Korea longer to capitalize on the increasing share of working-age population. The situation in India is completely different. Like China, India has benefited from an increasing support ratio since the 1970s, but compared with China, the increase was much more gradual. Nonetheless, India's rising support ratio contributed to its recent economic growth. The ratio is projected to continue rising before stabilizing, offering a further opportunity to take advantage of the favorable demographic change.

Several other emerging economies might also benefit from their increasing ratios of workers per dependent. As you can see

FIGURE 7.15 Due to its steep fertility decline, China benefited from a steep increase in the share of working-age population.

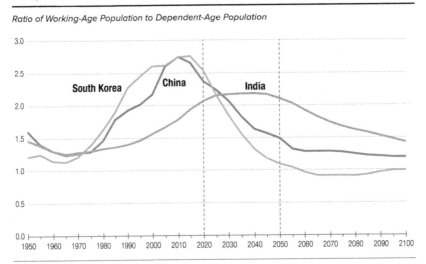

Ratio of Working-Age Population to Dependent-Age Population

Note: Working-age population = ages 15–64; dependent-age population = ages <15 plus 65+.

Data source: United Nations, *World Population Prospects 2019,* medium variant.

in Figure 7.16, Mexico and Bangladesh both had steeper increases in the support ratio than India. While Bangladesh is projected to see continued gains until around 2040, Mexico's window of opportunity is smaller. Unlike the economies with expected increases in their support ratios, Brazil will soon be on the downward part of the curve, facing an economic drag from its changing demographic mix.

Figure 7.17 shows the projected ratios for several countries with continued high fertility rates that are only slowly declining. While none will see a rising support ratio comparable to China's, these rapidly growing countries might still be able to leverage their changing demographics to achieve an economic benefit. Investments in health and education could make a difference. Faster reductions in fertility would further boost the support ratio.

Finally, in Figure 7.18 you can see how the largest economies have fared. It is no surprise that they all face the economic drag of declining support ratios, but it is useful to compare the nature of

FIGURE 7.16 For many emerging economies, the potential benefit of an increasing support ratio is projected to diminish.

Ratio of Working-Age Population to Dependent-Age Population

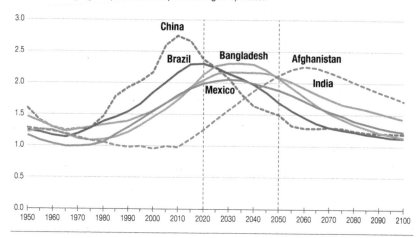

Note: Working-age population = ages 15–64; dependent-age population = ages <15 plus 65+. China and Afghanistan are included for reference.

Data source: United Nations, *World Population Prospects 2019,* medium variant.

FIGURE 7.17 Many young, fast-growing countries could benefit from an increasing ratio of workers to dependents. None will see the steep increase that benefited China.

Ratio of Working-Age Population to Dependent-Age Population

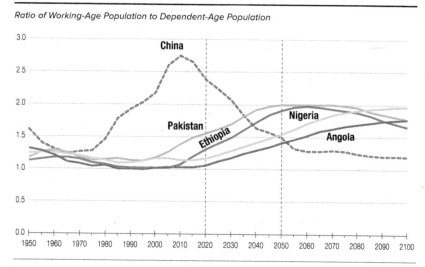

Note: Working-age population = ages 15–64; dependent-age population = ages <15 plus 65+. China is included for reference.

Data source: United Nations, *World Population Prospects 2019,* medium variant.

FIGURE 7.18   Older countries face the demographic drag of declining ratios of workers to dependents.

Ratio of Working-Age Population to Dependent-Age Population

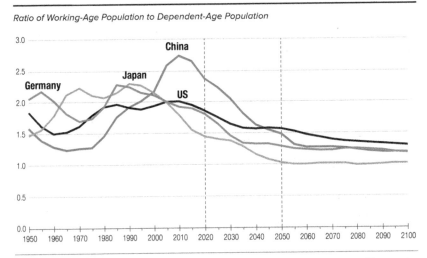

Note: Working-age population = ages 15–64; dependent-age population = ages <15 plus 65+.

Data source: United Nations, *World Population Prospects 2019*, medium variant.

the support ratios they face. China faces the steepest decline, while the US is projected to have the slowest decline, which will soon stabilize, at least temporarily. Japan has faced a relatively steep decline since the 1990s, and that decline is projected to continue. Although Germany's support ratio will continue shrinking, the change has been more gradual, and is projected to be less severe than in Japan, giving Germany more time to adapt.

We can reach two broad conclusions about the ratio of workers to dependents: First, young countries, where growth in working-age population will exceed growth of the dependent-age population, could benefit from an increasing ratio of workers per dependent. Depending on the political and economic environment, the increasing ratio could provide a boost to economic growth. Second, older countries with the opposite dynamic—where growth in the dependent-age population will surpass growth in working-age population—face an increasing burden of dependents. Absent major productivity gains or changes in labor and retirement policies, the demographic drag of aging could substantially constrain economic growth. In this environment, productivity-enhancing innovations will be increasingly important.

CONCLUSION

The landscape of successive workforce declines provides a useful framework for understanding the changes under way in several groups of countries.

First, the high-income countries, most of which have had low fertility for decades, now face shrinking workforces. Many have already seen declines, and others are dealing with much slower growth. A few, including the United States and Canada, may be insulated from workforce decline by continued immigration. But continued immigration is also being threatened. In general, all the large economies will need to adapt to much slower workforce growth.

The biggest disruption will come to the upper-middle-income countries. Because most had large and rapid fertility declines, they now can anticipate corresponding declines in their working-age populations. The surprise of China's shrinking workforce will occur in many other upper-middle-income countries.

Because they had slower fertility declines, many lower-middle-income countries, including India and the Philippines, will experience continued workforce growth for several more decades before growth slows.

Finally, it's no surprise that young, high-fertility African countries will see the fastest workforce growth.

Whatever the direction and magnitude of the coming changes, it seems clear that the workforce shifts will alter the public policy priorities of most countries, and that new policies will be needed to either compensate for shrinking workforces or to leverage growing workforces.

These projected changes in workforce growth show what lies ahead, giving countries—as well as their trading partners and allies—time to adapt.

LOOKING TO THE FUTURE

8 | THE SHAPE OF THINGS TO COME

"The End of the Population Pyramid"
The Economist, by P.J.W. and J.P., November 18, 2014

"Pyramids, Beehives, and Pillars. Oh My!"
Issues in Physics and Society (blog), February 25, 2013

"Demographic Turning Points for the United States"
Current Population Reports, US Census Bureau, March 2018

Now that you are armed with knowledge of the population drivers and key challenges, you can use demographic analysis to gain insights into how a country's changing demography will shape its advantages and vulnerabilities—and therefore its priorities—in the years to come. With these insights, you will be able to understand more than the headlines, as you'll have a grasp of what lies behind the news.

You have seen that declining fertility and rising life expectancy are the two main drivers of population change. Together, these drivers determine the natural increase in an area's population. Immigration, a third driver, also contributes to total population. We have seen how these drivers combine to change the population in each age bracket. You have also seen how these drivers differ in timing, pace, and magnitude across countries. It is these variations that determine how demographic changes will unfold differently around the world.

Although the three drivers are interrelated, so far we have looked at them individually to understand how each one affects a particular country at specific moments in time. And we have explored key challenges stemming from the overall age shift. In this chapter, we will consider how those various threads interact to create a country's overall demographic trajectory.

One of the most useful tools for understanding demographic change in a particular geographic area is the old-fashioned frequency distribution, or histogram, which illustrates the number of people by age and sex. As you have seen in previous chapters, each histogram—sometimes called an age pyramid—is more than just a static encapsulation of population data and more like a demographic time capsule, containing information about prior events and trends that have led to the current situation. The blips and bulges you will see result from social, economic, and political changes over time, which are in turn reflected in the population composition. Such changes might stem from economic booms, population policies, wars, diseases, or natural disasters. Like time capsules, individual histograms contain information about past events that have affected the population and that can offer insights for understanding an area's past and future demographic changes and challenges.

Each histogram is like a detailed snapshot of the situation at that time, but if you look at a histogram series, you can see how the demographic situation has evolved. You might think of a series of histogram snapshots as a flipbook, capturing the transformation over time. By studying the series, you can see not only how the overall picture evolves, but you can also stop to look closely at the individual frames to examine details at selected moments in time.

When exploring a histogram, you should note five features: the overall shape and size, the relative sizes of the three broad age groups, the median age, and any particular blips and bulges that might reflect demographic impacts of social and economic developments. Understanding these characteristics and how they change for our cast of characters will reveal how the drivers work to produce divergent outcomes.

The histogram *shape* indicates the overall age distribution, from young—pyramid shape—to old—inverted pyramid and cube. Changes in the shape generally reflect impacts of the key drivers on the population: declining fertility reduces the size of the base, as fewer children are born; while increased life expectancy will widen the size of successive bars, as more people survive to the next age level. Similarly, immigration can increase the population of various age brackets.

Changes in overall *size* of the histogram reflect the combined effects of the three drivers on total population.

Change in *relative size of the age groups* reflects changes in the support ratios; for example, number of workers per retiree, or number of workers per dependent. Investigating changes in these ratios can help to identify potential demographic dividends when ratios improve or potential drags when the ratios decline.

In a single number, *median age* captures data on the relative youth or aging of a population. You can think of this indicator as the center of gravity of the age structure. Changes in median age indicate the pace of aging.

By studying the *blips and bulges*, you can see how certain events or trends affect the population in particular age brackets, such as the immediate effects of a war or economic depression, or the longer-term results of a baby boom.

JAPAN'S RAPID TRANSFORMATION FROM PYRAMID TO CUBE

Japan is a good example of the three drivers converging to produce significant challenges of population aging and workforce decline. Indeed, Japan has one of the oldest populations in the world, and its workforce and total population are already shrinking. The histograms in Figure 8.1 present a visual narrative of dramatic and worrisome demographic developments unfolding in the world's third-largest economy.

1950: JAPAN IS YOUNG AND GROWING

As we look at the series of histograms for Japan, we can see how the demographic transition unfolds. In 1950, Japan's population was

FIGURE 8.1 Japan's age structure has rapidly transformed from the traditional pyramid to a top-heavy profile that reflects its aging population and shrinking workforce.

Total Population by Age and Sex, in Millions

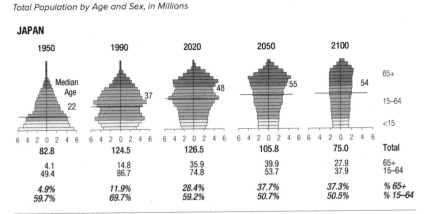

JAPAN

	1950	1990	2020	2050	2100	
Total	82.8	124.5	126.5	105.8	75.0	Total
65+	4.1	14.8	35.9	39.9	27.9	65+
15–64	49.4	86.7	74.8	53.7	37.9	15–64
% 65+	4.9%	11.9%	28.4%	37.7%	37.3%	% 65+
% 15–64	59.7%	69.7%	59.2%	50.7%	50.5%	% 15–64

Note: Population in millions by five-year age bracket with ages 0–4 on the bottom and 100+ on top; males at left, females at right.

Data source: United Nations, *World Population Prospects 2019,* medium variant.

relatively young, which is reflected in the pyramid shape of the 1950 histogram, with its broad base of young people and few old people at the top. This shape is typical of young, growing populations around the world, with the bars near the bottom reflecting an increasing number of births.

The blips and bulges of the histogram reflect the demographic impact of events that affected a particular age bracket. For example, the larger size of the youngest bracket at the bottom of the 1950 histogram reflects the increased number of births due to the post–World War II baby boom. An indentation further up the left side of the histogram, which depicts the male population age 25 to 40, likely reflects deaths of Japanese men during World War II.

2020: SHRINKING BASE OF CHILDREN

As you can see, Japan's histograms tell an interesting story. By 2020, Japan's pyramid-shaped histogram had morphed into a completely different shape, reflecting the impacts of declining fertility and increasing life expectancy. The country's fertility rate fell sharply after its 1949 post–World War II peak of 4.3 births per woman, and it has been at or below replacement rate for more than 50 years, registering only 1.4 births per woman in 2020. The narrowing base of the 2020 histogram reflects the declining number of births. At the same time, the top of the histogram has grown rapidly, as death rates have declined, and more people reach older ages. Because women have a higher life expectancy than men, more women than men reach the upper age brackets; thus, the right-hand bars of the upper age brackets are wider than the left-hand bars.

The 2020 histogram illustrates demographic results of various social and political developments. The bulge near the top, around age 70, represents the postwar baby boom; this baby boom cohort, which was in the bottom bracket of the 1950 histogram, has reached ages 70 to 74 in the 2020 histogram. As the fertility rate fell in the 1950s, the number of births dropped, creating what is known as a baby bust. An echo boom followed, as the postwar baby boomers started having families. This echo boom is reflected in the bulge around age 40 to 45. Fertility rates continued to decline, and the lower age brackets continued to narrow. Despite the narrowing of the base, the total population increased by 47 million, from 83 million in 1950 to a peak of 129 million in 2010. By 2020, the total population had declined slightly to 126 million. As a result of the fertility decline and life expectancy gains, the age distribution is becoming more cube-like, with a top-heavy age distribution punctuated by baby boom and echo boom bulges.

2050: SHRINKING TOTAL POPULATION, TOP-HEAVY WITH OLDER PEOPLE

As the base becomes even smaller and the top fills out, by 2050, Japan's age histogram will become almost inverted, or kite shaped. This top-heavy histogram reflects important projections. First, the number of births will continue to fall, even as the fertility rate stabilizes; and second, both the number and share of old people will increase. As a result, the age distribution will shift upward. Half the population will be age 55 or older (the median age) and more than one-third of the population will have reached age 65 and older. Not only will Japan's population markedly age over time, but by 2050, the total population will shrink. From 2020 to 2050, the total population is projected to decline by nearly 21 million, a decrease of 16%. The upward shift in the age mix associated with this total population decline is startling. More than 100% of the decline will occur in the working-age population, which is projected to fall by more than 21 million, a drop of 28%. The number of children will continue to decline, a change which is easily seen in the narrowed histogram base. While these two broad age segments are shrinking, the older population is projected to grow by 4 million, or 11%.

2100: A MORE EVEN AGE DISTRIBUTION

By the end of the century, according to UN projections, Japan's age structure will become cube-like, with its smaller population of only 75 million more evenly distributed across the age brackets. The cube is already partially visible in the 2020 and 2050 histograms, and it becomes more dominant as the echo boom bulge disappears. By 2100, total population is projected to be 40% smaller than the 2020 level, a drop of 52 million. Although 80 years might seem like a long horizon, it is useful to consider how the changes already under way might continue to evolve. The histograms of 2100 show how the future population might look for today's children.

ALMOST ZERO IMMIGRATION

As you have read, the third driver of population change is international migration—people crossing borders for economic, political, or environmental reasons. Migrants seeking economic opportunity are often concentrated in the working-age brackets of the population. Thus, in a histogram, such economic immigration would be reflected in the widening of those working-age brackets. Historically, Japan has not had a tradition of welcoming foreign workers, so immigration has not been an important demographic driver for the country. In 2013, Japan's foreign-born population was just 1.3% of its total, compared with 13% for the US. However, in late 2018, in response to the demographic pressures of a shrinking and aging workforce, Japan's parliament passed controversial legislation to allow more foreign workers. This significant policy shift indicates mounting concern about the challenges of an aging population, a shrinking workforce, and a decreasing total population.

DIVERGENT AGE STRUCTURES: PAKISTAN, MEXICO, AND SOUTH KOREA

One of the most startling things about Japan's demography is how fast the population composition morphed from a youthful pyramid to a top-heavy structure as the drivers took hold. In 1950, many young countries had pyramid-shaped histograms like Japan's, but since then, their histogram shapes have changed dramatically.

The histogram comparison in Figure 8.2 demonstrates how population change unfolds differently depending on the divergent timing and pace of the demographic drivers. In the comparison of Pakistan, Mexico, and South Korea, you can see how the demographic trajectories will unfold differently. All three had pyramid-shaped histograms in 1950, with median ages between 19 and 20, but by 2020, their shapes had diverged, and the median age difference widened substantially. Differences in the timing and pace of their fertility and mortality patterns have put them on different trajectories, leading to different demographic outcomes, with different consequences. By 2050, the differences will be even more stark.

Youthful countries like Pakistan, with high and only slowly declining fertility combined with relatively low life expectancies, may see some increase in their older age groups, but their overall populations will remain relatively young, and their age structures will remain pyramid-shaped, as population at all ages will continue to grow. Pakistan is projected to add 100 million people over the

FIGURE 8.2 Though similar in 1950, Pakistan, Mexico, and South Korea now face divergent demographic priorities.

Total Population by Age and Sex, in Millions

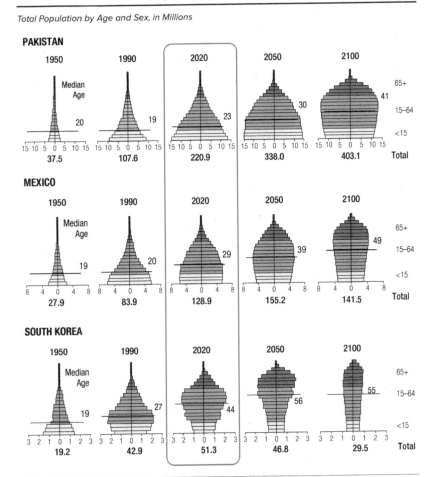

Note: Population in millions by five-year age bracket with ages 0–4 on the bottom and 100+ on top; males at left, females at right.

Data source: United Nations, *World Population Prospects 2019,* medium variant.

30 years from 2020 to midcentury. In some countries, including Pakistan, as well as many countries in sub-Saharan Africa and the Middle East, the high fertility rates and population growth will lead to potentially volatile "youth bulges." The large shares

of youth in situations with high unemployment, rapid population growth, and low economic prospects can spark civil conflict. There are other examples, including the Asian Tigers, where the youth bulges became a positive force, serving as economic fuel; by managing this demographic fuel, some countries were able to capitalize on the "demographic dividend" and achieve the economic benefits of an increased working-age population.

In contrast to Pakistan, "middle-aged" countries such as Mexico will see a more cube-like age profile emerge, driven by rapid fertility declines, which narrow the base, and increased life expectancy, which widens the top and increases the overall histogram width. Mexico has retained its young, pyramidal age structure until recently, when the steep fertility declines of the 1980s eventually caused the population base to square off and later narrow. The projected 10-year increase in median age from 29 to 39 reflects Mexico's rapid aging. The working-age population is projected to peak around 2050 and slowly decline after that.

Finally, South Korea and many other low-fertility countries with a high life expectancy will face shrinking workforces, rapidly aging populations, and shrinking totals. Countries like the Asian Tigers, which experienced steep fertility declines, will see their age structures become smaller at the base and increasingly top-heavy with old people. South Korea exemplifies the rapid demographic transformation that accompanies rapid economic development: its fertility decline was one of the steepest of any country, and consequently, it now faces a dramatically shrinking workforce. The working-age population is projected to fall by nearly a quarter over just the next 20 years. By 2050, the working-age population is projected to be one-third smaller than in 2020. South Korea also has the distinction of being one of the fastest-aging countries. By 2050, half the population will be over age 56 and nearly 38% will be age 65 and older.

Although they began the post–World War II period with similar pyramid-shaped age structures, these three countries have evolved differently due to divergent patterns of fertility declines and life expectancy gains. How these populations grow or shrink and how youthful or old they are should inform global relations and international strategies. Recognizing and addressing the differences will be critical.

CHINA AND INDIA—DIVERGENT WORKFORCE TRAJECTORIES

In 1950, India and China had youthful, pyramid-shaped age structures typical of developing countries with high fertility rates. Divergent changes in these two countries since then reflect differences in the pace and timing of their fertility declines and life expectancy gains. China's age structure is quickly becoming top-heavy with older people, and its working-age population is already shrinking. In contrast, due to its later and more gradual fertility decline, India's population retains a youthful profile with a small share of older people. The histograms shown in Figure 8.3 point to the divergent strengths and vulnerabilities of these two strategically important countries.

The Chinese histogram series is punctuated with many blips and bulges, most of which reflect various government population policies. In 1950 China's age structure was pyramidal, typical of developing countries with high fertility rates and successively larger generations. By 2020, 70 years later, the base of young people has narrowed significantly, due partly to the one-child policy begun in 1979, but also due to the steep fertility decline that began in the 1970s, well before the one-child policy. Moreover, improved living conditions and better health care sharply reduced childhood mortality and increased life expectancy, raising the number of people who survived to the next age bracket. These developments combined to make China's age profile square off at the base, while the upper brackets widened. By 2050, the rapid aging of China's population will make its age distribution top-heavy with old people; by then, the median age will be 48 years, and more than one-quarter of the population will be age 65 and older. By 2050, the older population will be more than double what it was in 2020, an increase from 172 million to 366 million. And by 2050, the UN projects that

FIGURE 8.3   China and India: Divergent workforce trajectories will drive different strategies.

Total Population by Age and Sex, in Millions

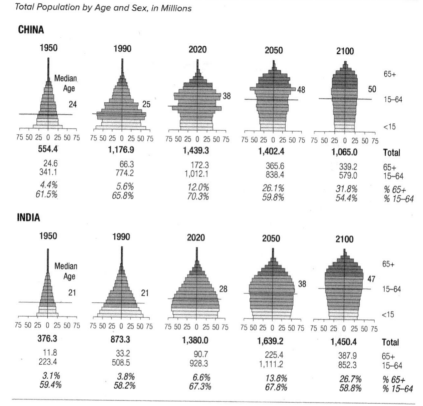

Note: Population in millions by five-year age bracket with ages 0–4 on the bottom and 100+ on top; males at left, females at right.

Data source: United Nations, *World Population Prospects 2019,* medium variant.

China's working-age population will be 17% smaller than in 2020, a decline of 174 million. By the end of the century, China's profile will become a narrow cube, with a much smaller population more evenly distributed across the age brackets. The rapidly aging population and shrinking workforce pose significant challenges for China and threaten its continued economic growth.

In contrast to China's more cube-like age structure, India's age profile remains closer to the pyramid shape typical of young developing countries. India's fertility has dropped much more slowly than China's and its base of children continued to increase until around 2010, reinforcing the pyramid shape. Nevertheless, India's declining fertility will gradually affect the age structure, causing the base to narrow. By 2030, India's total population will exceed China's. Despite the narrowed base, growth in the working-age population is projected to continue until around 2050, more than 50 years past China's peak in working-age population. India's large grow-ing workforce could be a major advantage propelling its economic growth. However, on the negative side, although life expectancy has increased, it still lags behind the steep gains made in East Asia.

It is revealing to compare the demographic trends in these two most populous countries and to highlight the stark differences. As shown in the histogram comparison, the similarities end with the 1950 pyramid! After that, China morphs more like an aging advanced economy with persistently low fertility, while India morphs like a developing country with only a gradual fertility decline. It will be informative in the future to monitor how they each adapt to their changing demographics: What will China do to compensate for its shrinking workforce? How will India capitalize on its large growing labor supply at a time when many large economies face declining workforces?

AFGHANISTAN—A DEMOGRAPHIC DIVIDEND?

Afghanistan's demography provides a useful lens for better under-standing its current political and economic situation and yields some insights about the coming challenges and opportunities. The histogram series in Figure 8.4 reveals two striking features. First is Afghanistan's youth. With a median age in 2020 of just 18, Afghani-stan ranks among the world's 20 youngest countries, most of which are located in sub-Saharan Africa. Second, we can see that the total population of Afghanistan more than tripled over the past 30 years, increasing from 12 million to 39 million. The squared-off base of the 2020 histogram stems from several dramatic improvements in the

FIGURE 8.4   The shift in Afghanistan's youthful age profile shows the impact of a steep fertility decline and the development of a potential demographic dividend.

Total Population by Age and Sex, in Millions

AFGHANISTAN

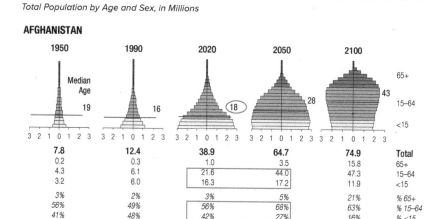

	1950	1990	2020	2050	2100	
Total	7.8	12.4	38.9	64.7	74.9	Total
65+	0.2	0.3	1.0	3.5	15.8	65+
15–64	4.3	6.1	21.6	44.0	47.3	15–64
<15	3.2	6.0	16.3	17.2	11.9	<15
% 65+	3%	2%	3%	5%	21%	% 65+
% 15–64	56%	49%	56%	68%	63%	% 15–64
% <15	41%	48%	42%	27%	16%	% <15

Note: Population in millions by five-year age bracket with ages 0–4 on the bottom and 100+ on top; males at left, females at right.

Data source: United Nations, *World Population Prospects 2019*, medium variant.

underlying demography over the past 20 years. Most importantly, the fertility rate declined sharply, from nearly 8.0 births per woman in 2000, a rate that had persisted for decades and was one of the world's highest, to 4.6 births per woman by 2020. This sharp drop in fertility points to an important societal transformation reflecting advances in maternal health and the improved economic role of women. Such a steep fertility decline is unusual in developing countries, especially poor countries like Afghanistan. To put this in perspective, the 20-year fertility decline was nearly as steep as the decline in China and the unexpected declines in Iran and Bangladesh. The decline in child mortality is another important advance during this 20-year period; as a result, total life expectancy at birth increased by 10 years, to 64 years. Even with such a significant improvement, life expectancy in Afghanistan is still relatively low, just matching the average for least developed countries.

As a result of the fertility decline, growth in the number of births in Afghanistan has slowed and the population of children under age 15 has stabilized—meaning the histogram base starts to square off, while the rest of the histogram grows more quickly. We see that from 1990 to 2020, the working-age population more than tripled, and it is projected to double by midcentury, from 22 million to 44 million.

This leads to two important observations about the current situation. First, the median age in 2020 was 18 years; that means that more than half the current population wasn't even born before the 9/11 terrorist attacks and had no experience of what life was like under the previous Taliban regime. More importantly, their lives have been shaped by Western values, which allowed women and girls to be educated and pursue careers. Second, the total population of Afghanistan, 40 million in 2021, has nearly doubled since the Taliban last controlled the country. This huge increase creates enormous governance challenges for the Taliban going forward. Furthermore, the predominance of youth in a country where economic development may be stalled produces important security threats for the region and for the world.

However, on the positive side, the shift in age structure that is currently under way could provide a potential "demographic dividend" to Afghanistan. The steep fertility decline leads to a lower proportion of children relative to working-age population. The base of children shrinks, and the midsection of working-age people becomes a larger share of the total population. You can see in the histogram data that the share of working-age population increases from 50% in 1990 to 56% in 2020, and is projected to increase to 68% by 2050. With relatively more working-age people, the support ratio of potential workers per dependent increases sharply and creates a potential demographic dividend. If managed appropriately, the increase in the relative share of working-age can boost economic growth.

The best examples of leveraging a demographic dividend are the Asian Tigers. They benefited from the increased support ratios by adopting economic and social policies that allowed them to effectively use the boost in labor supply to achieve higher economic growth. Such policies included investing in youth development through social and educational programs as well as through family-planning and reproductive-health policies that solidified their fertility declines.

Afghanistan faces a window of opportunity over the coming decades when the support ratio is projected to markedly increase. Because of its steep fertility decline, the potential demographic dividend could be especially large, paralleling the economic boost that occurred in China and the Asian Tigers. If the favorable demographic ratio is recognized and managed, it could be a significant advantage for Afghanistan. However, because girls' education would have to play a significant role, it's hard to be optimistic about the Taliban capitalizing on the favorable demographics.

The potential demographic dividend in Afghanistan presents an unusual situation. Most low-income countries have not experienced such steep or large fertility declines, and therefore don't face this type of significant increase in their support ratios. Amidst the humanitarian crisis and current political situation, it may be difficult to focus on leveraging the favorable demographics, but hopefully the benefits will not be wasted, even if somewhat delayed. Perhaps the Taliban can be persuaded that capitalizing on Afghanistan's favorable demographics would not only boost the country's economic prospects, but would also serve their political and national security interests.

THE UNITED STATES—FACING FAVORABLE DEMOGRAPHICS

If you look at the histograms of the United States in Figure 8.5, you can see that the United States has some competitive advantages: with a 2020 median age of 38 years, the US is relatively young compared to Europe (43 years old) and Japan (48); we have a growing working-age population; and the share of older people is increasing more slowly than elsewhere. However, our workforce growth depends heavily on continued immigration, which raises numerous challenges. Also, our more slowly aging population doesn't mean we don't face the social and economic challenges of a growing number and share of older people. But the gradual age shift combined with our economic strength positions us well to address the various challenges.

FIGURE 8.5 Relative youth and continued workforce growth give the US some competitive advantages.

Total Population by Age and Sex, in Millions

UNITED STATES

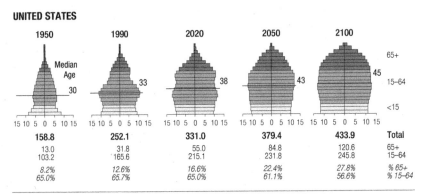

	1950	1990	2020	2050	2100	
Total	158.8	252.1	331.0	379.4	433.9	Total
65+	13.0	31.8	55.0	84.8	120.6	65+
15–64	103.2	165.6	215.1	231.8	245.8	15–64
% 65+	8.2%	12.6%	16.6%	22.4%	27.8%	% 65+
% 15–64	65.0%	65.7%	65.0%	61.1%	56.6%	% 15–64

Population in millions by five-year age bracket with ages 0–4 on the bottom and 100+ on top; males at left, females at right.

Data source: United Nations, *World Population Prospects 2019*, medium variant.

In 1950 near the beginning of the baby boom, the US population had a broad base of children, a big midsection of working-age people, and relatively few old people. By 1990, the situation had changed, as evidenced by the baby boom bulge in the middle of the working-age population, with the baby bust becoming evident as the bottom brackets narrow. The slight widening at the base is evidence of the echo baby boom. By 2020, the baby boom and echo boom bulges are still visible, but the overall population profile has morphed from the more traditional pyramid, with a broad base of young people, into a cube, with population more evenly distributed across the age brackets. The three demographic drivers have produced major changes: near-replacement fertility has created a stable base; increased life expectancy broadened the top of the histogram; and immigration has added population across many age brackets, as well as contributing to the higher fertility rate.

The change in age structure from pyramid to cube reflects aging of the population. The US population age 65 and older more than doubled from 1980 to 2020, from 27 million to 55 million, and is projected to increase to 85 million by 2050, with the share of old people increasing from 17% to 22%. Another feature of the changing age mix is the continued growth of the working-age population. Though workforce declines are projected for many other large economies, the working-age population in the US is forecasted to continue growing, albeit slowly.

With good planning and foresight, the competitive advantages of our youth and growing workforce can be leveraged to improve economic and social well-being. Continued and perhaps increased immigration is critical. Improved education of our valuable youth is even more critical. Another priority is retraining older workers so their skills are suitable for open positions. Still another is to consider what might be done in anticipation of the health care burden of the aging population—in particular, the cost and social burdens of Alzheimer's and other dementias. Finally, the dip in life expectancy must be addressed.

The histograms presented in this chapter give you insights into the different challenges and opportunities faced by countries at various stages of economic development. As you have seen, a time series of histograms provides a useful summary of how demographic changes are likely to unfold, and the country comparisons provide further information about the stark differences we can expect. The histogram shapes reveal a variety of challenges, ranging from youth bulges to aging populations, and the speed of the transformations points to how fast countries must adapt. Finally, from a global perspective, the differences between countries point to questions we should address about the implications of the new landscapes of demographic change.

9 | WATCH LIST

"Russia Doesn't Have the Demographics for War"
Foreign Policy, by Brent Peabody, January 3, 2022

"The Rising Toll of Famine and Conflict"
Ft.com, by Gideon Rachman, January 12, 2022

"China's Births Hit Historic Low, a Political Problem for Beijing"
New York Times, by Steven Lee Myers and Alexandra Stevenson, January 17, 2022

"Why Educating Girls Is Even More Important Than People Realise"
The Economist, August 19, 2021

This book has given you a framework for understanding how divergent demographic trends and challenges will likely unfold around the world over the coming decades. You have seen the way historical trends have combined to create the current situation, and you saw that these demographic trends point to major challenges for many countries around the world, including economic growth and national security. How countries adapt to their own demographic challenges and to the worldwide shifts will have enormous consequences for both their individual well-being and for global security. By using demographics as a window into the future, we can better prepare for the coming challenges. Since we can see the changes coming, we should be ready for them.

We should ask our policy makers how they plan to address these challenges, and we should closely watch how other countries are adapting and preparing for the coming changes. We saw that each country has different underlying demographics, as well as its own set of demographic strengths and weaknesses, so their priorities and strategies will differ. Because how our partners and adversaries adapt will affect our own economic growth and national security, we should pay close attention.

Some countries might seek out partners with complementary demographics; for example, countries with shrinking workforces might take advantage of available labor in faster-growing populations, or might encourage immigration where land is available but labor is scarce. Others might look for technology-enabled solutions that boost productivity and reduce labor needs. The demand for public spending will increase globally as countries need to make internal trade-offs among their top priorities—for example, elder housing, educational needs of children, workforce retraining, or more broadly, the allocation of resources between defense spending and health care, just to highlight a few.

We should also ask our business leaders what they are doing to anticipate these challenges. How do they plan to adapt to changing labor supply and aging populations? How will they prioritize education and retraining? How are they preparing for health challenges, such as the current obesity epidemic or another pandemic? What about immigration reform?

Similarly, we individuals should be developing strategies for ourselves, our families, and our communities that take into account the coming demographic changes, whether it be in our housing choices, education, careers, or caregiving. We should develop personal strategies for addressing the issues that directly affect us— adapting our homes or finding housing for older family members, better schools for our children, job retraining for our workers, or assimilation of economic migrants and political refugees into our communities.

We saw during the COVID-19 pandemic how individuals and institutions, as well as businesses and governments, stepped up to address the crisis; they mobilized resources and developed strategies for coping with the disruptions and uncertainties. Some have been more resilient than others; some got caught flat-footed. And I'm sure most of you have heard or read the recriminations about not being ready for a crisis that many scientists and policy planners long warned was likely.

The alarms being raised about demographic challenges may strike you as similar to warnings about future pandemics. But there is a big difference. Unlike with COVID-19, there is little uncertainty about the coming population shifts. Most of the changes and demographic disruptions that we expect are already baked into our societies. True, there is considerable uncertainty about how much international migration will likely occur, whether it be economic, political, or environmental, and there will be wild-card events that we can't predict. But based on what we already know about the key demographic drivers, we can be reasonably confident in the projections that account for changes in fertility and increasing life expectancy. This is not like earthquake forecasts that warn of destructive seismic activity coming within the next 30 years. Demographic changes are unfolding now—not starting sometime in the future. Even so, many of us are more prepared for earthquakes and hurricanes than for known transformations in our workforces and population age mix. Many Californians put together earthquake preparedness plans and emergency kits, and many companies regularly update their business interruption strategies. Likewise, we should all have plans for demographic preparedness. And these should not be emergency plans; they should be long-term strategies for adapting to what we know is coming. Our plans should also include how we might manage unexpected disruptions that affect our lives, such as political instability and humanitarian crises. For government, Demographic Preparedness strategies would include plans for managing major challenges, such as population aging, shrinking workforces, increased migration, greater food insecurity, and the consequences of climate change.

In thinking about how to anticipate and manage demographic dynamics, we should first consider our priorities. One top priority might be ensuring that the next generation can look forward to promising opportunities for health and economic well-being, as well as political stability. Those lofty goals can be achieved only if individual citizens and voters engage with policy makers and business leaders to address the coming challenges. A first step plan will be for everyone to educate themselves about the demographic transformations around the corner and what their consequences mean for economic, political, and social change.

To prompt your thinking about all this and help prepare you for productive discourse, I've put forward a set of questions rooted in the demographic trends discussed in this book. You'll see that the list includes both worrisome concerns as well as more hopeful questions that point to solutions already being implemented. As you now know, demographics matters for all aspects of our lives, so many of the impacts and solutions overlap. The list is broad but is not intended to be all-encompassing. Rather, it is meant to show you how you might use a demographic perspective to more fully understand the issues and challenges you will be reading and hearing about.

I hope in the future you will read the news with some of these questions in mind. More importantly, I hope the questions that interest you will prompt you to learn more about the demographics behind them so you can more fully understand how the world is changing and what it might take to address the pressing problems unfolding now and on the horizon.

The world tours in this book have equipped you with a demographic lens that can inform your worldview and further prompt your thinking. This lens will deepen your understanding of global events and can bolster your participation in civil discourse.

I've organized the questions into 11 categories:

1. Education
2. Economic Growth
3. Technology and Innovation
4. Immigration
5. Climate Change
6. Health Care and Wellness
7. Role of the Family
8. Population Aging

9. Women's Rights

10. National Security

11. Governance and Civil Society

You have already seen many of these questions in the news, and many will become paramount. You may want to zero in on particular areas that spark your interest, or you might choose to keep a broad perspective. Whatever your approach, you can use these queries as prompts to develop your own set of thoughtful, hard-hitting questions for your policy makers.

WATCH LIST:
ISSUES AND UNCERTAINTIES
TO CONSIDER AS YOU READ THE NEWS

1. EDUCATION

- What is the impact of girls' education on reducing fertility rates in Africa, as well as in other high-fertility, fast-growing populations like Yemen and Pakistan?

- How can governments, investors, and nongovernmental organizations (NGOs) support education in fast-growing developing countries?

- What are countries doing to encourage education and retraining for longer careers and for new occupations and industries?

- How can technology be developed and employed to improve education in developing as well as advanced economies?

- How are countries prioritizing education to address the diverse needs of children, workers, and older populations?

2. ECONOMIC GROWTH

- How are countries adapting to slower-growing or shrinking workforces? What policy changes are being adopted—increased immigration, older people working longer, greater labor force participation at all ages and for women, job retraining, or apprenticeship programs?

- Which countries are successfully maintaining economic well-being while facing slower workforce growth? Which countries stand out for successfully using productivity gains to offset slower growth in labor supply? What evidence is there that economic growth and incomes can be sustained as population growth slows?

- What new business practices are being instituted to address specific demographic challenges, such as leveraging the talents of older workers, or encouraging greater self-employment?

- How can older workers be encouraged to stay economically active and possibly retrain for new occupations? How can companies encourage labor force participation among older people? What practices are in place to transfer skills and experience? How can the expertise of older workers be leveraged?

- Which industries might relocate to countries with greater labor availability? Which of these might be attracted to Africa, where they could capitalize on the available labor?

- How can technology help to maintain growth in per capita income? How is technology being used to improve productivity?

- Which countries are promoting greater labor force participation of women as an effective tool for increasing or maintaining economic growth? What policies are being implemented to reduce the gender gaps in education, employment, and pay?

- How will young, growing countries manage growth in their working-age populations? Which developing countries might capture the potential demographic dividend stemming from an increase in their shares of working-age population? What policies and practices might help them leverage their favorable demographics?

- Which countries are more likely to see their youth bulges lead to political unrest and instability, rather than demographic dividends? What might countries do to reduce the potential unrest?

- How might countries use competitive advantages—in resources, manufacturing, or strategic location—to offset their demographic weaknesses, such as slower-growing and aging populations, or a mismatch in labor supply and needed skills? Which countries are pursuing partnerships that help leverage their attractive assets?

- Are economic forecasters optimistic about how countries will adapt to their changing workforces? What assumptions are they making about productivity growth and labor force participation? What is the outlook for how economic growth might shift geographically, and from the current large economies to emerging economies?

- What will China do to address its unfavorable demographics? What issues arise as China invests around the world through its Belt and Road Initiative? How is any of this outward interest intended to compensate for domestic weakness? How might China supplement its native workforce? Will an increasingly authoritarian state try to restrict out-migration? How might work rules change? What are the consequences for human rights?

3. TECHNOLOGY AND INNOVATION

- How might the widespread availability of broadband affect education and economic growth in developing countries?

- How are countries using technology when human labor is scarce? How does this change the way work gets done and where?

- How might the use of robots and other technologies, such as 3D printing, reduce the demand for low-cost labor in developing countries and thereby diminish their economic prospects?

- What is the evidence about how much technology innovations can increase productivity and boost economic growth? How will technology help developing countries leapfrog traditional business practices in manufacturing, communications, sales, and marketing?

- What are the possible social and financial impacts of new drugs that could reduce or eliminate diseases of old age, such as arthritis, Alzheimer's, or diabetes, to name a few? What about other health care innovations, such as improving artificial joints and using animal parts for human transplantation?

- How can technology help people age more functionally? How might technology be used to assist or possibly replace human caregivers?

- How will the rate of innovation and entrepreneurship be affected as societies age and both the percentage and number of young people decline? What policies might encourage innovation as societies age and possibly become more dependent on technological advances in caregiving and medical treatment?

4. IMMIGRATION

- If today's top host countries restrict immigration, what new host countries might benefit? If the US restricts immigration, will migrants from the Northern Triangle stay in their home countries or seek other destinations?

- Which countries are seeking increased economic immigration, and what policies are being implemented to manage immigration and support effective assimilation?

- How are countries changing their policies regarding political refugees, including criteria for asylum and the numbers being admitted? How will refugee flows shift?

- How will climate change affect international migration? Will climate-affected countries become large originating countries? How much climate-induced migration will likely occur inside a country's own borders?

- What might be done in the originating countries to improve prospects for native workers and dampen pressure to emigrate?

- How will internal migration and greater urbanization affect labor supply and economic growth? Can African countries spur urbanization to boost economic growth?

- How might companies and countries capitalize on Africa's youth and available labor? Which countries will seek to attract African migrants? Which if any of Africa's 54 countries are encouraging such possibilities?

- How likely are policy changes that would help the United States return to its past immigration levels of about 1 million per year? In the absence of migration, how would the US adapt to a shrinking population?

- What might happen in the Northern Triangle countries as their populations expand? Will they become more or less stable? Stronger or weaker economically? Will residents be under continued pressure to migrate to Mexico and the United States? How will Mexico and the United States adapt their migration policies?

- How might low-immigration countries like Japan change their immigration policies and work rules? What pro-immigration policies have been adopted in low-immigration countries?

- How might Russia or China seek to attract climate migrants from Africa and Asia? Can Siberia and other available land be made attractive to investors and migrants? What other places have land available for migrant resettlement?

5. CLIMATE CHANGE

- How might climate-induced migration evolve? What countries or regions are likely to be affected by drought or rising sea levels, and where might their residents move?

- What are the projections for the number of climate migrants? What are the underlying assumptions in these models of migration? What are the main points of disagreement across the estimates?

- As climate change becomes more concerning, will young people desire fewer children? How might having more children actually help address long-term climate challenges?

- Does population growth always cause environmental damage? How can population and economic growth be managed to mitigate environmental consequences?

- As industries adapt to climate change, how will workers be affected? What are the impacts on workforce management and migration?

- How can the challenges of increasing climate migration and shrinking workforces be jointly addressed? What countries are positioned or organized to use climate-induced immigration to meet their labor needs?

- Where are African climate migrants likely to move? Within their own countries, or to neighboring countries? Which countries are likely to accept international climate migrants from Africa? How can the migration flows be anticipated and managed to avoid the major disruptions of past refugee crises?

- How might the industry mix change in the oil-rich Middle Eastern countries if the use of fossil fuels declines? How might dependence on foreign workers, especially Asians, change? Where else might those Asian-born workers go?

6. HEALTH CARE AND WELLNESS

- What progress is being made, especially in developing countries, to reduce infant and childhood mortality? How will these advances affect overall health, life expectancy, and population growth?

- What trade-offs will societies make between health care spending on older people and policies that would improve the health status of younger people?

- What about the trade-off between health care and defense spending?

- How can countries ensure they have adequate health care for their aging populations?

- What are countries doing to address the global obesity epidemic? And the opioid crisis? How is life expectancy affected by these epidemics? How are workforces affected by these health issues? What are the economic costs?

- Which countries or communities are adopting wellness programs to reduce long-term health costs of chronic diseases, including heart disease, diabetes, and Alzheimer's and other dementias? Which countries are investing in prevention campaigns to reduce the prevalence of costly diseases such as Alzheimer's?

- How might countries implement wellness policies that incentivize people to get and stay fit, to allow them to work longer, remain productive longer, and reduce health care burdens? How might countries leverage wellness to offset declining workforces?

- As chronic diseases become more prevalent, especially in developing countries, how will health care practices and spending change?

7. ROLE OF THE FAMILY

- How will the living arrangements of older people change as family size shrinks and the number of childless and single people increases? What new housing options and investment opportunities might arise to complement existing congregate care arrangements?

- What events or trends might encourage, or discourage, an increase in the desired number of children? How might the desire for greater kinship encourage larger families?

- How will health scares, such as the COVID-19 pandemic, or political events, such as the 9/11 terrorist attacks, change the desire for children and kinship?

- What pronatal policies are being adopted and where? Is there evidence that such policies actually increase the number of children?

- How do childcare benefits affect female labor force participation? What is the evidence?

- How will lower marriage rates and higher age of marriage affect living arrangements? How are housing developers adapting their strategies?

8. POPULATION AGING

- How will aging societies with slower-growing or shrinking work-forces address their changing age profiles? How might interest in pronatal policies and increased immigration change as countries seek to supplement their labor supply?

- How are living arrangements for older people changing? What innovations in housing and services are being considered?

- How can countries manage the challenge of caring for aging residents, with fewer workers and caregivers? What are the implications for education, immigration, and housing?

- How are countries addressing the needs of older people who have not saved enough to support themselves?

- What innovations in social security policies are being adopted in young, developing countries?

- How will countries address the possibility of a humanitarian crisis of aging?

- How might politics change in aging societies? How might countries manage the generational warfare that some predict will occur as the increasing older population demands greater public services—perhaps at the expense of investments in the young?

- What does potential generational conflict mean for the burden of old-age entitlements at a time when educational opportunities for young populations are increasingly important? Is there evidence that older people won't support investment in education?

9. WOMEN'S RIGHTS

- How might greater female labor force participation affect economic growth? How can greater employment of women become the economic game changer that many have advocated? Where has such a trend been most effective in boosting economic growth? What about female entrepreneurship? What effect might growth in female-owned businesses have on local economies?

- How are women's economic roles changing in traditionally Muslim countries?

- What challenges must be addressed if female labor force participation increases? What about claims of gender discrimination? How are countries addressing these challenges?

- As the educational attainment and professional status of women improves, how will male employment change?

- What are the economic and social implications of countries having more older women than men, especially when older women might be financially disadvantaged by past caregiving responsibilities and income inequalities?

- How will gender imbalances affect the role of women? What are the implications for bride markets?

- Besides improving girls' education, what practices and policies are helping to improve reproductive health around the world?

10. NATIONAL SECURITY

- How might China's rise be affected by its demographic challenges, including its shrinking workforce and the growing burden of a large, rapidly aging population, to name a few?

- What problems are created for the rest of the world if Nigeria and Pakistan can't effectively manage their youth bulges?

- What will Russia do to cope with its population decline and relatively weak overall health? How will relations change among the former Soviet republics, which are each facing their own demographic challenges?

- How will countries address the trade-off between national security spending and spending on education, housing, health care and social security?

- As population growth slows, will national defense strategies rely more heavily on technological weapons than on conventional forces? How do militaries adapt to a shrinking supply of able-bodied recruits? Will there be greater investment in autonomous weapons to offset the reduced number of recruits?

- Will countries with fewer children become less willing to engage in conflict and more unwilling for soldiers to die? How do attitudes toward global engagement change as societies age? Is there evidence of a geriatric peace?

11. GOVERNANCE AND CIVIL SOCIETY

- What are the political consequences of the coming demographic changes? How might preferences change in the face of divergent generational priorities for education and health?
- How might the appetite for government intervention change as populations age?
- How will increasing diversity affect political preferences? How can democratic institutions protect the rights of minorities in societies with increasing racial and ethnic diversity?
- How can demographic change contribute to or counteract threats of authoritarianism? What countries are examples of those demographic impacts on democracy?
- How will rising climate, political, and economic migration affect democracies? How might anti-immigrant attitudes threaten democratic institutions, even as many countries with shrinking workforces recognize the economic need for greater immigration?
- Which countries have implemented orderly processes to support increased immigration as a means to fuel stronger economic growth? What are the key features of such policies?
- How can improved governance in young, growing populations reduce future out-migration through creation of educational and economic opportunities at home?
- What role might NGOs play where governance may be weak? What are other examples, besides Bangladesh, where NGOs have significantly contributed to improving health and education?
- How could countries restore confidence and trust in their governments in general and in democratic institutions in particular, and assure residents that their changing needs will be addressed?

APPENDIX
UN CLASSIFICATION OF COUNTRIES
AND AREAS

Note: This list shows the UN official names, but this book uses familiar names for the subregions and countries.

PART I: BY REGIONS AND SUBREGIONS OF THE WORLD

AFRICA

Northern Africa

Algeria
Egypt
Libya
Morocco
Sudan
Tunisia
Western Sahara

Sub-Saharan Africa

Eastern Africa
Burundi
Comoros
Djibouti
Eritrea
Ethiopia
Kenya
Madagascar
Malawi
Mauritius
Mayotte
Mozambique
Réunion
Rwanda
Seychelles
Somalia
South Sudan
Uganda
United Republic of
    Tanzania
Zambia
Zimbabwe

Middle Africa
Angola
Cameroon
Central African Republic
Chad
Congo
Democratic Republic of
    the Congo
Equatorial Guinea
Gabon
Sao Tome and Principe

Southern Africa
Botswana
Eswatini
Lesotho
Namibia
South Africa

Western Africa

Benin
Burkina Faso
Cabo Verde
Côte d'Ivoire
Gambia

Ghana
Guinea
Guinea-Bissau
Liberia
Mali
Mauritania

Niger
Nigeria
Saint Helena
Senegal
Sierra Leone
Togo

ASIA

Central Asia

Kazakhstan
Kyrgyzstan
Tajikistan
Turkmenistan
Uzbekistan

Bhutan
India
Iran (Islamic Republic of)
Maldives
Nepal
Pakistan
Sri Lanka

Western Asia

Armenia
Azerbaijan
Bahrain
Cyprus
Georgia
Iraq
Israel
Jordan
Kuwait
Lebanon
Oman
Qatar
Saudi Arabia
State of Palestine
Syrian Arab Republic
Turkey
United Arab Emirates
Yemen

Eastern Asia
(East Asia)

China
China, Hong Kong SAR
China, Macao SAR
China, Taiwan Province
of China
Dem. People's Republic of
Korea
Japan
Mongolia
Republic of Korea

South-Eastern Asia

Brunei Darussalam
Cambodia
Indonesia
Lao People's Democratic
Republic
Malaysia
Myanmar
Philippines
Singapore
Thailand
Timor-Leste
Vietnam

Southern Asia
(South Asia)

Afghanistan
Bangladesh

EUROPE

Eastern Europe

Belarus
Bulgaria
Czechia
Hungary
Poland

Republic of Moldova
Romania
Russian Federation
Slovakia
Ukraine

Northern Europe

Channel Islands
Denmark
Estonia

Faroe Islands
Finland
Iceland
Ireland
Isle of Man
Latvia
Lithuania
Norway
Sweden
United Kingdom

Southern Europe

Albania
Andorra

Bosnia and Herzegovina
Croatia
Gibraltar
Greece
Holy See
Italy
Malta
Montenegro
North Macedonia
Portugal
San Marino
Serbia
Slovenia
Spain

Western Europe

Austria
Belgium
France
Germany
Liechtenstein
Luxembourg
Monaco
Netherlands
Switzerland

LATIN AMERICA & THE CARIBBEAN

Caribbean

Anguilla
Antigua and Barbuda
Aruba
Bahamas
Barbados
Bonaire, Sint Eustatius
    and Saba
British Virgin Islands
Cayman Islands
Cuba
Curaçao
Dominica
Dominican Republic
Grenada
Guadeloupe
Haiti
Jamaica
Martinique
Montserrat
Puerto Rico

Saint Barthélemy
Saint Kitts and Nevis
Saint Lucia
Saint Martin (French
    part)
Saint Vincent and the
    Grenadines
Sint Maarten
    (Dutch part)
Trinidad and Tobago
Turks and Caicos Islands
United States Virgin
    Islands

Central America

Belize
Costa Rica
El Salvador
Guatemala
Honduras
Mexico

Nicaragua
Panama

South America

Argentina
Bolivia (Plurinational
    State of)
Brazil
Chile
Colombia
Ecuador
Falkland Islands
    (Malvinas)
French Guiana
Guyana
Paraguay
Peru
Suriname
Uruguay
Venezuela (Bolivarian
    Republic of)

NORTHERN AMERICA (NORTH AMERICA)

Bermuda
Canada
Greenland

Saint Pierre and Miquelon
United States of America

OCEANIA

Australia/New Zealand
Australia
New Zealand

Melanesia
Fiji
New Caledonia
Papua New Guinea
Solomon Islands
Vanuatu

Micronesia
Guam
Kiribati
Marshall Islands
Micronesia (Fed. States of)
Nauru
Northern Mariana Islands
Palau

Polynesia
American Samoa
Cook Islands
French Polynesia
Niue
Samoa
Tokelau
Tonga
Tuvalu
Wallis and Futuna Islands

PART II: BY INCOME

HIGH-INCOME COUNTRIES

Andorra
Antigua and Barbuda
Argentina
Aruba
Australia
Austria
Bahamas
Bahrain
Barbados
Belgium
Bermuda
British Virgin Islands
Brunei Darussalam
Canada
Cayman Islands
Channel Islands
Chile
China, Hong Kong SAR
China, Macao SAR
China, Taiwan Province of China
Croatia
Curaçao
Cyprus
Czechia
Denmark

Estonia
Faroe Islands
Finland
France
French Polynesia
Germany
Gibraltar
Greece
Greenland
Guam
Hungary
Iceland
Ireland
Isle of Man
Israel
Italy
Japan
Kuwait
Latvia
Liechtenstein
Lithuania
Luxembourg
Malta
Monaco
Netherlands
New Caledonia

New Zealand
Northern Mariana Islands
Norway
Oman
Palau
Panama
Poland
Portugal
Puerto Rico
Qatar
Republic of Korea
Saint Kitts and Nevis
Saint-Martin (French part)
San Marino
Saudi Arabia
Seychelles
Singapore
Sint Maarten (Dutch part)
Slovakia
Slovenia
Spain
Sweden
Switzerland
Trinidad and Tobago
Turks and Caicos Islands

United Arab Emirates
United Kingdom
United States of America

United States Virgin
  Islands
Uruguay

UPPER-MIDDLE-INCOME COUNTRIES

Albania
Algeria
American Samoa
Armenia
Azerbaijan
Belarus
Belize
Bosnia and Herzegovina
Botswana
Brazil
Bulgaria
China
Colombia
Costa Rica
Cuba
Dominica
Dominican Republic
Ecuador
Equatorial Guinea
Fiji

Gabon
Grenada
Guatemala
Guyana
Iran (Islamic
  Republic of)
Iraq
Jamaica
Jordan
Kazakhstan
Lebanon
Libya
Malaysia
Maldives
Marshall Islands
Mauritius
Mexico
Montenegro
Namibia
Nauru

North Macedonia
Paraguay
Peru
Romania
Russian Federation
Saint Lucia
Saint Vincent and the
  Grenadines
Samoa
Serbia
South Africa
Suriname
Thailand
Tonga
Turkey
Turkmenistan
Tuvalu
Venezuela (Bolivarian
  Republic of)

LOWER-MIDDLE-INCOME COUNTRIES

Angola
Bangladesh
Bhutan
Bolivia (Plurinational
  State of)
Cabo Verde
Cambodia
Cameroon
Congo
Côte d'Ivoire
Djibouti
Egypt
El Salvador
Eswatini
Georgia
Ghana

Honduras
India
Indonesia
Kenya
Kiribati
Kyrgyzstan
Lao People's Democratic
  Republic
Lesotho
Mauritania
Micronesia (Fed. States of)
Mongolia
Morocco
Myanmar
Nicaragua
Nigeria

Pakistan
Papua New Guinea
Philippines
Republic of Moldova
Sao Tome and Principe
Solomon Islands
Sri Lanka
State of Palestine
Sudan
Timor-Leste
Tunisia
Ukraine
Uzbekistan
Vanuatu
Viet Nam
Zambia

LOW-INCOME COUNTRIES

Afghanistan
Benin
Burkina Faso
Burundi
Central African Republic
Chad
Comoros
Dem. People's Republic of
   Korea
Democratic Republic of
   the Congo
Eritrea
Ethiopia
Gambia
Guinea
Guinea-Bissau
Haiti
Liberia
Madagascar
Malawi
Mali
Mozambique

Nepal
Niger
Rwanda
Senegal
Sierra Leone
Somalia
South Sudan
Syrian Arab Republic
Tajikistan
Togo
Uganda
United Republic
   of Tanzania
Yemen
Zimbabwe

No income data

available

Anguilla
Bonaire, Sint Eustatius
   and Saba

Cook Islands
Falkland Islands
   (Malvinas)
French Guiana
Guadeloupe
Holy See
Martinique
Mayotte
Montserrat
Niue
Réunion
Saint Helena
Saint Pierre and
   Miquelon
Saint-Barthélemy
Tokelau
Wallis and Futuna
   Islands
Western Sahara

PART III: LEAST DEVELOPED COUNTRIES

Afghanistan
Angola
Bangladesh
Benin
Bhutan
Burkina Faso
Burundi
Cambodia
Central African Republic
Chad
Comoros
Democratic Republic of
   the Congo
Djibouti
Eritrea
Ethiopia
Gambia

Guinea
Guinea-Bissau
Haiti
Kiribati
Lao People's Democratic
   Republic
Lesotho
Liberia
Madagascar
Malawi
Mali
Mauritania
Mozambique
Myanmar
Nepal
Niger
Rwanda

Sao Tome and Principe
Senegal
Sierra Leone
Solomon Islands
Somalia
South Sudan
Sudan
Timor-Leste
Togo
Tuvalu
Uganda
United Republic of
   Tanzania
Vanuatu
Yemen
Zambia

ABOUT THE AUTHOR

Adele Hayutin, an Annenberg Distinguished Visiting Fellow at the Hoover Institution, is a business economist specializing in comparative international demographics. Building on her experience in business and academia, Hayutin combines broad knowledge of underlying demographic data with analytical ability to distill and synthesize that data into practical, easy-to-understand language and implications. She has developed an innovative comparative international perspective that highlights surprising demographic differences across countries and that illustrates the unprecedented speed and impacts of critical demographic changes. She is skilled at developing compelling visual displays and presenting complex information to policy makers and business executives. As chief economist and director of research at the Fremont Group (formerly Bechtel Investments Inc.) and senior real estate analyst at Salomon Brothers in New York, she focused on issues and trends affecting business investment strategy. More recently, Hayutin was director of demographic analysis at the Stanford Center on Longevity, where she focused on the challenges of global and regional population aging, including shifting age structures, shrinking workforces, increasing diversity, and changing family structures. Hayutin received a BA from Wellesley College and holds an MPP and a PhD in economics from the University of California–Berkeley.

INDEX OF FIGURES BY COUNTRY

GENERAL INDEX

Page numbers in italics indicate tables and figures.

Afghanistan
  demographic dividend in, 262–265, *263*
  fertility rates in, *90*
  international migration and, *134,*
    163, 165
  working-age population in, *245*
  youthful age profile of, *263*
Africa
  Asia and, 53–54, *130,* 130–131
  fertility rates in, 21–25, *22–23, 25, 66,*
    66–67
  global population shift to Africa, *15*
  HIV/AIDS in, *115,* 115–116
  life expectancy in, 98, *98, 101, 115*
  older population in, *192,* 193
  population growth in, 21–28, *22–23,*
    25, 27
  population milestones in, *29*
  workforce growth and, 188, *219,* 235
  youth in, 277
    See also sub-Saharan Africa;
      specific countries
Albania, 45, *152–153*
Algeria
  fertility decline in, *230*
  international migration and,
    152–153, 155
  life expectancy in, *115,* 116
  older population in, *201*
  population growth in, *27*
Alzheimer's disease, 204, 210, 276
Angola
  fertility rates in, *73*
  life expectancy in, *109*
  population growth in, 25–26, *27*
  total population ranking of, *52*
  working-age population in, *231, 245*
Argentina, 37–38, *38, 198*
Asia
  Africa and, 53–54, *130,* 130–131
  fertility rates in, 61, *66*
  international migration and, 165–168
  life expectancy in, *98, 101*
  older population in, *188, 192*

population growth in, 15, 22–*23,* 28–29,
  29, 31, 32–34, *33*
shrinking workforces in, *235*
workforce growth and, *219*
  See also specific countries
Asian Tigers
  demographic dividend and, 243, 259
  fertility decline in, 73, *80*
  gulf oil states and, 79–82, *80, 82*
  older population in, *197*
  working-age population in, *231*
    See also specific countries
Australia
  international migration and, *132,* 133,
    139, 141, 142, 149–150, *176*
  life expectancy in, *106, 111, 123*
  as traditional immigration country,
    149–150
  workforce growth and, *223, 241*

Bangladesh
  fertility rates in, *31,* 72, *86,* 86–87. *230*
  international migration and, *134,*
    152–153, 157, 163, 165, 176
  older population in, *197, 201*
  population growth in, *31*
  total population ranking of, *52*
  working-age population in, *231, 233, 245*
Belize, 36
Belt and Road Initiative, 275
Benin, *73*
birth rates. *See* fertility rates
Bosnia and Herzegovina, 45, *73*
Brazil
  fertility decline in, 77, *230*
  international migration and, *176*
  life expectancy in, *111*
  net international migration and, *172*
  older population in, *198, 201*
  population growth in, *38, 40,* 54
  shrinking workforce in, *223*
  total population ranking of, *52*
  workforce growth and, *227, 231,*
    241, 245